Cultivating Learning Within Projects

Cultivating Learning Within Projects

Andrew Sense

© Andrew Sense 2007
Foreword © Derek H.T. Walker 2007 and Richard J. Badham 2007

All rights reserved. No reproduction, copy or transmission of this publication may be made without written permission.

No paragraph of this publication may be reproduced, copied or transmitted save with written permission or in accordance with the provisions of the Copyright, Designs and Patents Act 1988, or under the terms of any licence permitting limited copying issued by the Copyright Licensing Agency, 90 Tottenham Court Road, London W1T 4LP.

Any person who does any unauthorized act in relation to this publication may be liable to criminal prosecution and civil claims for damages.

The author has asserted his right to be identified as the author of this work in accordance with the Copyright, Designs and Patents Act 1988.

First published 2007 by
PALGRAVE MACMILLAN
Houndmills, Basingstoke, Hampshire RG21 6XS and
175 Fifth Avenue, New York, N.Y. 10010
Companies and representatives throughout the world

PALGRAVE MACMILLAN is the global academic imprint of the Palgrave Macmillan division of St. Martin's Press, LLC and of Palgrave Macmillan Ltd. Macmillan® is a registered trademark in the United States, United Kingdom and other countries. Palgrave is a registered trademark in the European Union and other countries.

ISBN-13: 978–0–230–00691–1 hardback
ISBN-10: 0–230–00691–4 hardback

This book is printed on paper suitable for recycling and made from fully managed and sustained forest sources. Logging, pulping and manufacturing processes are expected to conform to the environmental regulations of the country of origin.

A catalogue record for this book is available from the British Library.

A catalog record for this book is available from the Library of Congress.

10 9 8 7 6 5 4 3 2 1
16 15 14 13 12 11 10 09 08 07

Printed and bound in Great Britain by
Antony Rowe Ltd, Chippenham and Eastbourne

*Whatever you can do or dream you can, begin it.
Boldness has genius, power and magic in it.*

Johann Wolfgang von Goethe (1749–1832)

Contents

Foreword   x
Preface   xiii
Acknowledgements   xv
List of Figures   xvi
Glossary of Abbreviations   xvii

1 Introduction   **1**

  1.1 Why it is important to learn and understand learning within projects   2
  1.2 Developing a project learning libido   7
  1.3 Important methodological and contextual information concerning the contents of this book   8
  1.4 The structure of this book   15

2 Conceptualizing Learning Within a Project   **17**

  2.1 Organizational perspectives on learning   17
    The cognitive perspective of OL   20
    The behavioural perspective of OL   21
    The sociological perspective of OL   21
  2.2 The relationship of OL to individual learning   23
  2.3 The cognitive dimension of learning   25
  2.4 The situated dimension of learning   30
    Situated learning theory   30
    Communities of practice   35
  2.5 Why focus on the situated dimension of learning for cultivating learning within projects?   42

3 Sociological Perspectives and Learning in Projects   **45**

  3.1 A view from within the field   46
  3.2 A view from outside the field   52
  3.3 Concept of a project team from a learning perspective   56
  3.4 The pentagon of project situated learning behaviour   63

4 Cognitive Style — 66

- 4.1 The theory of cognitive styles — 67
  - How does cognitive style relate to learning style? — 69
- 4.2 The methods of understanding cognitive styles — 71
  - Cognitive styles assessment in the project team case study — 80
- 4.3 How did the cognitive styles of project participants in this project case impact their situated learning behaviours? — 84
  - The match/mismatch of cognitive style to project information-processing demands — 85
  - Participants individually and collectively selecting situations which align with their cognitive style — 86
  - Predominance of a particular cognitive style type across a team — 88
- 4.4 Summary — 90

5 Learning Relationships and Pyramid of Authority — 93

- 5.1 Learning relationships — 94
  - The importance of understanding the learning relationships — 94
  - How did the learning relationships exhibited in this project case, impact participants' situated learning behaviours? — 97
- 5.2 Pyramid of authority — 108
  - What is a pyramid of authority? — 108
  - The importance of managing politics for learning in projects — 110
  - How did the pyramids of authority of project participants in this project case impact their situated learning behaviours? — 115
- 5.3 Summary — 132

6 Knowledge Management and Situational Context — 136

- 6.1 Knowledge management — 137
  - Managing knowledge flow in projects — 137
  - How did the project participants' knowledge management approaches impact their situated learning behaviours in this case study project team? — 143
- 6.2 Situational context — 149
  - Situational context and situated learning — 149
  - How did the situational context of this project case impact the situated learning behaviours of project participants? — 151
- 6.3 Summary — 164

7 The Project Learning Opportunity: Where to Now? **167**

7.1 A summary of the key issues for project learning 167
The conceptual issues 168
The methodological issues 173
7.2 Limitations of this study and recommendations for future research 175
7.3 Some questions to further stimulate your thinking on this topic 177
7.4 Summary 178

References 181

Index 198

Foreword

The pressing need of competitive advantage bears down on all organizations. They are either pressured by cutting costs through being more efficient (less waste, less re-work and working smarter) or they need to be more effective (providing differentiated or unique value-adding quality service). Both efficiency and effectiveness strategies require organizations to effectively harness the knowledge of work groups and individuals to learn how to be both efficient and effective. But knowledge is not enough. Knowledge is passive whereas learning is active, and action from learning can transform. One significant key to competitive advantage is the ability for organizations [including temporary organizations such as projects] to learn.

Cultivating Learning Within Projects is a book based upon rigorous case study research and explains how situated learning may be effectively deployed and promoted within project teams. It uses a model of situated learning behaviour to describe the extent to which project learning may occur through: the interaction of individuals' cognitive style characteristics; the way that the power and authority of sponsors/leaders and followers is structured to encourage or deter learning; the situational context – involving an organization's internal-political and external-impinging factors that act upon the support infrastructure to limit or enhance 'real' support and culture for learning; the way that knowledge is managed within a project and the organization; the learning relationships – involving participants' attitudes towards reflection and public disclosure and their preparedness to explore their relationships. This model was derived through in-depth action research in an engineering organization that attempted a project to achieve transformational management change through organizational learning. There are few documented examples of organizations (or project teams) attempting to achieve such a transformation.

This book is intensely practical while being rooted in rigorous theory of how individuals and organizations learn. Its practical value is derived from its explanation of the process of project-based learning as it became revealed through the research. This book uses reflections from inside the organization as the project team lived the experience, and so it exposes the reality of the tasks and challenges faced by project participants. This differentiates it from other texts that only offer theoretical models of what is optimal or what is desirable for developing learning in organizations or in project teams.

It is for this reason that this book should be of value to academics who wish to explore findings from a real practical example. Perhaps more importantly, practitioners who wish to look beyond rhetoric to find the substance of real experience will find great value from absorbing the content of this book. The data used to ground the theory developed and tested in this book came from a traditional and large 'blue-collared' heavy industry organization, and so its attempts at becoming a learning organization make it a particularly brave and interesting example. There is much in this book that readers will find themselves returning to time and time again, and so it should be the kind of book that will be referred to and passed around colleagues working together. Hopefully, its potential impact will be realized through practical people gaining value from its deep insights.

Derek H. T. Walker
Professor of Project Management, RMIT University

Anyone reading *Cultivating Learning Within Projects* will no longer be able, in good conscience, to adopt a partial, fragmented or reactive approach to learning in projects. The author draws on his experiences as a manager as well as a broad interdisciplinary coverage of the learning literature to uncover the factors that enable (and obstruct!) learning in project practice. This is well captured in the in-depth case study that illustrates the main arguments of the book. The outcome of his reflections is a five-fold model of the factors affecting learning, which involves the influences of Cognitive Styles, Learning Relationships, Knowledge Management, Pyramid of Authority and Situational Context. This model is of major value for any researcher wishing to step outside the confines of narrow disciplinary approaches to learning to cover the broad spectrum of conditions that affect how project-based learning occurs in practice. Equally important however, the author's model provides an accessible and stimulating framework for practitioners to reflect on their practice. Anyone seeking to really improve learning in projects will omit any of the influences outlined by the author at his or her peril.

I am most happy as a colleague and friend to recommend Andrew's work to the broadest possible audience. His energy, enthusiasm, commitment to learning and above all practical focus have produced a work that has the potential to push the frontiers of research and practice in the area of project-based learning. I am certain that you will find this book an interesting and extremely beneficial read.

Richard J. Badham
Professor of Management, MGSM, Macquarie University

Preface

The motivations behind this book

I have been motivated to develop and publish this book for two key reasons. First, when critically reflecting on my many years of industry experience as a project manager, manufacturing manager and engineer, I felt that generally project practitioners did not learn well because project learning activity, whilst on the job, was more opportunistic than it was deliberate. I then conjectured that this situation came about because project practitioners did not really understand (or were unaware of) what learning on the job involved, and did not fully appreciate its potential impact on project performance and their project management skills development. Such ambiguity about learning meant that they may not know or were not inclined to do anything about it within their project situations. Furthermore, taking the time to critically reflect on (particularly in a communal fashion) or to challenge a project process or intended outcome was generally avoided – as such actions were perceived as unnecessary or wasteful digressions while in the process of seeking to deliver a project on time and to specification. These determinations clearly stress the notion of systematic learning within projects as being considered both a foreign and often intrusive activity that is not considered an essential process within the management activities of projects. If I and other colleagues in industry, for example, did not feel that we had learnt well during a project, then what was the resultant impact on project performance and our skills development? From these humble and critically reflective beginnings, my desire to better understand what I felt was an important topic for project management grew. Hence, it became my passion to seek out ways that would help fellow practitioners to practice learning within their project management activities. Thereby, they might begin to realize the value in pursuing a systematic learning agenda within their projects, which, in turn, would positively contribute to their immediate project outcomes and their personal project management skills development.

The second stimulus for this book involves my desire (as an academic) to make a contribution to scholarly knowledge and debate about the dynamics of learning within the project-based environment. Drawing on a case study investigation of project learning, this book makes a contribution to project management knowledge, by articulating the importance of learning within a project and by revealing and explaining the pragmatic and conceptual difficulties faced in pursuing it. In so doing, it draws together or references theories and concepts from different scholarly fields in attempting to explain the dynamics of project-based learning. This material offers a fresh perspective on learning in projects and provides an impetus and new points of theoretical departure for project management researchers to further investigate the learning phenomenon across different project environments. This book also makes a contribution to the increasing volume of organizational learning literature that recognizes the significance of the social dimension of learning. Moreover, it makes a contribution to the literature on workplace learning through emphasizing within the practice learning activity, rather than a focus on more formalized and remote training and development activities that are disconnected from the peculiarities of specific workplace contexts. It also adds to the chorus of knowledge management theorists arguing for the social dimension of knowledge to assume at least an equal, if not a more dominant, role over the technical dimension in knowledge management practices.

Through this book's dual coverage of the conceptual and pragmatic aspects of learning within the project environment, it is my hope that through your reading of it you too will better understand learning in project settings. I particularly hope you finish this book with a greater appreciation and understanding of the sociological moderators of project practitioners' learning behaviours, and also the need for practitioners to take a more systematic and purposeful approach towards learning activity within their project practices.

Happy reading!

Acknowledgements

My thanks to my family for their support while writing this book – yet another project brought to fruition. Thanks also to the editorial team at Palgrave for their professionalism and assistance in completing this project.

Thanks also go to the real Bill, Len and Steve who are mentioned throughout this book. Without your project experiences and actions, this project would just be a fanciful idea.

List of Figures

2.1 The relationship between the situated and cognitive
    dimensions of learning 43
3.1 A typical project team 61
3.2 A preferred project team 62
3.3 Pentagon of project situated learning behaviour 64
4.1 Cognitive style in perspective 69
5.1 Len's view of the project team hierarchy 131

Glossary of Abbreviations

CC	Coal conversion
CLT	Cokemaking Leadership Team
COP	Community of practice
COPs	Communities of practice
CSA	Cognitive Styles Analysis
CSI	Cognitive Styles Index
E	Extraverted person
F	Feeling person
I	Introverted person
IL	Individual learning
J	Judging person
LO	Learning organization
LPP	Legitimate peripheral participation
LSQ	Learning style questionnaire
MBTI	Myers-Briggs Type Indicator
N	Intuitive person
OL	Organizational learning
P	Perceiving person
PAR	Participative action research
PMBOK®	Project Management Body of Knowledge
PMI®	Project Management Institute
S	Sensing person
SLT	Situated learning theory
T	Thinking person
VI	Verbal-Imagery
WA	Wholist-Analytic

1
Introduction

Building on a recent study by the author, this book provides a deep insight into the sociological dimension of learning within the practice of project management, and identifies how to improve our knowledge and learning practices within such an environment. Drawing on a project case study, it identifies and explores how situated learning activity (which involves the social and practical aspects of learning while on the job) within a project team may be supported or stifled by five sociological elements within a project environment. These constraint/enabler elements are identified as: *cognitive style*; *learning relationships*; *pyramid of authority*; *knowledge management*; and, *the situational context*. Combined, they form a model of project situated learning behaviour – as depicted by Figure 3.3 and explained in Chapter 3. These elements serve as a starting point to conceptually focus participants in project teams, and researchers in the field, on the pragmatic and complex social issues involved in learning within projects. They also provide a framework to aid practitioners' systematic reflection on their learning activities.

Furthermore, as is argued in this book, the processes of public exposure and communal reflection on these five constraint/enabler elements by project team participants, and their improved understanding of them, cultivate situated learning activity (or builds a learning practice) within projects. Such actions also aid the development of the learning-how-to-learn skills of project participants. That is, such actions help participants to develop a deep understanding of their approaches and biases to project learning opportunities or problem situations, which then enables them to configure their future situations or actions to become more effective and more purposeful learners. In so doing, situated learning and pragmatic-individual competency and learning development are no longer consigned to a peripheral and opportunistic project activity.

Consequently, the contents of this book confront some commonly held prejudices and limited perceptions of learning in the project management context, and, in particular, challenge project practitioners to consider situated learning as a critical and systematic project action that requires their intentional focus and energy.

This book illustrates the complex dynamics of situated learning within a project through providing rich empirical examples and vignettes from a case study of project-based learning. This project case (in an iron and steel producing company) was an organizational change project which articulated learning to be one of its explicit project goals (see further details in Section 1.3). In utilizing material from this case and weaving together relevant theories, this book addresses a noticeable empirical and theoretical gap in knowledge concerning the social dynamics of project-based learning.

The next two sections of this chapter identify and discuss some broad, and yet core, questions or issues about learning in a project environment. These sections may also pose contemplative challenges to you, the reader, about your current attitudes and approaches towards project learning, or about your research initiatives within project settings. This discussion establishes the broad rationale for pursuing learning *within projects* and provides the platform on which to build the arguments contained within the following chapters. Section 1.3 then outlines important methodological information concerning this study and provides context information on the case study project team referenced throughout this book. As you progress through the book and view the numerous empirical illustrations provided, you can then relate those illustrations to a specific case context and draw comparisons or differences with your own situations or experiences. The final section in this chapter simply articulates the structure of the remainder of this book and therein the goals of each of the chapters to follow.

1.1 Why it is important to learn and understand learning within projects

To ensure survival and growth, organizations attempt to adaptively respond to dynamic and unstable competitive markets and the human, political and technological conditions that they confront (Hedberg, 1981; Leonard-Barton, 1992, 1995; Choo, 1998; Boud and Garrick, 1999; Kezsbom and Edward, 2001). Organizations engage different structural arrangements to meet these challenges, for example different organizational structures such as self-managing work teams, outsourcing functions, networked organizations and temporal organizational arrangements such as projects and project teams. In these dynamic business-operating environments, projects are used to accomplish a diverse and often complex set of technological and cultural changes that would otherwise be less obtainable by the permanent organization (Lundin and Hartman, 2000; Antoni and Sense, 2001; Ayas and Zeniuk, 2001), particularly where the fast speed and high quality of goal achievement is highly desirable, for example new product development projects. This new diversity and expectation of projects have challenged the traditional view of projects and project teams. Lundin and Midler (1998a) observe that the traditional project paradigm involved a project being complicated only in terms of size and detail, whereas now, in addition, they are also becoming increasingly complex in terms of interrelationships and changing performance measures or expectations. This may include, for example, using the project vehicle to deliver both a project outcome and also to be seen as a cultural change engine – as has been the case with some socio-technical projects and total quality management projects. In utilizing projects to achieve such diverse goals and the very nature of them being temporary structures mean that a number of phenomena within the project environment are constructed differently, or are accentuated forms of structures and activities found in traditional organizational systems, or within the traditional project paradigm. For example, emphasized micro-political dynamics, accelerated development of internal and external relationships, complex interdisciplinary learning requirements and high demands on information coordination activities (Antoni and Sense, 2001). Within the diverse raft of projects that organizations pursue, different project organizational structures are employed to achieve the project goals and to effectively utilize the organizational resources in pursuit of those goals, for example traditional functional support structures or matrix project structures (Wheelwright and Clark, 1992; Van Der Merwe 1997; Cleland, 1999; Gray and Larson, 2002; Gido and Clements, 2003). However, regardless of the different project organizational structures applied across all this project variety, the increasing use of projects to achieve important organizational goals suggests a necessity to better understand these project environment phenomena and their interaction within a project setting. This is particularly so, if one seeks to respond effectively to the challenges of complex business and social operating environments.

A further organizational response to environmental challenges is to embrace organizational learning as a means to successfully cope with and lead change (Ingelgård *et al.*, 2002). The reliance on and development of intellectual capital to successfully engage with dynamic environmental conditions has meant that managers in any context need to foster learning rich organizational contexts (Boud and Garrick, 1999; Watkins and Cervero, 2000; Saint-Onge and Wallace, 2002). Underpinning the ability to initiate and foster such learning rich contexts is a broadly developing realization of the need to understand how a person learns within specific contexts, so as to enable development of the individual as well as the development of satisfactory organizational outcomes (Bresnen *et al.*, 2003). Core to that understanding and outcome is paying systematic attention to the learning environment. Any learning environment (which includes social, physical, formal and informal attributes) requires deliberate attention, commitment and resources to invite, encourage and support individuals and teams to learn (Lave and Wenger, 1991; Mumford 1994; Salaman and Butler, 1994; Antonacopoulou, 1997; Ayas, 1998; Starkey, 1998; Wenger, 1998; Matthews, 1999; Matthews and Candy, 1999; Senge *et al.*, 1999; Billett, 2000; Ayas and Zeniuk, 2001; Billett, 2001a; Järvinen and Poikela, 2001; Wenger *et al.*, 2002).

In support of attending to the learning environment, for example, Senge (1990) posits that team learning will remain poorly understood and a product of opportunism until there are reliable methods for building teams that can learn together. Salaman and Butler (1994) question whether managers, because of their roles, are trained, rewarded and encouraged in ways that actually obstruct or restrict their capacity to learn. When considering the likely impact and significance of these and many other environmental aspects on learning activity across any organizational setting, and the potential to waste vital organizational resources on ill-conceived approaches to address them, it also seems important to develop a deeper understanding of the learning phenomenon and the learning environment influences. Such improved understanding may lead to the development of individual and organizational learning and ultimately the capability of the organization to be successful (Senge, 1990; Leonard-Barton, 1992; Amit and Schoemaker, 1993; Kim, 1993; Dunphy *et al.*, 1997; Frame, 1999; Saint-Onge and Wallace, 2002).

With this increasing focus on the learning development of individuals and the organization, coupled with the use and further development of project teams and structures to achieve organizational goals, it is clearly important to develop a better understanding of the learning phenomenon specifically associated with projects. From a project management perspective, a better understanding of, and systematically enacting, learning processes within project team settings may be an important aid in the development of projects and their outcomes, as well as in the development of the learning and project skills capability of individuals within projects. Indeed, as Ayas (1996) suggests, learning is actually a key strategic variable for project management. However, despite this strategic significance, there is a dearth of empirical research into the complexities of the learning phenomenon in projects, that is learning in relation to the goals of a project and the professional development of participants. Literature on this specific cross-disciplinary topic is also limited. For example, in the project management literature that embraces the sociological aspects of project management, there is a very limited and generally rather shallow coverage of learning and its challenges within project team environments. This coverage is usually limited to expounding the virtues of learning in the project and promoting normative post-project review processes. This book attempts to directly address these deficits or opportunities.

In seeking to develop a better understanding of learning and to stimulate it within projects, a number of questions about facilitating it in project teams emerge. For example, what social mechanisms shape one's individual approach to learning in this particular context? What local factors influence or constrain project team efforts to learn? These questions and others emerge, I suggest, from a commonly held practitioner-perception within the project management community, that some focus on learning is valuable and yet confusing, and learning (within a project) is mostly accepted as a random, opportunistic and coincidental act grounded in experience. This view of the complexity of learning is also reflected in the following comment from a project team participant reported on in this book. That is, 'So learning has to be key to what we do. We have to change...we have to learn to change our behaviours, change our thinking, change our recognition, and change what is normal. Normal should be robust argument rather than polite acceptance. So how do we actually make that happen? I'm not sure many of us are doing too much thinking along how can we make that change.'

This quotation also highlights the dilemma faced by many project team participants when confronted with the learning challenge, that is while they usually recognize that the potential value of learning it is not a focal point of the project and they are unsure about how to proceed to harness the opportunity.

One typical and traditional approach to supposedly foster learning in project teams is to conduct post-completion reviews on projects (or, as often referred to by practitioners as post-mortem reports or project-end reviews). Whilst these formal reviews or formal audit processes can be seen as important learning tools for future project performance, they fail to encourage a systematic learning process during the project. Worse still, in some experiences of the author and other colleagues in industry, post-completion reviews have been used as a blame tool, where problems experienced in the project are made explicit and the culprits responsible are identified and publicly vilified. In such a circumstance, the process was not about learning but about laying blame. Alternatively, these processes have been seen as necessary organizational, political or procedural compliance matters, which confirm the apparent success of a project against its original hard objectives. Furthermore, developing systematic intra-project learning processes have not generally been considered as one of the key inputs to project success. This situation reduces the effectiveness of any learning processes employed within a project, and subsequently also impedes the quantity and quality of the outcomes of any post-completion review.

Moreover, as Keegan and Turner (2001) illustrate, even when organizations have such post-completion review practices in place to try and capture and codify such project learning, some time after the actual event as it were, project team participants rarely have the time to reflect and articulate their limited learning and to receive critical feedback – which reduces the effectiveness of such learning practices. In that light, Busby (1999) refers to learning emanating from a post-project review process as propositional knowledge – knowledge that essentially you can pronounce, but not necessarily practise. He urges project review processes to encourage a deep diagnosis and an examination of the bigger system beyond the immediate confines of the project (Busby, 1999). In effect, Busby offers support to a notion that post-project review processes should look beyond the obvious (including cost, quality and time parameters), and look deeply and broadly at the system of issues impacting a project. Such broader reviews should also provide an appropriate context that encourages team member reflection and understanding, that reduces defensive routines which inhibits the post-project team learning process, and provides a context that is systematically structured and inclusive – rather than being an exclusive process (Barker and Neailey, 1999). In attending to the environment to nurture such a process, the opportunity for real and meaningful learning for the review participants is created and made explicit. However, this learning process whilst valuable, if run broadly and inclusively, can be limiting, since such an evaluation is adversely time affected (in relation to the project process) and may be sanitized to appease current organizational expectations. Some authors commenting on post-project review processes suggest that, in seeking to minimize memory loss and to maximize the gathering of key experiences and learning in real time, a project manager's work should also include a systematic, concurrent and continuous learning assessment of projects throughout their life cycles (Lundin and Söderholm, 1998; Wilemon, 1998; Schindler and Eppler, 2003). Any concurrent and continuous or post-project learning processes necessarily require the socio-cultural environment of a project to be supportive of conducting them, and any employment of concurrent and continuous learning processes suggests that traditional conceptions of project teams and their learning processes and limitations be challenged.

1.2 Developing a project learning libido

One core theme implicit in the discussions and arguments presented throughout this book is that learning should be a more prominent, deliberate and systematic within-project action. However, such activities are progressed only by participants who are interested and motivated enough to want to pursue such goals. In that sense, practitioners first and foremost must develop a project learning libido (or passion for learning within projects) as a harbinger to cultivating a learning practice within a project.

In seeking to develop such a learning libido and to stimulate learning activity, the primary challenges for project participants is in conceiving projects as 'vehicles for learning' (Smith and Dodds, 1997: 8) and in conceiving themselves as learners as well as traditional project task achievers. A project team participant reported on in this book echoed this challenge, with his comment that, 'The value in teaching and learning is still a pretty tough dimension – the alligators are biting at our heels wanting all sorts of rational things done...but yet, we still need to move on from that. We need to convey to people the value in learning and understanding what is going on in the business.' Wenger (1998) suggests that one of the reasons people do not think of their job as learning is that what they learn is their practice, and that learning is not reified as an extraneous goal or as a special activity. Similarly, Raelin (2001) suggests that whilst we learn in everyday work activity, we are not subjecting that learning to conscious activity as doing so might impede our performance. Yet, projects are rich with significant personal learning opportunities (Smith and Dodds, 1997; Arthur *et al.*, 2001), and therefore project team participants may need to redress this perception of their learning just being their practice (i.e. going about the tasks of their project) to enable them to develop a systematic learning practice conjoined to their project management practice – what Björkegren (1999: 138) defines as 'a dual approach to project management'. This potential duality of the project role is not something easily embraced from within traditional project management practice/cultural perspectives. However, for practitioners to make this conceptual shift to consider themselves as learners and to conceive project teams (and project situations) as rich learning entities constitute a crucial leap towards stimulating a desire or passion to learn within project team environments. Alongside of other research publications concerned with learning and knowledge management within a project environment, perhaps this book can serve as a catalyst in helping to shift these conceptual perspectives of project practitioners.

Although crucial, building this desire to learn within a project practice is not on its own, however, enough to make learning happen. A vital next step, and the primary trajectory of this book, is to gain a deep insight into the project environmental influences or conditions that impact how project team participants construct their learning processes or activities. By implication, this insight is particularly concerned with the practical and social aspects of learning in a project context. Actions in this regard will identify and help address a range of sociological elements within a project team environment that may constrain or conversely support the learning of participants and the development of a systematic localized project learning practice. Identifying such elements presents opportunities for personal and project team capability development (Senge, 1990; Kim, 1993; Dunphy *et al.*, 1997; Frame, 1999; Saint-Onge and Wallace, 2002) as well as greater intellectual, creative and practical contribution towards immediate project outcomes. This is not to suggest that there may not be conflicts between personal and project learning goals, since the two orientations may be substantially misaligned. Regardless of the focus or emphasis of the learning activity however, if the project environment influences on learning are not known, then intra-project learning would remain rather obscure and opportunistic.

1.3 Important methodological and contextual information concerning the contents of this book

This study was informed and guided by a social constructivist perspective on learning. Within that epistemological framework, the arguments and conceptual ideas contained in this book are built on a qualitative and longitudinal participative action research case study of project-based learning. The empirical illustrations provided were also derived through that action research process. Action research is a human-focused social research strategy (Pasmore, 2001; Alrichter *et al.*, 2002) which has a simultaneous dual customer focus on developing practical social change for the client group and in developing and refining theory for social science (Carr and Kemmis, 1986; Argyris and Schön, 1991; Gummesson, 1991; Cunningham, 1993; Denscombe, 1998; Dickens and Watkins, 1999). One of its great strengths is that learning is such an integral and explicit part of the action research cycle which then facilitates the development of grounded and practically relevant theory. It targets both individual and group levels to prompt social change and serves as a bridge between theory and practice (McNiff, 1988).

Participative action research (as compared to other forms of action research) has a predominant emphasis on genuinely involving and researching with the participants of a community – as co-researchers having ownership of both the research activities and outcomes (Chein *et al.*, 1948; Whyte, 1991a; McTaggart, 1997; Argyris, 1999; Reason, 1999; MacIntosh, 2001). In this process, reflection and continuous learning is an explicit collective activity. It is also an idealized process characterized by: participants being emancipated from the traditional constraints of their contexts to empower them to find voice in decision-making; a continuous learning experience where organizational learning is enhanced; cooperatively changing individuals' attitudes and values and the institutional practices of the community in which the practitioners reside, and is not simply a quest for knowledge; posing challenges to the prevailing culture and practices and power bases in changing existing practice and social organization; self-critical communities of people which involves them in theorizing about their practice and producing knowledge for those in the practice and external to it (Argyris and Schön, 1991; Whyte, 1991a; Whyte *et al.*, 1991; Reason, 1994; McTaggart, 1997; Dickens and Watkins, 1999; Reason, 1999; Borda, 2001; Heron and Reason, 2001; MacIntosh, 2001). Given this long list of attributes, it becomes apparent that participative action research is not normal work as it involves systematic and collaborative data collection, it is not simple problem-solving as it poses problems during the process and it is not a method of policy implementation, nor is it a scientific method applied to social work (McTaggart, 1997).

This methodological approach was applied to a case involving an active project team pursuing an organizational change project, that is a complex 'process innovation' type project (Bresnen *et al.*, 2003: 163).

It presented a number of advantages for investigating learning in this case study context. First, it provided access to real, raw and rich data from the practice of a project and facilitated the author 'getting dirty with the data' (Dawson, 1997: 389). It also provided participants in this case study multiple opportunities, over time and at multiple levels, to become self-critical and reflective, to learn, to learn-how-to-learn, and to develop ownership and empowerment of the research process – which helped further fuel the inquiry activity. It also provided the opportunity for them to safely (relative to the organizational cultural condition), collaboratively and honestly explore learning in their project, so that valuable individual tacit knowledge was exposed and shared. Consequently, this participative action research methodology employed provided a broader (as in number of participant investigators) and deeper (as in the cooperative opportunity to source rich data) insight into the real sociological influences impacting learning in this project team case.

The empirical data from the case was accumulated over 18 months and across three major participative action research cycles (involving planning, acting, observing and reflecting), which were adaptively developed and applied in response to the shifting dynamics of the project environment. The data collection processes broadly involved: extensive researcher participation and observation of project participants in the project team meetings and reflection sessions; participants' multiple and collaborative observations of each other's behaviour in the project; serial semi-structured interviews and feedback sessions with the project team participants; serial learning workshops development and facilitation; and, documentation reviews. For a detailed and insightful discussion of the participative action-research methodology and specific research actions employed in this study (including an analysis of any methodological conundrums experienced), see Sense (2005b).

In addition to a brief introductory discussion on the methodological approach employed in this study, it is also important to convey a sense of the genesis and contextual situation of the case study project. This is important because the illustrations presented and the conclusions drawn in this book are infused with, or influenced by, the specific contextual situation of the project. Therefore, through becoming aware of these conditions, you may relate the empirical illustrations provided to the specific project conditions, and then reasonably compare and contrast the illustrations and conclusions presented in this book with your own experiences or situations. That in itself may help initiate reflection and learning for you as you progress through the chapters that follow. Hereafter, for the purposes of this book, the company name and location and the names of the participants are pseudonyms, but the descriptions provided are a completely real and accurate account of the actions of participants and of the contextual conditions associated with the case study project.

This study was undertaken in a major multinational heavy engineering company called Antarctic Steel. This company was and still is a leading steel company in the Asian region and it manufactures steel products in a number of countries. Since the late 1990s, this company has embraced a new corporate strategy involving substantial change and performance improvement across its operations, so as to remain competitive in the world steel market. Enveloped by this overarching corporate change activity, the specific setting in which this research was conducted involved an individual operational unit on the site of one of the company's major integrated steel-making facilities. This facility is home to an array of continuous and batch-processing operations, which are scattered over the 8 square kilometres of land that is home to these integrated operations. These large, technically complex physical facilities require high levels of long-term capital investment and a relatively high level of employee skills to both operate and integrate the processes used in the manufacture of steel. One of the operational stages in manufacturing steel at this site involves the conversion of raw coal into metallurgical coke (which involves a continuous process of blending, crushing, oiling and then heating coal in a battery of ovens) so that it can be used in the steel-making process, or exported. This can be referred to as the coal conversion (CC) operation. This plant occupies a geographical area of approximately 350,000 square metres and employs over 400 people. Given the long history of the plant, the site and the parent company, it follows that it was a traditional engineering-dominated and hierarchically organized operation. One external consultant report characterized it as a culture of rationality, masculinity, eroding paternalism, increasingly insecure public service career paths for managers, a silo mentality between departments and divisions, and low trust relations between management and employees (Badham and Sense, 2001). Internally, within the Antarctic Steel organization at this site, this CC operation was perceived as the lowest status unit in the entire integrated works, as having a total authoritarian and disciplinarian approach to management, and having a poor safety record and an unsatisfactory working environment which resulted in a high frequency of industrial disputation. Because of these conditions, there was a policy of no forced transfers of people into the CC operation within the site (Internal company report, 2000: 1).

In June 1998, a new plant manager (and the dominating political thrust behind the local change programme) transferred to the plant, possessing strong workplace culture change credentials from his work at two other plants within the same company. Armed with the recognition that there was a developing charter for change within the broader organization, and with a self-referent position that the process of change must be broader, deeper and more inclusive, more learning-oriented and more implementation-focused (i.e. avoid elite groups simply talking about change), the new manager set about to initiate processes to redesign the organization and operation of the plant. The plant manager felt that his previous approaches to managing change at other sites resulted in inadequate understanding and engagement by the workforce, as well as gaps in detailed implementation. He felt there was too much focus on reaching decisions and too little learning, and that led to a lack of sustainability of change, particularly within middle management. He felt that middle managers were not modelling the new way of operating, were not acting as leaders supporting and inspiring initiatives from below their level, and they were undermining the motivation of lower level employees by seeming to protect their turf and resisting change (Badham, 1999). Additionally, he was attempting to initiate this process in a traditional organization harbouring a culture where risk and change from tradition were avoided. Alongside these historical socio-cultural factors embedded in the organization, his goal was also being pursued in a broader business context of competition from cheap overseas producers, alternative cost-saving technologies in steelmaking (i.e. direct pulverized coal injection), pressures from the community and the government to dramatically reduce environmental emissions, and a need to involve a workforce that traditionally had a low self-image and low trust in management.

The low trust culture of Antarctic Steel typically encouraged a tendency to look to outside experts for solutions to in-house problems or opportunities. In this case, however, the plant manager decided to establish a series of innovative forums at the CC operation involving people from senior, middle and shop-floor levels. His idea was to involve a much wider set of people in the change process and enhance their abilities to reflect on the ways in which they approached their concerns about work. Several of these new forums began to occur on a weekly basis, with others happening less frequently, and new ones evolving steadily for the first two years of the change initiative. The forums ranged in length from two to eight hours, involved as few as three and as many as seventy individuals from across the plant. The plant manager stated his intention was to spur debate in these forums about which actions would be most in line with creating the new organization, without the political hierarchy of the old culture. His intention aligned with Coopey and Burgoyne's (2000) argument that political change needs to be part of organizational learning, in that he frequently reiterated the need to replace a hierarchical Christmas tree structure with a more amorphous, oak tree-like structure to nurture learning.

These forums were meant to work within the vision, mission and values that had been more or less imposed by the new plant manager and senior management in the company. The vision had been articulated by the senior management team as 'World class people working together to make world class coke' (CC Working Party, 2001: 45). It was intended that this vision involved people being willing to embrace new ideas, being reliable and dedicated to the organization, being team oriented, highly skilled and motivated to achieve a high quality product in the most effective manner. The values included such things as sharing information, respect for others' viewpoints, being honest and open, and being optimistic about what can be achieved. The mission, as decided by these managers, was 'to secure the future of the CC business' (CC Working Party, 2001: 11). Within that mission, the strategic objectives consisted of eight items concerned with: meeting a particular benchmark coke price; achieving environmental discharge license requirements; optimizing community relationships to allow them to continue to operate; achieving zero accidents; establishing a proud work force where ideas are valued and efforts are aligned with the business goals; meeting customer expectations on quality, quantity and delivery needs; meeting employee expectations; and, optimizing the use of assets (CC Working Party, 2001).

The broad goal of the forums was to engage discussion on everyday events at the plant, to question existing practices and clarify the vision and principles behind the change initiative. While participants in these forums did discuss detailed and concrete issues in relation to the operation of the plant and change in the organization (such as shiftwork patterns), the forums were neither simply nor predominantly decision-making settings. The plant manager expressed the hope that they would stimulate participants to launch their own initiatives, establishing spin-off forums to pursue changes that they were passionate about.

One of these spin-off forums, or project team, provided the empirical base for this research. This project team, located within the CC operation, was originally named Coke Inc., and initially consisted of three core-manufacturing managers, that is the superintendents. They occupied the most senior managerial roles within the coke-making operation and they reported directly to the plant manager. They had successfully and proudly resided for many years in the traditional organizational culture, and in those roles, they were also the high profile gatekeepers for the change processes. If they did not change the way they worked through strongly developing their learning and leadership competency then the entire change process would stall. Therefore, these superintendents needed to reconstruct their own roles and responsibilities to assist the change process, and for later, when the culture change became embedded in the organization. Their specific aims for their project were defined as: first, to redefine their roles and their relationships and responsibilities in accordance with the new vision and values of the organization; secondly, to practise new leadership skills; and, thirdly, to explicitly and mutually learn through this project team process. After some six months, the composition of the project team changed to involve up to 16 members in the team, which included the project sponsor and lower level managers in the organization. Also accompanying this change was a project name change to the Cokemaking Leadership Team – or, as it was referred to as, the CLT. These changes were a direct response to context issues surrounding the project.

In this project team, and despite all the superintendents' previous and extensive training and development activities and project management experience, attempting to make learning and learning-how-to-learn such a deliberate part of their everyday project practice posed an immense challenge to them from their existing cultural frames of experience. Focusing the research on these three participants in this dynamic project setting as they jointly and explicitly confronted these ambiguous project-learning challenges presented an exciting and valuable opportunity to collaboratively explore and then develop a rich understanding of project learning. Henceforth, the learning behaviours and activities observed and experienced by these three core members of this project team (i.e. Bill, Len and Steve) while they participated in the project, both separately and then with the other 13 members of the team, constitute the rich empirical data and illustrations presented in the chapters that follow. These reported empirical examples also embody the learning dynamics observed across the full membership of the case study project team.

1.4 The structure of this book

In an orderly way, the seven chapters within this book introduce and discuss a raft of conceptual and pragmatic issues about learning in the project environment. In the majority of the chapters hereafter, the conceptual discussions are intermingled with the rich empirical illustrations (quotations, vignettes and stories) from the project case study. This approach, as well as intending to help you become quite conversant with the challenging conceptual issues presented, will help your understanding of the practical implications or manifestations of those issues in the field. In presenting the material in this way, it is also intended that this book be considered approachable by both practitioner and academic audiences interested in learning in project settings.

Following the introduction provided in Chapter 1, Chapters 2 and 3 establish the key conceptual frameworks that informed and guided this research. As such, these chapters constitute a highly appropriate review of the cross-disciplinary literature relating to the topic under focus. Specifically, Chapter 2 provides an analysis and discussion on key conceptual frameworks in the learning field, for example the cognitive and situated dimensions of learning. In so doing, you are introduced to the learning literature landscape relevant to learning within projects. Since it critically underpins the conceptual arguments posited in this book, this chapter proceeds to explore the situated dimension of learning in some detail. It also discusses the relationship between the cognitive and the situated dimensions of learning – which is important, since the trajectory of this book moves away from a notion of learning as only being primarily a cognitive activity. The chapter closes off by arguing that this situated dimension of learning offers the greatest potential avenue to improve the quantum and the quality of the total learning activity within projects.

Chapter 3 first provides an analysis and discussion on literature concerning sociological perspectives and learning from within and external to the project management field. These sections articulate and elaborate on the limited literature focused on learning in project management and help establish the contribution that the findings from this study make to project management knowledge. The next section in this chapter then introduces a conceptualization of a project team from a learning perspective. This conceptualization challenges traditional conceptions of project teams as characteristically being discrete, temporal and rational entities where learning and acting are considered disconnected. It is the intention in this section to convey to you a view of project teams as being both task and learning-focused where learning and action are intimately entwined and embedded within a complex system of social and contextual relationships. This conception also encapsulates a notion of learning between project participants as being mediated by local sociological elements, and as such, this section provides the final important piece of the conceptual framework that underpins the discussions contained in the chapters that follow. The final section of this chapter then builds on the preceding discussion to articulate and illustrate a model of project situated learning behaviour. This model incorporates five sociological constraint/enabler elements that impacted situated learning activity in the case study project (see Figure 3.3). It also establishes the framework for the detailed discussions provided in forthcoming chapters.

Chapters 4, 5 and 6 continue to stress the importance of the situated dimension of project learning through elaborating on the key empirical findings from this research, that is the five sociological constraint/enabler elements. Specifically, Chapter 4 provides an insight into the impacts on the situated learning activity of project participants resulting from the intrapersonal constraint/enabler element of cognitive style. Chapter 5 explores the interpersonal constraint/enabler elements of learning relationships and pyramid of authority. Chapter 6 details the infrastructural constraint/enabler elements for project situated learning, being, knowledge management and situational context.

Chapter 7 draws together the core findings or issues for situated learning as identified in this study, and emphasizes the implications they have for practice and for further research in the field. This chapter also comments on the limitations of this study and the opportunities for future research. To partially close off, and as a means to further stimulate your interest in project situated learning, this chapter then provides some probing questions on this topic for your reflective assessment. Through your consideration of these questions, you may develop some indication of your propensity and approaches towards cultivating situated learning in project contexts.

2
Conceptualizing Learning Within a Project

This chapter helps to conceptualize learning within a project context by introducing and appraising some core conceptual frameworks concerning learning, and to convey a sense of their relationship to each other. It begins by presenting a focused discussion and analysis of different organizational perspectives on learning, and then, in following sections, moves this conceptual discussion onto learning at the individual and group levels. At that juncture, it first explores the key cognitive learning theories – which spotlight how the cognitive dimension of learning is intimately located within social practice. The discussion then moves onto situated learning theory and explores the key constructs in this theory. In the final section of this chapter, the relationship between the situated and the cognitive dimensions of learning is elaborated on, and the reasons established as to why situated learning theory was the prime conceptual input that informed and guided the work of this study. Consequently, given the analysis provided in this chapter, and coupled to the findings presented in forthcoming chapters, this book challenges readers to consider that learning is not only a cognitive activity, but rather it is primarily a social and practical activity that requires deliberate and systematic attention if one seeks to improve the quantum and the quality of learning activity within a project (or in any other context).

2.1 Organizational perspectives on learning

As organizations confront the globalization of competition, changing economic and social values regarding knowledge and intellectual capital, restructuring and de-layering of management structures, and computerization and other high technology infrastructures, they need to respond to those challenges in an adaptive and flexible way – which places a premium on learning to facilitate survival and growth (Hedberg, 1981; Leonard-Barton, 1992, 1995; Schein, 1993; Miner and Mezias, 1996; Tsang, 1997; Choo, 1998; Denton, 1998; Starkey, 1998; Kezsbom and Edward, 2001; Ingelgård *et al.*, 2002). Not surprisingly then, organizational learning (OL) conceptualizations are the focus of considerable attention, and are addressed by a broad range of disciplinary literatures covering organization theory and development, sociology, industrial economics and management, strategy, economic history, business management, innovation studies, cultural anthropology and psychology (Dodgson, 1993; Garvin, 1993; Easterby-Smith, 1997; Mitki *et al.*, 1997; Ingelgård *et al.*, 2002). Despite this growing popularity of the term OL, and the acceptance of its importance for organizational survival in dynamic and unstable operating environments, there is little consensus in terms of definition, perspective, conceptualization and methodology (Shrivastava, 1983; Fiol and Lyles, 1985; Nicolini and Meznar, 1995; Tsang, 1997; Crossan *et al.*, 1999; Teare and Monk, 2002).

As an abecedarian plunging into these choppy waters of OL literature from a springboard of project management, one is promptly exposed to this diversity of thought and differing perspectives in this field. This diversity in part can be understood in the observation that while general principles and aspirations of OL are fairly well established, OL research is diverse and unfocused and should be considered a multidisciplinary field (Easterby-Smith, 1997). Hence, as Easterby-Smith *et al.* (2000) suggest, the OL landscape is both dynamic and continually evolving. Crossan *et al.* (1999) suggest that this diversity has resulted because different researchers have applied the concept of OL in different domains. For example, Huber (1991) takes an information-processing perspective in effecting behavioural change, Nonaka and Takeuchi (1995) deal with product innovation, and March and Olsen (1975) explore the limitations on learning of the cognitive limitations of managers (Crossan *et al.*, 1999). More broadly, Richter (1998) suggests that much of the literature on OL till now developed theory on the functioning of an organization's perception and thinking, its rational brain or memory systems. She (and others) suggest more empirical work in different types of organizations is needed in order to develop a deeper understanding of an organization's circulatory system, the veins and capillaries of OL, and how the work of the circulatory system (i.e. involving the actual learning practices) affects the functioning of the body in general (Shrivastava, 1983; Miner and Mezias, 1996; Richter, 1998). Likewise, Weick and Westley (1996) emphasize the value in more closely examining the workings of cultural systems involving language, material artefacts and action routines to better understand learning and learning tensions in organizational settings. Or, as Garvin (1993: 78) puts it in raw terms, 'Beyond high philosophy and grand themes lie the gritty details of practice.' This book attempts to make explicit some of those gritty details associated with learning in a project team situation.

As part of the process of delving specifically into OL, one needs to very briefly explore the associated term of learning organization (LO) in a bid to achieve clarity between these often interchangeably used terms (Gherardi, 1999). Generally speaking, OL is a concept used to describe certain types of learning activity that take place in an organization, while the LO tag refers to a particular type of organization which is good at OL (Tsang, 1997). Tsang (1997) contends that this distinction between LO and OL is based on the dichotomy between descriptive and prescriptive research (Gherardi, 1999). Tsang postulates that prescriptive writings on the LO are concerned with how an organization should learn, as they target an action-oriented practitioner audience. Therein, this literature adopts definitions incorporating actual behavioural change, but lacks methodological research rigour. Descriptive researchers on OL are concerned with how an organization does learn, and they strive for scientific rigour (Tsang, 1997; Easterby-Smith *et al.*, 2000; Sun and Scott, 2003).

Perhaps because of the prescriptive orientation of the LO literature as posited by Tsang (1997), people tend to see the LO as a journey which is difficult and hazardous (Smith and Saint-Onge, 1996), murky and confusing, and difficult to penetrate (Garvin, 1993; Gold, 1997). The reason managers might see this journey as hazardous and confusing is that the concept of the LO ranks more on the level of a powerful ideological slogan for developing organizations, which provokes emotive and differential commitment and meanings between people (Garvin, 1993; Dunphy *et al.*, 1997; Steiner, 1998). Hence, accompanying this ideology has been a focus on the outcomes of learning, rather than on an OL process focus that provides frameworks for learning action (Dodgson, 1993).

Various definitions of LO prevail (Ellinger *et al.*, 2002), but essentially they all revolve around a theme of an LO being one that is 'continually expanding its capacity to create its own future' (Senge, 1990: 14). This theme incorporates a notion of organizational competence and development through continuous learning, by individuals within the organization and by the organization itself (by way of altering organizational norms, behaviours, values and communal mental maps). Continuous learning thus increases the knowledge and understanding of the organization, its relationship with its environment, and its ability to adapt and transform its behaviours and practices, and perform better over time (Pedler *et al.*, 1989; Senge, 1990; Galer and Van Der Heijden, 1992; Dodgson, 1993; Garvin, 1993; Kim, 1993; Pearn *et al.*, 1994; Gephart *et al.*, 1996; Watkins and Marsick, 1996; Dunphy *et al.*, 1997; Tsang, 1997; Mumford, 2000; Ellinger *et al.*, 2002; Saint-Onge and Wallace, 2002). Clearly, the learning and learning processes of individuals and groups (being the agents of OL), and the utilization of that learning in developing new systems and practices for the organization are central to this theme of an LO (Galer and Van Der Heijden, 1992; Dodgson, 1993). Put simply, and in unison with Tsang (1997), OL activity is a pre-requisite for an LO. Therefore, for the purposes of this book, OL and LO are unambiguously linked terms, and can be considered a conjoined whole within the broad theoretical landscape enveloping this study.

The different views on OL congregate around three broad perspectives. These perspectives include: *Cognitive*, which includes organizational higher and lower level cognition processes (i.e. operational and conceptual levels of organizational learning); *Behavioural* (action), which has an outcome focus by wanting to see a change in organizational actions as a result of learning; and, *Sociological*, wherein, meaning and actions and learning are a result of collective social practice. These three perspectives provide a broad structure on which to group and understand the OL literature, whilst helping to minimize the confusion resulting from the diversity of definitions provided by researchers in the field. These perspectives are borrowed from and reflected in the work of Fiol and Lyles (1985) and Tsang (1997).

The cognitive perspective of OL

Tsang (1997) considers the cognitive perspective to be generally concerned with knowledge, understanding and insights, that is the organization gaining knowledge regardless of whether that knowledge is converted into actions. As such, it forms an information-processing view of OL (Richter, 1998). Fiol and Lyles (1985) extend this definition to suggest that this perspective involves the extent of cognitive development, or the level of learning that takes place. Fiol and Lyles (1985) refer to lower levels of learning, where adjustments are made to parameters within set rules and structures that remain unchallenged, and higher levels of learning, where those determining rules, structures and values are challenged and redefined. This is similar to Senge's (1990) distinction between adaptive and generative learning and Dodgson's (1991) tactical and strategic learning, wherein, the lower level is assumed to be the normal state of the organization and the higher level is assumed to be the desired state (Easterby-Smith, 1997).

At an individual level, this definition also aligns to Argyris and Schön's (1978) discussion on single, double and triple loop learning (learning-how-to-learn) and Kim's (1993) levels of learning that he terms as operational and conceptual levels linking thought and action. Or, put more broadly at the individual level, 'the cognitive aspect views learning as the transformations of internal cognitive structures' (Wenger, 1998: 279). In a project team situation, lower-level learning might include using standardized procedures to solve problems; using standardized procedures to manage subcontractors; using formalized routine project process rules without question. Higher-level learning could include challenging the norms of the project process and developing new frames of reference, for example challenging and changing the scope of the project, actively seeking new information and input from stakeholders, or pursuing new customized approaches to dealing with subcontractors. This double loop or higher-level learning results in a change in the values of theories-in-use as well as in the underlying system strategies and assumptions that exist within a context (Argyris and Schön, 1978). This double-loop learning also then involves changing the organization's knowledge base and its specific competencies and routines (Dodgson, 1993).

The behavioural perspective of OL

Fiol and Lyles (1985) suggest that the organizational behavioural outcomes, which they define as the content of learning, reflect the patterns and/or the cognitive associations that have developed, that is the organizational behavioural changes resulting from the learning. This stimulus – response perspective highlights an important issue about the differences between cognition and behaviour, that is an organization can change behaviour without any cognitive development, and alternatively knowledge may be gained but is not translated into any accompanying change in behaviour (Fiol and Lyles, 1985). Similarly, Tsang (1997) defines the behavioural perspective as consisting of a change in behaviour by the organization, and it can be either an actual change or a potential behavioural change (consisting of the lessons learnt that would have an impact on the organization's future behaviour).

The sociological perspective of OL

This social-constructivist perspective on OL provides a challenge to the traditional idea that learning takes place only within the heads of individuals, or in organizational systems and structures (Easterby-Smith *et al.*, 2000). This social-constructivist perspective suggests that we consider organizations as interpretive systems which are created to make sense of the world, and that products or services get produced as a by-product of collective sensemaking processes (Richter, 1998). Weick (1995) defines sensemaking as an ongoing individual and social process which involves people making retrospective sense of the situations they find themselves in, while they construct their identities. Proponents of this sociological perspective suggest that individual and OL occur through the conversations and the interactions between people as they negotiate meanings and their identities, while they participate within a community revolving around a practice (Brown and Duguid, 1991; Lave and Wenger, 1991; Cook and Yanow, 1993; Wenger, 1998; Dixon, 1999; Gherardi, 1999; Gherardi and Nicolini, 2000; Wenger *et al.*, 2002). This focus on the mutually determining interactions of individuals within their socio-cultural settings has shifted learning perspectives from an epistemology of possession (i.e. the cognitive and behavioural dimensions) to one of evolving practice, and thereby introduced a stronger emphasis on socially oriented approaches to the understanding of learning and knowing (Easterby-Smith *et al.*, 2000). Wenger (1998: 96) succinctly sums up this relationship between learning and practice (with all its social interactional processes) as: 'Learning is the engine of practice, and practice is the history of that learning.' The notable symbolic interactionist George Herbert Mead (1934: 223) also captures this sentiment in stating that 'mind can never find expression and can never come into existence at all, except in terms of a social environment'.

Whilst many ongoing debates on OL prevail (e.g. the levels of analysis being the individual or the organization, double and single loop learning, and the nature and location of learning and how to investigate it (Easterby-Smith *et al.*, 2000)), the current and potentially the most fruitful ideas in contention in the field revolve around the social-constructivist perspective of learning – for individuals and organizations. This perspective sees practice and activity as the new units of learning analysis and suggests that the traditional emphasis on the individual, the formal team or the institutionalized organization as the key unit of analysis may be rather less appropriate (Easterby-Smith *et al.*, 2000). Such a focus on work practices offers future operational consequences. That being, developing an understanding of how learning happens in the workplace may help devise better ways of sustaining and fostering learning processes, particularly since organizations are becoming increasingly difficult to think of as stable entities with defined boundaries (Easterby-Smith *et al.*, 2000). This field severely challenges long-held views of how people learn and how the social and material context relates to the learning of an individual and an organization. The authors in this sociological field are suggesting (and in my opinion, correctly so) that the social relations and context take a predominant position in the learning process, and by that recognition require significant understanding and facilitation to promote learning. As might be readily appreciated, when you open a door on context and relationships, a whole new array of less explored issues emerge on the learning front, for example politics, organizational structures, informality and formality, language and emotions, conversations, narrative, storytelling and dialogue, identity and the interrelations of objects and artefacts with learning (Easterby-Smith *et al.*, 2000).

2.2 The relationship of OL to individual learning

There has also been a longstanding debate about the relationship of OL to individual learning (IL), and, is OL simply the sum of what individuals learn? There appears to now be some consensus that IL is the point of departure for OL and is a contributor to it, and also that OL resides in the systems and structures and processes of an organization (Hedberg, 1981; Shrivastava, 1983). As Hedberg (1981: 6) suggests, 'it would be a mistake to conclude that organizational learning is nothing more than the cumulative result of their members learning...Members come and go, leadership changes, but organizations' memories preserve certain behaviours, mental maps, norms and values over time.'

There are two main themes revolving around this OL–IL relationship. These include:

- *Individual learning is the prerequisite for OL* since people are the agents of organizational action and therefore OL (Argyris and Schön, 1978; Hedberg, 1981; Senge, 1990; Kim, 1993; Probst and Buchel, 1997; Crossan *et al.*, 1999; Dixon, 1999; Andrews and Delahaye, 2000).
- *Dialogue and conversational learning and storytelling* (Gold, 1997; McKenna, 1999; Tenkasi and Mohrman, 1999; Baker *et al.*, 2002) *helps to bridge the IL–OL divide*, since they generate individual understanding and collective actions, and thereby individual knowledge can become embedded within an organization's collective memories, structures and processes (Argyris and Schön, 1978; Crossan *et al.*, 1999; Dixon, 1999; Oswick *et al.*, 2000). In effect, those processes are the transfer vehicles for IL to be part of OL.

These themes of dialogue, conversational learning and storytelling are an increasingly popular process for stimulating OL and IL, and in stimulating social change through group inquiry across multiple contexts and situations (Fulmer *et al.*, 1998; King and Rowe, 1999; Tenkasi and Mohrman, 1999). Clearly also, these themes are highly employee-centred methods for stimulating OL and IL. For example, Gold (1997) examines the way learning may occur in organizations through ways of talking or storytelling within nets of collective action, and how the centrality of language, discourse and storytelling is a key feature of an approach to understanding social constructionism. Baker *et al.* (2002) (while also being strong proponents of experiential learning) assert that much of the learning that occurs through experience emerges out of the social and interactive dimensions of conversation amongst people. They define conversation (in all its forms, e.g. verbal and written) as a process of interpreting and understanding human experience, and conversational learning as learning that embraces differences as a source of new understanding, and when it questions assumptions, it can be called deep learning.

Coombs and Smith (1998) see these conversations at two levels – one internal, involving internal reflection framed by an individual's mental models, and the other, external, which is governed by social relationships with other people. Tacit and explicit dimensions of knowledge interplay in conversational-learning processes (consistent with Nonaka and Takeuchi's [1995] seminal work on knowledge creation) and within that process, an opportunity to build trust (the fundamental source of tacit knowledge) and share experiences presents itself. The repeated sharing of experiences from a basis of mutual trust is at the heart of conversational learning (Baker *et al.*, 2002). Baker *et al.* (2002) contend that whilst there is much agreement between the concepts of conversation and dialogue, there are also important differences. In their review of the meanings of these two words, Baker *et al.* (2002: 10) describe the meanings for conversation as emphasizing the communal, sensual and emotional aspects of conversation, and that dialogue is more related to 'opposing voices in search of a truth', which emphasizes conflict and rhetoric and involves the exploration of thinking and language. These authors refer to their conversational learning approach as a process of reaching interpersonal understanding, where all participants' contributions are equally valued, and it does not involve the transmission of pre-existent meanings from one person to another (Baker *et al.*, 2002).

Therefore, one might conclude that attending to the environment to enable and facilitate dialogue and conversations is vitally important for the IL-OL exchange to occur. Moreover, organizations have the opportunity to engage and manage their learning more integrally and more effectively within their daily workplace situations (and thereby support IL and OL), rather than it being an opportunistic, isolated or hindered activity (Hedberg 1981; Jones and Hendry, 1992; Dodgson, 1993; Garvin, 1993; Mumford, 1994; Nonaka and Takeuchi, 1995; Antonacopoulou, 1997; Argyris, 1999; Dixon, 1999; Gherardi, 1999; Hong, 1999; Senge et al., 1999; Billett, 2000; Hager, 2001; Keegan and Turner, 2001; Teare and Monk, 2002).

In sum, this section of the chapter has provided an illustrative account of the different organizational perspectives on learning within the OL-LO literature field, that is cognitive, behavioural and sociological perspectives. Given its fundamental and broad influence on learning in any context and in consideration of the aims of this research, this study embraced the sociological perspective of OL. Such an engagement places a focus on the relationships, the practices and the context of the project environment to facilitate learning. Or, as Easterby-Smith *et al.* (2000) have suggested, learning perspectives have moved to an epistemology of evolving practice, which then opens up to scrutiny a plethora of less-explored sociological issues impacting learning activity. Organizations (including temporal organizations like project teams) have opportunities to purposefully manage these sociological environments, to both enable and positively stimulate the social learning processes between people and to develop participant learning skills – and thereby directly influence IL and OL. In this study, this perspective has encouraged direct engagement with the project practice (and activities therein) as the unit of learning analysis. It has also placed an emphasis on identifying ways to support and promote dialogue, conversations and storytelling between participants as the principal processes necessary to cultivate learning within a project.

2.3 The cognitive dimension of learning

This section and the remainder of this chapter move away from the more global theoretical discussions involving OL/LO to levels which provide a more direct theoretical input or comparative theoretical background for the research reported on in this book. Such a focus initially draws our attention to cognitive learning theory, which has emerged as the predominantly recognized and generally accepted individual learning theory. This has primarily come about through the publication of the seminal works of some notable authors in the learning field, for example

Argyris and Schön (1978), Kolb (1984) and Senge (1990). The following discussion on cognitive learning theory will, therefore, focus only on these pre-eminent authors in the field, as their collective work provides a sufficient analysis of the theory for the purposes of this book.

The cognitive theories presented include Kolb's (1984) experiential learning theory, Argyris and Schön's (1978) theory-of-action perspective, and Senge's (1990) five disciplines perspective. In forecasting some of the discussion that follows, cognitive learning may be viewed as an individual cerebral or psychological process, intimately engaged in reciprocal determination with the context and its sociological aspects. Therein, individuals try to make sense of their experiences by running them past their cognitive maps or mental models, possibly reforming their models and deciding on their behavioural actions to be taken, in accordance with the conditions of their context.

Underpinning psychological or cognitive theories on learning is an assumption that conflict (caused by error or different information) is an essential condition for learning and acts as a motor driving the learning process (Dodgson, 1993). That is, variation occurs in experiences, which then prompts individuals into reflection on the events and adjustments to their perceptions and actions. Coombs and Smith (1998) consider an individual's internalized stimulus of reflection as a free-will act of conversational constructivism – a constructivist learning event, wherein the personal constructs operate as a reflective process and are underpinned by the reflective skills of the learner (Coombs and Smith, 1998). This process is reflected in the works of Kolb (1984), Dewey (1938), Lewin (1946) and Piaget (1953), where they offer slightly different versions of a common experiential learning cycle, involving phases of having an experience, reflective observation, abstract conceptualization and active experimentation. David Kolb (1984) actually synthesized the experiential work of John Dewey (higher education), Jean Piaget (cognitive development) and Kurt Lewin (organizational development), and consequently formed a unique perspective on learning and development (Kolb et al., 2002). These works of Dewey, Piaget and Lewin have also provided the basis for applications of experiential learning in areas such as social policy and action, competence-based education, adult development programmes and career development, experiential education and curriculum development (Kolb, 1984). However, for the purposes of this book, in relation to presenting a valid and economical discussion on this literature field, and given Kolb's work is a synthesis of these three founding fathers of experiential learning theory, I will only specifically elaborate on Kolb's (1984) experiential learning cycle.

Dixon (1999: 41) sums up the essence of Kolb's experiential learning theory as: 'learning is about interpreting what we experience in the world and that we each create our own unique interpretation and that interpretation mediates our actions'. Kolb (1984: 38) simply describes experiential learning as 'the process whereby knowledge is created through the transformation of experience'. Some authors have offered criticisms of Kolb's learning model surrounding its apparent ignorance of the sociological aspects impacting an individual's learning process, that is the human need to interact with each other and with their social and cultural environments to enhance the learning processes (Holman *et al.*, 1997; Miettinen, 2000). However, even with such significant limitations, Kolb's approach is the most widely used descriptive model for learning as a continuous process. Kolb has also been criticized for taking experience as the point of departure, where perhaps a better interpretation might be that the learning cycle describes the production of experience in the process of learning, rather than experience being the starting point (Järvinen and Poikela, 2001). Despite these criticisms, what is important for this discussion is that Kolb's learning cycle includes experience as a key component in the individual knowledge-creation process. This ability to learn from experience can be divided into two questions: 'How does what is outside get in? And, how does what is inside get out? [] Learning from experience thus involves balancing surrender and mastery, taking in experiences and others' views of them, and expressing one's own conclusions in thoughts and action' (Baker *et al.*, 2002: 2).

As well as being continuous and grounded in experience, Kolb (1984) also posits that learning requires the resolution of conflicts between dialectically opposed modes of adaptation to the world, for example the conflict between concrete and abstract concepts, and involves transactions between the person and the environment. As such, the experiential learning process is not strictly only a person-centred psychological view of learning, but one indicating that individual behaviour is a function of both the person and the environment and a result of this reciprocal interpenetrating determination (Kolb, 1984; Beard and Wilson, 2002). Similarly, Jean Piaget, the French developmental psychologist, presented a theory that described how intelligence is shaped by experience, that is intelligence is a product of the interaction between the person and the environment (Kolb, 1984). In this condition, existing cognitive structures and the knowledge they engender are continually challenged by new knowledge which does not fit, and these structures are eventually reorganized so that new knowledge is better integrated

(Dodgson, 1993). Also, when discussing social learning theory, Bandura (1977) claims that the psychological functioning of an individual is a result of the reciprocal determination between personal characteristics (e.g. mental models, cognitive styles), environmental influences (e.g. social frameworks, political imperatives, physical and psychological support systems) and behaviour (actions). That is, each of those factors influences the others in an interlocking fashion (Bandura, 1977; Kolb, 1984). These transactions between the person and the environment highlight the interdependency of both the individual and the environment in affecting change, behaviour and learning processes.

Specifically, Kolb (1984) describes two dialectically related modes of grasping one's experience. These consist of apprehension, where one grasps tangible felt experience without any need for inquiry or analytical confirmation, and comprehension, where one grasps an experience by drawing abstract symbolic conceptualizations about it and making the experience communicable between people. He also describes two dialectically related modes of transforming experience, consisting of intention, where one learns the meaning of an experience to oneself by internally reflecting on the experience, and extension, where one actively experiments with the previously grasped experience, that is one actively intervenes in the learning milieu and a new experience results in further movement through the learning cycle (Kolb, 1984). In that cycle, 'Learning, the creation of knowledge and meaning, occurs through the active extension and grounding of ideas and experiences in the external world and through internal reflection about the attributes of these experiences and ideas' (Kolb, 1984: 52) (see Kolb's experiential learning cycle diagram in Kolb [1984: 42] and Baker *et al.* [2002: 53]).

Moving from the experiential learning theorists onto other major contributors to this field of cognitive learning theory brings us to the popular OL theorist, Peter Senge (1990). He stresses the need to take a systems approach to learning, and his focus is predominantly on individual cognition, where we 'learn by using our brains and our ability to think in the abstract about the world' (Elkjaer, 2001: 155). Specifically, Senge (1990) attributes OL primarily to the personal learning attributes of organizational members – involving five disciplines. These consist of: Systems thinking – where an individual views the world and its processes as an abstract integrated whole rather than a series of isolated parts; Personal mastery – where a person becomes committed to their own lifelong learning and involves clarifying and deepening their own personal vision and focusing individual energies; Building a shared vision – where a leader unveils shared pictures of the future held by individuals that will foster genuine commitment and engagement, and a common sense of identity; Team learning – which involves the capacity of team members to suspend assumptions and enter into a genuine thinking together and engaging in dialogue; Mental models – which are the individual's deeply ingrained assumptions, viewpoints and generalizations about the world which guide how we interpret that world and how we take action (Senge, 1990).

This theme of mental models and their influence on our interpretations and behaviours is also a predominant attribute in Argyris and Schön's (1978) theory-of-action perspective on OL. Argyris and Schön (1978) contend that sustained achievement of the values of OL is seen as depending on the engagement of double-loop learning processes, wherein defensive routines of the players are exposed and evaluated in workshop situations (Dunphy et al., 1997). Agyris and Schön (1978) find that people are socially conditioned to use the cognitive model they refer to as Model I. That model is characterized by the need to control, maximize winning, suppress emotions and be rational. The consequences for people in that approach tend to be defensive behaviour, miscommunication and single-loop learning. Alternatively, Argyris and Schön's (1978) Model II behaviour is based on directly observable data and requires that people support their advocacy of positions with illustration and with inquiry into other peoples' views – thus, increasing learning by publicly challenging existing frames or assumptions. Model II attempts to test and make explicit individuals' assumptions about the dynamics going on in their organizations.

Argyris and Schön's (1978) argument is that people should aim to move from a Model I position to a Model II position. Therein, they challenge existing theories and reject unilateral control, as compared to Model I and its governing variables of rationally defining goals and controlling the environment in pursuit of those goals. The consequence of pursuing the path to Model II is that there would be an emphasis on double-loop learning, where individuals confront their basic assumptions behind their views of others and the world, and invite confrontation of their own assumptions and test these publicly (Argyris and Schön, 1978). In achieving this desired theory-of-action state, people and organizations will learn. If individuals do not know how to double-loop learn, then they do not know how to discover new knowledge, to invent new ways to discover and learn, to produce the learning interventions and to evaluate and to generalize the value and performance of their interventions (Argyris and Schön, 1978). Given this brief discussion on both Senge's (1990) and Argyris and Schön's (1978) perspectives, it is obvious that they attribute OL primarily to the learning of the individual, mediated by individual personal attributes (Dunphy *et al.*, 1997). However, underpinning the activation of these critically reflective individual processes are the context conditions. Therefore, establishing conditions that aid these reflective activities to proceed are also vitally important for the individual cognitive learning process.

In sum, in addition to providing a comparative theoretical base on learning, the principal contributions from this section on cognitive learning theory to the arguments presented in this book involve two items. First, experiential learning is a process which involves having an experience, which we interpret and reflect on, from which we then develop abstract conceptualizations and action processes, which we later enact within the learning environment and create another learning experience. Therefore, having an experience within an environment is a key component of an individual's cognitive knowledge-creation process. Second, cognitive learning being a continuous and individual cerebral process is also mediated by individuals' personal cognitive attributes such as their mental models. Sustained learning is considered to involve critical reflection processes, wherein individuals confront, challenge and alter their prevailing mental models and assumptions that guide their behaviours. However, cognitive learning is intimately linked to social practice (and not divorced from it) through individuals having experiences (including critical reflection experiences) within some form of environment. Therefore, in addition to an individual's personal cognitive attributes impacting knowledge creation, this linkage highlights that multifarious sociological influences within an environment also impact or mediate the critical reflective processes and the cognitive learning processes of individuals. Therein, it implicates the importance of organizing the sociological environment to assist the total knowledge-creation process of individuals.

2.4 The situated dimension of learning

Situated learning theory

This section presents and discusses situated learning theory (SLT), which provides the theoretical framework to interpret the findings from this study. Building on conclusions reached in previous sections of this chapter, learning can always be considered a practical accomplishment that takes place amongst and through other people (where learners construct their meanings and understandings and learn through their social interactions within a context) and is not simply and only an individual cognitive activity (where learners as individual actors possess and process information and modify their mental models) (Gherardi *et al.*, 1998; Richter, 1998; Gherardi and Nicolini, 2000). After reading this section, and coupled to the previous discussions in this chapter, one should develop an appreciation of the dual (and yet complementary) dimensions of learning, that is being a situated, socially constructed process, as well as a cognitive activity in the minds of individuals (Gherardi *et al.*, 1998). This duality should not cause confusion – merely confirm and highlight the double dimension of learning and the importance of dealing with the situated dimension if one seeks to pursue the full learning potential present in any project situation.

Lave and Wenger (1991) see situated learning theory simply as an analytical perspective on learning, or a way of understanding learning (Fox, 1997) which acknowledges that most learning occurs on the job in culturally embedded ways within a community of practice (Lave and Wenger, 1991). The main characteristic of SLT has been its discussion of the concept of context, in contrast to cognitive learning theory, which regards context as the container of impersonal, detached, asocial, apolitical and ahistorical de-contextualized knowledge (Gherardi, 2001). The primary focus of this theory of learning is on learning as social participation, which refers to a more encompassing process of being active participants in the practices of social communities (Wenger, 1998; Park, 1999; Senge and Scharmer, 2001). Expanding on this primary focus, Wenger (1998) also nominates four components of a social theory of learning. These include:

> *Meaning* – concerns the way we experience our life and the world as meaningful (Wenger, 1998). This involves two conjoined processes involving: participation, where people take part in a community and its activities and interact with others in this process, and; reification, which involves people projecting their meanings of their practice into the world and then perceiving them as existing in the world, for example a smoke signal, words, a formulae (Wenger, 1998).
> *Practice* – concerns the way of talking about the shared historical and social context, frameworks and perspectives that can sustain mutual engagement in action by providing structure and meaning to what we do (Wenger, 1998).
> *Community* – concerns the way our social configurations are defined as worth pursuing and our participation is recognizable as competence

(Wenger, 1998). Community involves three dimensions. These include: mutual engagement, which determines a person's membership in a community of practice; joint enterprise, which involves members of a community of practice developing relations of mutual accountability around their negotiated actions; shared repertoire, which results from people in a community of practice being mutually engaged in a joint enterprise and in developing a shared repertoire of routines, words, tools, stories, actions and concepts (Wenger, 1998).

Identity in practice – concerns the way learning changes who we are, and creates personal histories of becoming full participants in the context of our communities in which we participate (Wenger, 1998). An identity in practice is a layering of events of participation and reification by which our experience and its social interpretation inform each other. In this interplay of participation and reification, our experience of life becomes one identity. Identity is a negotiated experience involving: community membership, where an individual becomes competent within a community of practice; learning trajectory, where learning is an event on an identity trajectory through which people give meaning to their engagement in practice; nexus of multi-membership, which involves the practices of people being involved in multiple communities of practice and how those experiences influence them in different communities of practice; the relation between the local and the global, which implies that we do not simply relate to only local practice issues but are concerned about connections to broader constellations of communities (Wenger, 1998).

Expectantly perhaps, these four components of a social theory of learning highlight the significant themes of SLT. Those being: knowledge and learning reside within a practice; the participation and interaction of people within a domain of practice; collective sensemaking (Weick, 1995) activities; and, the development of peoples' social and technical competencies and identities to function effectively within the practice. These notions of participation and interaction around a practice, the development of competency (particularly technical competency to perform tasks within a workplace) and the mutually determinant relationship of learning with the sociological aspects of contexts are also reflected either explicitly or implicitly in the workplace vocational learning literature (for examples, see Marsick, 1987; Marsick and Watkins, 1990; Garrick, 1998; Marsick and Watkins, 1999;

Matthews and Candy, 1999; Solomon, 1999; Billett, 2000, 2001a,b; Järvinen and Poikela, 2001).

In a similar vein to the workplace vocational learning literature, it is also worthwhile noting at this point that an increasing number of authors in the knowledge management field are also focussing their attention on the social dimension of knowledge management. Therein, they recognize and argue that knowledge is complex and multidimensional and in constant interactive social development within and between humans within their contexts (for examples, see Nonaka and Takeuchi, [1995], Davenport and Prusak, [1998], Lundin and Söderholm, [1998], Baumard, [1999], Swan et al., [1999], Andrews and Delahaye, [2000], Brown and Duguid, [2000], Wenger et al., [2002], Bresnen et al., [2003], Fernie et al., [2003]). Brown and Duguid (2000) for example, in their book on the social life of information, highlight how information is embedded in social relationships and institutions, and that this social dimension is just as important as the technical dimension of information technology. In contrast, the technical aspects of knowledge management, whilst important, play only a supporting role in knowledge creation and management processes – which perhaps presents a somewhat contrary view to that generally perceived in the wider project practitioner community at this time. Thus, the establishment and maintenance of the conditions or environments to support the dynamic social processes of participation, interaction, collaboration and dialogue between humans, as detailed for example by Nonaka and Takeuchi (1995), is therefore an essential harbinger for supporting knowledge-creation and effective knowledge-management processes. The arguments offered in this book may add to the burgeoning chorus within the knowledge-management community that declares attention to the situated and social relationships, and the sociological environment, to be critical for effective knowledge-creation and knowledge-exchange processes – at both the individual and organizational levels.

In helping us to understand learning (and in unison with those views expressed by Wenger [1998]), SLT, therefore, draws our attention to learning that takes place in everyday life, and within those contexts, the learning process is part of the activities and practices, and therefore, the social interactions of people within communities of people (Raelin, 1998; Fox, 2000; Billett, 2004). Knowledge resides in the social relations of the practice, and developing one's identity is part of becoming an insider in a community of practice (Gherardi, 2001). In an earlier work, Brown and Duguid (1991) also argued that learning, working and innovating were interrelated and complementary, and were neither conflicting nor problematic forces – hence, they see practice as essential to understanding work, knowledge being conjoined to practice, and learning being the connection between work and innovation. Practice connects knowing with doing and is highly improvisational, and is therefore considered a bricolage of material and mental, social and cultural resources, where people and the world are active bricoleurs, and therefore not docile or passive (Brown and Duguid, 1991; Gherardi, 2001).

This perspective is also reflected in the following comment from Agashae and Bratton (2001: 92), 'In the real world, competency and knowledge is acquired in the swampy lowlands of messy and ill-defined problems found in the indeterminate zones of practice. Through the concepts of knowing in action (tacit knowledge) and reflection in action (rethinking tacit knowledge) the individual develops competency (Garrison, 1991: 295).' Hence, learning as a practical activity is always a socially structured activity where the conditions and forms for learning are established unintentionally and tacitly by the community that shapes the practice – which makes learning evasive to many forms of planning (Gherardi *et al.*, 1998). In more specific and pragmatic terms, McLellan (1996) summarizes the key components of this situated learning process as involving: stories; reflection practices; cognitive apprenticeship – which attempts to enculturate people into authentic practices through activity and social interaction; collaboration; coaching; multiple practice – where learners engage repeated activities to develop knowledge and skills; articulation of learning skills – where learners articulate their knowledge, reasoning and problem-solving processes; and, the use of various technologies to support these learning processes.

The profound significance of this theoretical perspective on learning in a project setting can best be highlighted by summarizing the main themes of SLT, and then briefly commenting on their potential impact on learning in a project team. These themes include:

- Knowledge is conjoined to practice and therefore contextually situated and influenced by the social and cultural conditions of the practice (*project knowledge is therefore a direct result of the project practices and local mediating socio-cultural conditions*).
- Social participation and interaction within a practice are essential for learning and knowledge development (*learning and knowledge development and social/technical competency development of participants within a project team will be suppressed unless participants can actively participate together and interact*).

- SLT involves collective sensemaking (Weick, 1995) or meaning-making processes which help participants make sense of their world of practice and enable them to operate productively within it (*making sense of a project practice is always a collective process involving people, which then enables participants to develop individual ways of operating to successfully contribute to the project team*).

- The development of the identity of participants within a practice is a negotiated process, which involves both their experiences and perceived social competencies within a practice (*as an individual project team member develops both technical and social competencies within a project setting, they develop an identity within the team, which has been mutually negotiated through their interactions with other team members*).

Therefore, SLT moves beyond the limitations of cognitive learning theory to directly involve the complex mediating sociological aspects of a context in the learning or knowledge-creation process. This theory therefore provides a social-centred theoretical framework in which to interpret and understand the findings presented in this book.

Communities of practice

General issues

Situated learning theory and its construct of a COP are facilitating attempts to understand how different social contexts impact (i.e. facilitate or frustrate) learning (Brown and Duguid, 1991; Lave and Wenger, 1991; Wenger, 1998, Saint-Onge and Wallace, 2002; Wenger *et al.*, 2002). The seminal works on this topic generally remain unchallenged in terms of providing a basis for understanding this social dimension of learning. Therefore, at this point, it is appropriate to mention the definitions for COPs that are provided by the principal authors in the field. Wenger *et al.* (2002: 4–5) define a COP as 'groups of people who share a concern, a set of problems, or a passion about a topic, and who deepen their knowledge and expertise in this area by interacting on an ongoing basis. Communities of practice are everywhere... we belong to a number of them at work, at school and in our hobbies.' Lave and Wenger (1991: 98), in their seminal book on situated learning, offered the following definition of a COP,

> A community of practice is a set of relations among persons, activity and world over time and in relation with other tangential and overlapping communities of practice. A community of practice is an

intrinsic condition for the existence of knowledge... participation in the cultural practice in which any knowledge exists is an epistemological principle of learning.

Essentially then, this construct of a COP involves people participating within a practice, and over time, they negotiate and develop their own competencies and identities and common meanings. Within that process, a person moves from a legitimate peripheral role within the community to a more central role as they develop full competency to function effectively within the community. The development of the competence of individuals to participate and contribute fully to their communities is also conjoined to the development of the common practice that represents a community's learning history (Lave and Wenger, 1991). Therefore, this enculturation around a practice is not simply a one-way process, where individuals are forced into the existing practices of the community. It is rather a two-way process, where individuals also contribute to the ongoing development of the community itself, by challenging the prevailing norms of the community, and co-creating new values, symbols and artefacts (Wenger, 1998).

This co-determining feature of communities of practice (COPs) was illustrated in a relatively popular movie. The example I refer to is the movie titled *Patch Adams* (based on the book *Gezundheit!: Bringing good health to you, the medical system, and society through physician service, complementary therapies, humour, and joy* [Adams, 1993]). In this movie, Patch was the rebel trainee doctor in a Medical School, wherein he saw patients as whole people, and not just as slabs of meat or problems to be quickly solved. That prevailing community of practice in which Patch participated, that is the Medical School, was bound in tradition and elitist norms of behaviour. It strongly forged the identities of the students to comply with long-held traditional views of the medical doctor being revered as an expert, and the patient to be seen as a problem to be solved. In the book and in the movie, Patch (the newcomer to the community) saw it differently. He saw the patient relationship with the doctor as core to a holistic medical treatment of a patient's problems. Patch, being the newcomer to the community, was pushing the commonly understood boundaries of the COP, that is the norms, values, traditions and their perspectives on the world. Patch sums up this nexus in his book by writing the following manifesto and hanging it on the wall of the school, 'I came to school on two legs, but left on four wrapped in wool... the school emphasized how we looked, not how we act.... They gave us an image. We ironed it right in, stay-press. We carry it around with us to impress our friends, better still our patients' (Adams, 1993: 11). Whilst this may appear as an impediment to change in the context of the movie and the book, it does highlight how participants become enculturated into a COP and mutually define and share communal values, beliefs and views on the world – or, as Raelin (2000: 75) suggests, 'people unite in a common enterprise, develop a shared history as well as particular values, beliefs, ways of talking, and ways of doing things', and come together in the process of doing a job. The movie and the book also highlight that the practice and the shape of the community is dynamic and continues to evolve, as new people join and challenge existing community boundaries or norms as they go about establishing their own identities or competence within a domain of practice (Wenger, 1998).

Whilst off the cuff most people can think of similar and various COPs that they might belong to – for example the jogging club, the university department, the pottery class – Fox (2000) suggests that the concept of a COP is mostly left as an intuitive notion (where the boundaries are rather fluid and porous [Wenger, 1998; Wenger *et al.*, 2002; Garrety, Robertson and Badham, 2004]), and as such requires more rigorous evaluation. Communities of practice are essentially informal, and form around the engagement within a practice because, as Wenger (1998) notes, they are concerned with content, that is about learning as a living experience of negotiating meaning – not about form. A practice may (by default) align to institutionally defined boundaries, for example a department or unit, but the practice may develop despite the constraints of the institutionally defined boundaries (Wenger, 1998). Hence, COPs cannot be legislated into existence or defined by decree – they can be recognized, supported, encouraged and nurtured by an appropriate infrastructure, but they are not reified, designable units (Wenger, 1998; Wenger and Snyder, 2000). Similarly, Gherardi *et al.* (1998: 277–8) state that a COP 'is not a way to postulate the existence of a new informal grouping or social system within the organization, but it is a way to emphasize that every practice is dependent on social processes through which it is sustained and perpetuated, and that learning takes place through the engagement in that practice'. Consequently, organizations should recognize the power of COPs for knowledge creation and sharing (Peansupap and Walker, 2005) and provide the infrastructures to support them since they often lack organizational legitimacy and budgets and integration within the broader organization (Wenger and Snyder, 2000).

Fox's (2000) opinion on COPs requiring more rigorous evaluation is biased towards evaluating the relations of power – which he considers is undeveloped within such a domain. That is not say that these relations of power and politics in COPs do not achieve some coverage from some authors (see, for example, Lave and Wenger [1991] and Wenger [1998]), simply that more investigation of specific phenomena within the COPs might be valuable. In particular, Richter (1998) suggests that this social practice of learning and knowing in COPs requires more empirical evaluation so as to better understand the impact of COPs on knowledge creation and transfer within organizations. Broadly what these authors recognize is that this notion of COPs, whilst clearly valuable for developing an understanding of the social dimension of learning, can appear somewhat ambiguous or incomplete. As such, the concept of a COP could benefit from more and deeper evaluations undertaken from multiple perspectives across different empirical settings. Through conducting such evaluations, one may find different trajectories of relationships and power within a COP across different social settings compared to that established in antecedent research conducted by the seminal authors in the field, for example the master–apprentice relationship illustrated in Lave and Wenger's (1991) work.

Whilst acknowledging these more recent conversations on developing a greater understanding of COPs, perhaps more fundamentally important to note, however, is that a COP involves both explicit and implicit activities. In this vein, Saint-Onge and Wallace (2002) refer to COPs as the knowledge-exchange venues, where tacit knowledge and lessons learned from experience are exchanged between people, and where explicit and tacit knowledge blend together to enable people to take effective action and to create knowledge within their circumstances. This view of the importance of presenting the opportunities for tacit and explicit knowledge to commingle within a setting is also consistent with those sociological perspectives on knowledge-management practices expressed by prominent authors in the knowledge-management field, for example Nonaka and Takeuchi (1995). Saint-Onge and Wallace (2002: 16–17) refer to 'knowledge objects' (explicit material such as tools and documents) as codified explicit knowledge that is stored and available for people to access, and see the interaction of these knowledge objects and COPs (the venue fostering the knowledge-exchange processes and access to the tacit knowledge of the members of the community) as the pillars of their knowledge architecture. In sum, they see COPs as high trust vehicles to increase capabilities, and as a place where people assist the flow and generation of (explicit and tacit) knowledge in an organization (Saint-Onge and Wallace, 2002).

Furthermore, as in project teams, participation in a COP is essential, as things need to be done – relationships formed, processes redesigned, situations interpreted, actions developed and artefacts produced (Wenger, 1998; Hildreth *et al.*, 2000). However, participation within a COP is not detached from the outside world. Rather, the connections to the outside world (e.g. other COPs) are vital for the community to function, and to change. Wenger (1998) refers to the boundaries of a COP as containing two types of connection to the world outside. The first type of connection is through boundary objects, which include artefacts, documents, terms, concepts and other reifications around which a COP interconnects with other COPs, and therefore such objects serve multiple constituencies. For example, this could include standardized project review procedures, safety audit documents, insurance claim forms. The second type of connection is through brokering, which involves interpreting and importing artefacts directly from one COP to another through connections provided by people (via their multi-membership of other COPs) – an import-export role. For example, this could include changing a procedure in one COP (or in a project team) to that used in another, based on the direct input from a participant who is a member of both. This brokering role is complex, as it involves the processes of translation, coordination, and an alignment of differing perspectives across the various COPs involved (Wenger, 1998).

The essential elements of a COP

Building on the definitions previously provided, at an elemental level, three interacting elements define a COP. These involve a *domain* of knowledge, which defines a set of issues that members experience: a *community* of people who care about this domain, wherein the community creates the social fabric of learning; a *shared practice* that they are developing to be effective within their domain (Wenger *et al.*, 2002). A *domain* establishes the common ground and a sense of common identity for all COP participants (Wenger *et al.*, 2002). A *community* consists of a group of people who interact, build relationships, learn together, and in the process develop competence, a sense of belonging, and mutual commitment and accountability (Wenger *et al.*, 2002). A community's *shared practice* is a product of the past, as it embodies the history of the community and the knowledge it has developed over time (Wenger *et al.*, 2002). Practice specifically involves a set of historical or social resources or frameworks, ideas, tools, information, styles, community language and shared world views, stories, symbols, roles, tacit conventions, routines and documents that the community develop and share and maintain to sustain mutual engagement in action (Wenger, 1998; Wenger *et al.*, 2002). Being home to such an eclectic mix of implicit and explicit artefacts for learning, COPs clearly represent significant venues for learning and knowledge creation.

A further elemental consideration of a COP concerns its social reproduction via communities of practitioners (Fox, 1997) over a longer-time cycle than the work practice cycle. This differential time factor between work practice and social reproduction, and the negotiated process of joint learning which develops a history that constitutes a practice are important distinguishing factors for COPs in comparison to other groups such as project teams. For example, project teams traditionally exist to accomplish specified tasks, are held together by the project goals and milestones, and are usually considered to have clearly defined boundaries – whereas, COPs exist to create, expand and exchange knowledge over a longer-time cycle, and are held together by the passion, commitment and identification with the group. Such comparative distinctions between COPs and other structures are further explored in Wenger *et al.* (2002). In relation to this study however, whether a project team can be considered a form of COP and the implications of that notion for learning in a project team will be further explored in Chapter 3.

Legitimate peripheral participation

A sub-element and analytic unit of the COP literature revolves around the construct of legitimate peripheral participation (LPP). LPP conceptualizes how a person participates and learns within the social world of a COP, and how they develop competency to participate fully within a practice, over time. Therein, LPP refers to both the development of knowledgeable people or identities within a COP, and also to the reproduction and transformation of COPs, that is the people and the practice are in mutual development since LPP is the way a COP reproduces itself over time (Lave and Wenger, 1991). In any community of practice, this reproduction process (being historically constructed and ongoing) needs to be deciphered, to enable us to understand different forms of LPP over time (Lave and Wenger, 1991). For example, in the case of Patch Adams (the movie), future medical students in that story may achieve differing competencies and different legitimacy, compared to those in the period prior to Patch's arrival at the Medical School. In that sense, their learning is a result of the structural characteristics of the current COP, which resulted from the prior reproduction of the community, wherein Patch and his colleagues attained legitimacy, but at the same time influenced change around what constituted competency and legitimacy within the practice.

Lave and Wenger (1991) and Brown and Duguid (1991) define LPP as a way of understanding learning across different settings (both social and physical) and across different historical periods and different methods. When new members join any COP, they are often given specific assignments and tasks that actively involve the tacit dimension of knowledge residing within the community, in the workplace practices, in the social interactions and in the power relations. Such assignments enable them to participate in the social context and to learn, as they become competent members of a COP (Gherardi *et al.*, 1998). Such participation involves problem-solving in goal-related activities, and relationships with more experienced others, which assist and guide the newcomers' development towards full participation within the community (Billett, 2000). Lave and Wenger (1991) and Hildreth *et al.* (2000) describe legitimacy as a way of belonging to a community, whilst Gherardi *et al.* (1998) consider that legitimate, emphasizes the journey that an individual would undertake in reaching the full membership of a COP. Lave and Wenger (1991) and Hildreth *et al.* (2000) describe peripherality as multiple and inclusive ways of being located in the field of participation or social practice, as defined by the community. Gherardi *et al.* (1998) see peripherality as the path that a new member must travel towards becoming a full participant within a community. Although broadly encapsulated by Lave and Wenger's (1991) descriptors of legitimacy and peripherality, Gherardi *et al.*'s (1998) views perhaps indicate a more purposeful intent about actions to be pursued by participants within a COP. Hence, LPP can be considered as a newcomer's progressive involvement in a community, through increasing their mastery of the practices of the community and their membership of that community (Gherardi *et al.*, 1998). Therein, learners learn to function within a community, to share its world-view and to speak its language, and therefore workplace learning is about 'becoming a practitioner not learning about practice' (Brown and Duguid, 1991: 69). Similarly, project-based learning deepens as participants move from more peripheral (and still legitimate) roles into more central positions within a project team setting (DeFillipi, 2001). The implications of this construct for this study revolve around conceptualizing how a project team participant can move from a peripheral learning role within a project practice towards full-learning participation, and the development of the project team as a purposeful, and yet temporary, learning community.

In summary, a COP consists of a community of people, who, over time, share a concern about a topic and participate and interact within a domain of practice around that topic. What COPs emphasize is that every practice and learning within a practice is dependent on social processes. In that way, a COP is both an outcome of the social practices of a community and, at the same time, a process for creating and sharing knowledge. COPs may be anywhere on a continuum of formality, as they are focused on content and not form, and therefore may emerge in spite of formal organizational constraints. The boundaries of a COP tend to be fuzzy and fluid as the community and those within it change over time. The practice is not static but dynamic, and is constantly changing by engagement with other communities as elements of one practice migrate into another.

By participating and interacting in a COP on an ongoing basis, people develop their competencies to fully participate within such a practice, and they mutually define their identities and shared meanings on issues while creating and exchanging knowledge. Consequently, a COP demonstrates a shared knowledge and discourse that reflects a particular perspective on the world, that is a shared world-view. A COP also produces a shared practice consisting of collective historical artefacts such as tools, routines, stories, documents and a common language, which contain the tacit and explicit knowledge of the community. Placing a learning focus on participation within a COP presents two broad implications for learning: that is for individuals, learning is an issue of effectively participating in, and contributing to the day-to-day practices within a community; and for communities, learning is an issue of refining their practices and ensuring a new generation of competent community members (Wenger, 1998).

2.5 Why focus on the situated dimension of learning for cultivating learning within projects?

Conventional views on learning primarily reflect the cognitive dimension of learning (Lave and Wenger, 1991) where learning is seen as mainly cerebral, unproblematic, and involves the transmission and assimilation of de-contextualized information around or through the minds of individuals. This view also tends to ignore or leave unexplored the nature of the learner and their world and their relationships and interactions within that context (Lave and Wenger, 1991). On the other hand, SLT views learning as a socially located and co-constructed process, which is contingent on human relations and practices within a context. On the surface, these two seemingly quite opposite views of learning appear to be in ontological conflict. Contrary to that perception however, both these viewpoints are complementary for a complete understanding of how learning occurs in natural work situations (Shani and Docherty, 2003). The cognitive dimension of learning is not, and cannot be divorced from situated or social practice within the context in which the cognitive learning process of an individual is enacted. It can be concluded then that cognitive learning theory spotlights the cognitive aspect of a situated learning process, and thus the context and its myriad sociological aspects mediate the cognitive learning activities of an individual and are an integral part of the learning or knowledge-creation process (Antonacopoulou, 1997; Coombs and Smith, 1998; Billett, 2000; Gherardi and Nicolini, 2000). As depicted in Figure 2.1, this primal influence of the situational relationships suggests that the situated or social dimension of learning always frames the cognitive dimension, or as Gherardi *et al.* (1998: 274) state, 'cognitive and practical activity can thus be pursued only within this world, and through this social and cultural network'. Therefore, learning can always be considered a practical accomplishment that takes place amongst and through other people (where learners construct their meanings and understandings and learn through their social interactions within a practice context) and is not simply and only an individual cognitive activity (where learners as individual actors possess and process information and modify their mental models) (Gherardi *et al.*, 1998; Richter, 1998; Gherardi and Nicolini, 2000). Hence, if one seeks to better understand and improve the complete learning activity of participants within any context, then paying systematic attention to the encompassing situated dimension of learning is of primary value.

This social constructivist view of learning encourages us to understand project learning through the experiences and interactions of project participants. Therein, individuals make sense of project activities

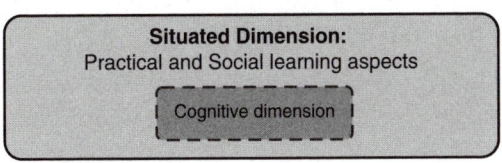

Figure 2.1 The relationship between the situated and cognitive dimensions of learning

and develop their own learning activities in interaction with their specific (and changing) project environments (Burrell and Morgan, 1979; Schwandt, 1994; Thomas, 2000). This perspective also suggests a need to develop localized views of learning, as the nature and process of learning activity may be different in different contexts and cultures (Dodgson, 1993; Easterby-Smith, 1997). Consequently, we need to consider: project teams as dynamic constructors of learning processes in accordance with their specific project contexts; that project knowledge is conjoined to practice and therefore contextually situated and mediated by the sociological conditions of the practice, and; social participation and interaction within a community of practice as essential for learning and for the development of one's identity within a practice. This theoretical framework and these considerations both informed and guided the conduct of this research and the analysis and theory building activities reported on in this book.

3
Sociological Perspectives and Learning in Projects

This chapter presents an analysis and discussion on the project management literature that encompasses the sociological perspectives and learning perspectives in project teams. The first section of this chapter overviews this project management literature that is primarily targeted towards an audience within the project management field. Given the audience, this section may therefore be considered *a view from within the field*. Conversely, such literature which is directed primarily towards an audience external to the project management field, and contributes to the views those people have of project management can constitute a perspective on project management from *outside the field* – as presented in the second section of this chapter. These contrived, high-level literature groupings enable me to discuss with some clarity the diverse project management literature which has relevance to the issues reported on in this book. Furthermore, it is also representative of what is currently occurring in this literature field. That is, there is a steadily increasing volume of literature on the sociological aspects of project management appearing in other, external to the field publications – which are signalling an increasing and diverse interest in project management. Meanwhile, there is also an increasing literature within the field focused on an array of sociological aspects of project management.

Building on the notion of a project team being a dynamic sociocultural entity, the third section of this chapter reviews literature specifically concerning the concept of a project team from a learning perspective. After appraising the traditional conceptualizations of a project team, this section then introduces a conceptualization which builds on situated learning theory and communities of practice. This constitutes the final key piece of the conceptual framework of this study.

This alternate conceptualization of a project team moves beyond a technical and task-oriented conception, and within that shift of perspective comes an entirely new way to conceive learning and learners in project team environments – that which is consistent with the sociological and constructivist thrust evident in preceding chapters. Embracing this new conceptual framework and incorporating the findings from the case study project, the final section of this chapter then articulates and illustrates a model of project situated learning behaviour.

3.1 A view from within the field

Within the field of project management literature, many authors (i.e. Morris, 1994; Lientz and Rea, 1995; Lock, 1996a,b; PMI®, 1996; Cleland 1999; Gido and Clements, 1999; Keeling, 2000; Smith, 2000; Kerzner, 2001; Kezsbom and Edward, 2001; Mantel Jr et al., 2001; Gray and Larson, 2000, 2002) present an array of sub-topics on project management which fall into what Gray and Larson (2002) refer to as the technical and sociological dimensions of the project management process. The technical dimension contains such items as the strategic perspective on projects, planning for and defining the project, scheduling project resources and activities, tracking and controlling, feasibility studies and managing risk, cost planning and performance, contracts management, terminating projects, and project management software. The sociological aspects include organizational structures for project work, leadership and the skills for project leaders, politics and conflict management, communication and negotiation processes and customer management, project quality, and attaining and maintaining project team performance. In large part, this array of topic areas appears broadly consistent with the knowledge areas prescribed in *A Guide to the Project Management Body of Knowledge (PMBOK® Guide)* (PMI®, 1996). This guide is used by the Project Management Institute (PMI®) (and other organizations) to provide a consistent structure for its professional development and certification programmes. The purpose of this guide is to identify and describe 'knowledge and practices that are applicable to most projects most of the time, and there is wide spread consensus about their value and usefulness' (PMI®, 1996: 3). Therefore, in all the nine knowledge areas identified within the guide, it raises central issues that project managers should address in building their competencies (PMI®, 1996). This guide details (as well as time, scope and cost management and other primarily technical competencies) human resource management, communication management and project integration management as core competencies or knowledge areas for project managers to develop. Given its development history and general acceptance within (and by) the profession, I believe it to be reasonable to suggest that this guide is considered a bible in regard to identifying and articulating the core competencies (particularly the technical competencies) required by the project management profession.

A project team is usually focused on some predefined, time limited and specific objective, which involves the management of an amalgam of non-routine and interdependent tasks (Frame, 1995; Morris, 1998; Turner, 1999; Gray and Larson, 2000; Wenger *et al.*, 2002). In managing those non-routine tasks, the authors of the guide suggest that the Project Management Body Of Knowledge (PMBOK®) overlaps with general management in many areas such as accounting, organizational design, organizational behaviour, human resource management, and managing work and people. Hence, they consider that these general management skills provide the foundation for building project management skills (PMI®, 1996). They exhibit candidness if you like, in expressing an avuncular link between PMBOK® and general management theories. From a perspective of building competencies, and with this focus on the human aspects of the project management process, one can reasonably conclude that the PMBOK® guide partakes in a sociological approach towards the management of projects.

In addition to the PMBOK® guide, the publications relating to those authors acknowledged above tend to have a voluminous bias towards the technical dimension of project management, and yet there appears to be a clear recognition and attention paid by those authors towards the social and cultural aspects of projects and the impact of those aspects on project performance. In contrast to that technical bias, other authors within this literature field (see, for example, Block [1983], Verma [1995], Briner *et al.* [1996], Smith and Dodds [1997], Blomquist and Packendorff [1998], Lundin and Midler [1998a], Pinto [1998a, 1998b], Pinto and Slevin [1998], Björkegren [1999], Frame [1994, 1995, 1999], Pinto and Millet [1999], Hartman and Lundin [2000], Lechler [2000], Thomas [2000], Boddy [2002], Gray and Larson [2002], Lewis [1998, 2003]) take a distinctive sociological approach to project management or project leadership. For example, Lechler (2000) concluded from a study of 448 projects in Germany that project success is very highly influenced by the human side of project management as opposed to the technical or more formal aspects of project management. Consistent with that conclusion, Verma (1995) and Lewis (1998, 2003), in addition to emphasizing the determining element of project success being people, explore the skills required to make the project manager an effective facilitator of the human resources associated with a project. On a larger canvas, but echoing the same perspective about building skills and competency, Frame (1999) expounds the necessity for project individuals, project teams and project organizations to learn and concurrently develop their competence in project management.

Other authors take a different (but nonetheless sociological) viewpoint on projects. For example, in evaluating the barriers and bearers on knowledge transfer between projects and the organization in which projects are executed, Björkegren (1999) uses a metaphor of projects as learning experiments (an objective in itself compared to the traditional internally focused and technical view of projects involving planning, controlling and evaluating), with a focus on action, learning and the exploration and exploitation of knowledge in organizations. Consistent with this perspective of learning and a preparedness to experiment, Lundin and Midler (1998a) see projects as significant opportunities for learning and continuous renewal in organizations. This notion of projects and their participants being involved in learning experiments, involving action and exploration for knowledge, echoes in Thamhain's foreword to Verma's (1995) trilogy of books on the human aspects of project management, in which he describes project managers as 'social architects who can work across levels and functions of the organization, continuously improving the business process and fostering an ambiance conducive to innovation, risk taking, self directed teamwork, commitment, quality and self improvement' (Verma, 1995: 7, citing Thamhain, 1995). If project managers are to become those creative designers and active facilitators of project social systems that support risk-taking, innovation, continuous business and self-improvement, they will require an experimental and explorative learning attitude in how they approach the management of projects.

In papers presented in a special issue of one of the leading journals in the project management field (i.e. the *International Journal of Project Management* – Volume 21, Number 3, 2003), the management of knowledge (both explicit and tacit) in project environments was explored (also note that some of these papers have been reproduced in revised form in Love *et al.* [2005]). A general and strong consensus within many of those papers concerned the impacts of social factors in enhancing knowledge-management capabilities across projects. These social factors, combined with the creation and management of social networks and the recognition that knowledge is a situated activity and therefore embedded within specific contexts, make the management and creation of knowledge in projects quite a complex project ambition (Bresnen *et al.*, 2003; Fernie *et al.*, 2003; Huang and Newell, 2003). As Fernie *et al.* (2003: 184) posit, 'Any approach to knowledge-sharing must be predicated on engaging the individual. If knowledge-sharing between individuals is to take place, it is necessary to facilitate dialectic debate within a socialized setting.' These conversations about the social dependency of knowledge creation and management between projects also resound in the work of Björkegren (1999), Antoni (2000) and Fong (2003). What is very relevant to this study is the clear recognition in this literature of the social and situated, and therefore dynamic nature of learning and knowledge management within project environments. I note, however, these authors make limited references to situated learning theory – which incidentally, generally supports their findings as presented.

Authors such as Block (1983), Frame (1994) and Pinto (1998a,b) further highlight the diversity of focus in this sociologically oriented literature from within the field. Separately, they define and explore project politics and offer guidance on how practitioners can better manage the political dimension of projects. Given these diverse interests within the field, perhaps what is useful then at this point is to attempt to broadly categorize this sociologically oriented project management literature. The works of those authors mentioned earlier in this section, and which primarily appear to offer guidance to project practitioners, tend to congregate into one of the following nominated categories:

- Human resource management skills for effective project leadership.
- Managing and integrating the project within the internal and external contexts.
- Managing and developing the competence of people and their performance in the project team.
- Power and political influence both internal and external to the project team.
- Designing supportive project team social structures.
- Knowledge development, transfer and management across project environments.
- Projects as systems which integrate with complex social environments.
- Communication and interaction between project team participants

What is also clearly apparent in this review is that there is a very limited literature within the sociologically oriented project management literature that specifically elaborates on aspects of, *within* project learning. At the time of writing this book, there are currently only 14 such publications within the field (see Lientz and Rea [1995], Anell [1998], Ayas [1996, 1998], Blomquist and Packendorff [1998], Boudès et al. [1998], Huemann and Winkler [1998], Lundin and Midler [1998b], Müllern and Östergren [1998], Kotnour [1999], Sense [2003a,b, 2007a], Sense and Antoni [2003]). Yet, implicit in the writings of the authors taking a predominant sociological perspective towards projects and project teams is some expectation that learning occurs. That being: that learning is the forerunner to individual and team competence development; that team processes (e.g. conflicts and decision-making) are reflected on and new actions are undertaken and tested; that project managers actually become leaders and facilitators through formal and informal learning processes; that project teams aim to effectively integrate their projects within the broader organizational context conditions.

Frame (1999) and Morris (1994), for example, suggest that building competence in an individual, the team and the project organization is vital for project success, and implicitly underpinning that viewpoint must be a perception of some form of learning activity. Some authors within this field, that do venture onto this learning topic, do so at the post-completion phase where the project review process supposedly captures the learning from the project, and which is then able to be referred to by other project teams and the organization at large. In these works, the values and issues involved in performing such reviews are expounded and suggestions are offered as to how one might perform such a review process (see Lientz and Rea [1995], Collier et al. [1996], Frame [1998], Wilemon [1998], Barker and Neailey [1999], Busby [1999], Keegan and Turner [2001]). For example, Frame (1998), in discussing closing out a project, suggests that to convey lessons learned a number of techniques may be helpful. These include such items as the distribution of written lessons to project people, embedding lessons in revised project methods, creating a lessons learned data-bank, personalising the sharing of lessons in meetings, maintaining a stable and experienced workforce and highlighting important lessons at each project startup. As mentioned previously in Chapter 1, this learning aspect, while valuable, can be limiting, since such an evaluation is adversely time affected (in relation to the project process), can be limited in scope to core review items of cost, quality, time and handover, and can be highly political, exclusive and sanitized.

Some other authors (i.e. Lundin and Söderholm, 1998; Wilemon, 1998; Schindler and Eppler, 2003), in writing on the post-project learning process, also suggest that the handling of learning and storing of knowledge for future use are desirable but formidable challenges for project managers. As mentioned previously in Chapter 1, they posit that systematic, concurrent and continuous learning assessment of projects throughout their life cycles (in addition to post-project evaluations) should also become part of the project manager's work (Lundin and Söderholm, 1998; Wilemon, 1998; Schindler and Eppler, 2003). Furthermore, like Lientz and Rea (1995), Lundin and Söderholm (1998), for example, do not offer guidance on specifically how a project manager might support learning during the project – they simply posit that it should be done. In this analysis, there is a recognition within this literature sub-field of the opportunity for learning from projects, a focus on post-project review processes as a means to address that learning opportunity, and some suggestions that progressive and seemingly formal reviews would be a valuable aid to learning in a project – but offer no detailed suggestions on how one might facilitate such a process.

In summary, within this literature field, there is a clear recognition of the sociological variables within a project, the impacts they have on project performance, and the subsequent necessity to try to effectively manage them. It is also apparent (and one might suggest a logical expectation in this literature field at this time) that there is a voluminous bias towards literature involving the technical dimension of project management. This section also identified authors that displayed a distinctive sociological interest in project management. They represent quite a diverse picture of topic areas, varying from politics through to team building, and they principally attempt to provide guidance to practitioners to assist their project management processes. Many of these authors are extending the traditional ontological boundaries of this literature field, that is incorporating social constructivist perspectives into a traditionally positivist-oriented field.

As recently discussed, one learning aspect that has had some attention within this literature field has been post-project review processes. These, I suggest, are typically approached from a rational frame of reference and such a review is an expected part of the rational linear project process model. While acknowledging that post-project review processes only offer some limited value for learning from projects, some authors have proposed that systematic and continuous learning within a project life cycle, in conjunction with those review processes, would greatly assist project learning and knowledge generation. It is also abundantly clear that there is a very limited literature within this field that ventures more deeply into the specific topic of learning and its associated challenges within a project environment. Some of those publications emphasized the situatedness and dynamic nature of learning in project contexts. Therein, they either implicitly or explicitly suggested a necessity to attend to the sociological factors of a project environment if one is to encourage learning activity. That is, in various ways they emphasized the importance of effectively harnessing the context conditions to learn. Moreover, most authors identified within this category expound the importance of learning for the project and the project management profession. However, none, except the author of this book and his co-authors in identified publications, has attempted to develop and articulate a theoretical understanding of specific sociological factors that facilitate or impede learning within a project. Therefore, this book makes a significant contribution to knowledge in this project management area.

3.2 A view from outside the field

The small number of authors identified in this section have written about sociological and learning aspects of project management, and their work is directed towards audiences external to the project management field, that is they publish in media targeted towards other fields, such as management learning or organizational change management.

While the literature residing in this sub-field is quite limited in volume, it is of high value, in that it directly addresses the learning opportunities associated with project teams and their environments. Implicit in the items presented in this section is an epistemological positioning within social constructionism and recognition of the situated nature of project learning. There are four journal items that have delved into learning in projects, and three of these have been published in a management learning journal and one in an industrial training journal. Further, there is one book which takes a somewhat reverse approach to discussing learning and project teams, that is these authors examine the value in using projects as developmental tools for managers. These articles warrant some specific explanations, since they provide valuable theoretical contributions that support many of the arguments raised in this book. At this point, I should also note that I have excluded six of my own journal article publications from this list as they embrace the information presented in forward sections of this book (see Antoni and Sense [2001], Sense and Badham [2006], Sense [2004, 2005a, 2006a, 2007b]). These articles (and other publications such as conference papers) have evolved from this research, and whilst I exclude them from the presentation below, it is appropriate to at least mention their contribution to this nominated literature field – particularly given the limited number of items identified.

First, Ayas and Zeniuk (2001) present what they consider to be the distinguishing features of project-based learning. These features include items such as: there is a sense of purpose; the environment fosters an individual's psychological safety; there is a supportive learning infrastructure; and, there is systemic and collective reflection when opportunities present themselves. They also discuss the ways in which attending to those features of project-based learning can contribute towards building a community of reflective practitioners, and how such a community, will in turn, promote reflective learning in and across projects, develop learning capabilities, and cultivate habits of reflective practice (Ayas and Zeniuk, 2001). Therefore (in their analysis), they see projects and project teams as vehicles for creating a context in which participants develop inquiry skills (that better enable them to understand their assumptions and the consequences of their actions) and reflective practices at all levels in the organization. The effectiveness of the work of project team participants (and by implication their learning activity) is dependent on them deliberately crossing those community-constructed boundaries of individual teams, groups or divisions (Ayas and Zeniuk, 2001). Thus, to carry on their project work effectively, project participants need to develop the capability of managing across social and organizational boundaries and to expand their sphere of influence and credibility beyond the immediate project, that is they are unavoidably part of a wider web of complex social relationships. In doing so, as well as engaging with the project practice, they deal with the boundary issues that are inherently socially oriented and socially resolved (Ayas and Zeniuk, 2001).

Whilst Ayas and Zeniuk (2001) delved into the potential for learning in projects, Keegan and Turner (2001) investigated the actual practices adopted for project learning across 19 project-based firms in the United Kingdom. They concluded that time pressures (i.e. minimal time to perform reflective learning actions), centralized planning and control of projects (i.e. centralization promoting knowledge retention over variation, and therefore exploitative learning over explorative learning (March, 1991)) and the deferral of assessment practices until after a project was completed, all contribute towards an emphasis on the quantity of projects completed rather than an emphasis on the quality of the project learning and reflection practices (Keegan and Turner, 2001). Further, they also concluded that centrally mandated learning practices distract attention away from the necessity to nurture and facilitate learning at the project team level, and as a consequence of their study believe that learning continues to evade project-based firms (Keegan and Turner, 2001). At a broader level, they consider project-based learning practices to be an immature subset of organizational learning practices, since the promotion of variation, and therefore exploratory learning, between projects is lean – hence also, an opportunity to learn from organizational learning practice (Keegan and Turner, 2001).

Consistent with Ayas and Zeniuk's (2001) view that project team participants need to manage across multiple social and organizational boundaries, and the notion expressed by Keegan and Turner (2001) that the physical/organizational environment in which a project is embedded can have significant effects on project learning activity, Arthur *et al.* (2001) present project-based learning as an interplay of an individual's career capital and the project sponsoring company's accumulated non-financial capital. The company's non-financial capital consists of the cultural (e.g. values and beliefs), human (e.g. tacit and explicit knowledge) and social (e.g. the resources available to an organization through its relationships) aspects of the company environment. The accumulated individual career capital consists of an individual's past interconnected learning experiences of knowing-why, which represents a disposition to participate; knowing-how, which represents an individual's emergent repertoire of skills; and, knowing-whom, which reflects an individual's accumulated human network both internal and external to the project field (Arthur *et al.*, 2001). Through this interplay they see projects not only as 'one-shot, time bounded, goal driven [and performance] activities', but also as personal and organizational learning opportunities (Arthur *et al.*, 2001: 99–100). This perspective is also consistent with that held by Morris (2002), who argues that projects are particularly powerful vehicles to facilitate knowledge creation, knowledge management and organizational learning.

Thus, Arthur *et al.* (2001) see projects as learning episodes, and within these episodes individual career capital can be invested and returns on that investment accumulated. They consider the project forum a mixing pot, where the defined individual and organizational capitals blend together to create new capital output – a very social constructivist perspective on learning in projects. These outputs can accrue to the individual project participant, the project organization and those parties external to the organization that have links to those participants in the project team. Therefore, project success can be determined in terms of the standard project performance goals and also in the generation of project participant and company learning (Arthur *et al.*, 2001).

Through their evaluation of their cases, the provisional lessons posited from their research included: the importance of community building as a mechanism for promoting project-based learning; the need for learning agendas to be explicit and credible and hierarchically supported within the project and the organization; the opportunity to extend the learning boundaries beyond the host organization via the network relationships; and, the need to organize a project for successful knowledge capture, that is organize the systems and structures to assist knowledge generation and exchange (Arthur et al., 2001).

Raelin (2001) extends this discussion on learning in projects, by appraising the virtues of public and critical reflective practice in a project environment and how that process contributes to self and organizational learning. He reflects on the skills required for reflective practice, and suggests that public reflection is the key to unlocking learning within projects and beyond a project to other levels of the organization and society (Raelin, 2001). Clearly, this focus on learning resulting from reflective practice within and surrounding a project team necessarily confronts an array of sociological issues, for example power and organizational culture. So, whilst the notion of public reflective practice in itself is a sociological perspective on learning in project teams, the field in which such reflection takes place is riddled with sociological issues that impact any project learning process.

Smith and Dodds (1997: ix) (in both their book and journal article on the same topic) take a perspective that projects are a natural and powerful vehicle for performing and learning within a context of continuing change. Their promotion of a project being a vehicle for learning, and their relating of how learning can be realized through project opportunities (e.g. establishing and managing infrastructures for learning, coaching and mentoring, action learning approaches, interpersonal and inter-team relationships, and cross-cultural aspects) suggest a strong sociological perspective on how project teams can assist management development through learning. They suggest that the espoused benefits of using project teams as management development vehicles are twofold – for the managers, in terms of personal growth, and for the organization, in terms of achieving change and organizational learning. Their publications primarily targeted the people development specialists, that is human resource management, management training, and training and development practitioners.

In summary, the project management literature that casts a sociological view of project teams into other academic or practitioner communities, external to the project management field, is very limited.

This may be because of the artificial boundary I have established at the start of this section. Perhaps also, that is to be expected, given a general perspective of the project management literature field as being young compared to the more established fields of, for example, organizational learning. Nevertheless, such issues should not detract from the value offered in the works of those authors outlined above. As well as expressing and exploring the potential and value for learning in project teams, these authors managed to convey a number of other important points. One paper identified three practices in project management that seemed to impede project learning activity and instead placed an emphasis on the quantity of projects completed. Other authors identified a number of lessons (from their research) for promoting learning in projects. For example, one identified lesson was the importance of community building to support learning. This lesson also echoed in the work of other authors (both in this section and in previous sections) who argue that project teams are not independent entities but are embedded in complex webs of social and contextual relationships. Because of that, they stress the importance of building a community of reflective practitioners (Ayas and Zeniuk, 2001), and in developing the skills to manage across these potentially difficult social boundaries. This theme of reflective practice reverberates in the work of Raelin (2001), who expounds the value in public reflective practice for learning in projects. Finally, and perhaps contrary to the project itself focus offered by the preceding authors, Smith and Dodds (1997) promote a view of projects as learning and development tools for management development. Many of the themes presented in this literature field resonate strongly with the findings of the study presented in this book. As such, the findings of this study (to be presented in future chapters) make a further contribution to understanding projects as prime avenues for systematic and continuous learning activity. Furthermore, in seeking to activate such learning activity, and in unison with many of the authors in this field, the findings presented in this book also progress powerful arguments for attending to the sociological aspects of learning in projects.

3.3   Concept of a project team from a learning perspective

This section discusses literature that presents a concept of a project team from a learning perspective. A conceptualization of a project team from a traditional implementer perspective predominates in the many definitions of a project, a project team and project management. There appears to be only one article which attempts to conceptualize project teams from a learning perspective. That one article is a work of the author of this book, and the conceptualization offered is of some importance to the empirical findings presented in forthcoming chapters. The following discussion briefly elaborates on definitions of projects, project management and project teams, and from those definitions articulates the implicit attributes of the traditional conceptualization of project teams. The second part of this section explores in limited detail the author's paper, which utilizes SLT (as previously presented in Chapter 2) to depict a conceptualization of a project team from a learning perspective.

In attempting to establish the concept of a project team from a learning perspective, it is comparatively useful to first define a project, project management and a project team. *A Guide to the Project Management Body of Knowledge* (PMI®, 1996) defines a project as 'a temporary endeavour undertaken to create a unique product or service. Temporary means that every project has a definite beginning and a definite end' (PMI®, 1996: 4). It also defines project management as 'the application of knowledge skills, tools and techniques to project activities in order to meet or exceed stakeholder needs and expectations from a project' (PMI®, 1996: 6). Some authors simply report those definitions or slight variations from them when describing their definitions of projects and project management (for examples, see Cleland [1999] and Verma [1995]). Other authors (for examples, see Frame, 1995; Morris, 1998; Turner, 1999; Gray and Larson, 2000, 2002; Wenger *et al.*, 2002; Gido and Clements, 2003; Turner and Müller, 2003) not only support those sweeping definitions, but also highlight that projects are non-routine processes that involve the coordination of interrelated activities. For example, Turner (1999: 3) states, 'A project is an endeavour in which human, financial and material resources are organized in a novel way to undertake a unique scope of work, of given specification, within constraints of cost and time, so as to achieve beneficial change defined by quantitative and qualitative objectives.'

Lundin and Midler (1998b) consider that a project is a social construct by which a singular problem is extracted from a messy context of ongoing processes and events, and that it is this separation which creates social involvement and a focus on a given issue. This separation process can elicit diversified and contingent responses in terms of project activities in different project situations – supporting a notion that there is no one best way for all projects. Lundin and Midler (1998b) suggest that the essentials of project management revolve around the social phenomenon of sensemaking (Weick, 1995), mutual understanding, leadership and learning capacity – those things which reflect the project as a collective creative process of cooperation. This social constructivist perspective on project management is also reflected in the project management theory development work of Thomas (2000), where she evaluated two different orientations towards the function of project management. Those being either control, which views a project as a closed rational system, or sensemaking (Weick, 1995), which views a project as a means of organizing, and refers to the deliberate social interaction between humans working together on the project task. The latter orientation emphasizes the complex, negotiated and emergent nature of the project activity.

Turner (1999: 3–4), who adopts a similar social orientation to project management, considers 'project management is about managing people to deliver results' and offers a panoptic definition of project management being, 'Project management is the art and science of converting vision into reality' – the imprecise nature of this definition reflecting the need to perform work in transient, structured, yet novel and creative ways to produce tangible outcomes. Briner et al. (1996) places the standard three constraints of project management (involving cost, specification and time) in a context consisting of organizational politics, personal objectives and external or commercial pressures. This structuring contributes to their definition of project management being, 'managing the visible and invisible team to achieve the objectives of the stakeholders' (Briner et al., 1996: 10). Their definition shifts the focus of project management strongly onto the people-centred issues and the organizational context of the project – an orientation also strongly supported and explored by Boddy (2002) and Lechler (2000).

In most definitions of projects the characteristic emphasis is on: separation and temporality, that is a separate process with a finite time to complete; the uniqueness or specificity of objective and of the project activity in comparison to ongoing operations such as a functional department in an organization; and, the flexible management or coordination of many interrelated activities and resources of the project, by the people associated with the project. Project management definitions appear primarily socially oriented, which therefore suggests that project management is primarily about managing people (i.e. a complex sociological and constructivist activity) and not rational tasks to achieve a project's objectives. These constituent features of these definitions provide the broad framework in which to conceptualize about a project team.

Drawing on that framework, and in crude terms, the traditional view of project teams and those managing them is one of implementers, that is to make things happen (Frame, 1994). In more sophisticated terms, project teams are traditionally conceived to be a group of people that develop a perceived common identity (mobilized around a project objective) so that they can work together using a set of values or norms or behaviours (derived from past custom and practice) to deliver a project's management system and the project objectives (Block, 1983; Cleland, 1999; Turner, 1999). These descriptions convey a conception of a project team as some type of separate social form that maintains a rational output focus on achieving a particular tangible project outcome. This ostensibly limited conception is somewhat representative of the positivist foundation of the project management field. One might conclude that this conceptualization of a project team is highly inadequate in capturing the messy, dynamic, social and contextual character of learning in projects. Faced with such a conundrum, SLT may offer ways in which to build a conceptualization of a project team that embraces these attributes of learning – which are arguably, a neglected part of the project context.

This section now explores in limited detail a paper produced by the author of this book, which used SLT to conceptualize a project team from a learning perspective. This conception includes project teams being considered an amalgam of many different communities of practice (Lave and Wenger, 1991; Wenger *et al.*, 2002), which then simulates an embryonic form of a new community of practice. In his analysis, the author (see Sense, 2003b) summarized that project teams differ from communities of practice in the following ways:

- They have different time horizons, that is a defined start and finish point, compared to an open-ended horizon of a community of practice. Subsequently, a project team does not normally have a collective past or a collective future.
- They have different purposes, that is project teams are focused on a specific task and not normally on the development of a long-term participant practice.
- The individual identities of members of the project team are primarily forged external to the project team and those members reflect other communities' views of the world.
- They do not share a common negotiated perspective on the world (as in communities of practice), but instead serve as a knowledge exchange venue for multiple communities of practice. Therein, focused expertise is brought into this learning milieu and the multiple communities of practice act as conduits for project participants

to access other external sources of distributed knowledge. This perspective also being consistent with Lindkvist's (2005) consideration of a project team as a collectivity-of-practice.
- They do not develop a mutually negotiated shared practice consisting of an array of new and unique (to that project) artefacts that persist over time. Rather, through community of practice boundary exchanges, they tend to become a dumping ground for others' artefacts, which are then incorporated into a project team's temporal practice.

Sense (2003b) then assessed whether one might consider a project team as an embryonic form of a community of practice. He concluded that a project team can be considered an embryonic form of a new community of practice since:

- It provides a focal point on a topic that people have an interest in, and is therefore a causal prompt for a community of practice to form and grow, that is it is a potential community of practice. This potential for a project team to morph into a community over time, also being acknowledged by Lindkvist (2005).
- It necessarily engages team members in the following:

    Negotiating boundary objects – creating temporary artefacts relevant to the project from the different perspectives of project team members.
    Brokering – interpreting and importing artefacts directly into the project team from the multiple communities of practice associated with the different participants in a project.

Both these actions aim to establish the artefacts such as the tools, the information, and the context in which the project team can undertake their project activities.

- It provides opportunities for individuals and the team to learn and develop individual and team capabilities – provided the focus of project teams and their practice is explicitly shifted to include learning. In that sense, a project team can be considered an infant community of practice.
- It possesses the potential to contribute to the development of the identity of team members and to the development of a practice – that which may be considered mobile and also constitute learning between projects.

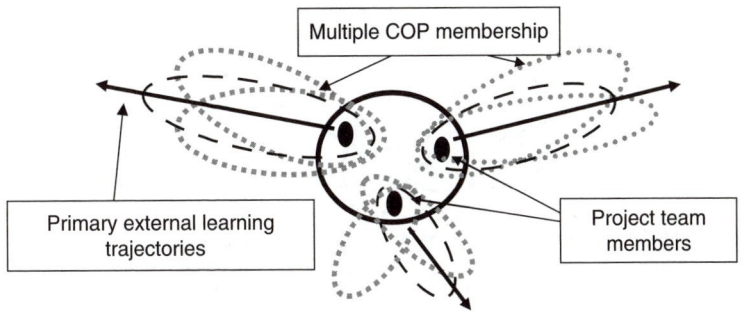

Figure 3.1 A typical project team

Based on this analysis, Sense (2003b) developed a new conception of a project team from a learning perspective. This includes a project team acting as a knowledge exchange venue for multiple communities of practice, and as a dumping ground for other communities of practice artefacts, whilst members' identities and work relationships are primarily forged external to the project team setting. Figure 3.1 illustrates this concept of a project team, which involves a conglomeration of communities of practice (attached to each project participant) coming together around a particular project purpose. For pictorial clarity, the communities of practice boundaries in both figures are shown as well defined, but in practice these boundaries are often fuzzy and flexible. In this figure, the multi-layered community of practice person joining a project team, by virtue of their external memberships and established external identities and practices, has a primary learning trajectory or bias external to the project team. Due to that alignment, a team member spends only the required time on an inward learning trajectory, that is towards the project team grouping – enough perhaps to exchange knowledge and dump other communities' artefacts into the project milieu to get the project done as specified. This lineament means that members migrate towards the periphery of the project team learning potential, as they are attracted towards their more familiar external communities of practice.

An inward learning trajectory or bias results in a movement towards the centre of the diagram by the team members as shown in Figure 3.2. This is representative of the adoption of an additional purpose by the project team to now include a focus on learning and the development of individual learning capabilities within the project. When these multiple communities of practice for each individual collide or abut each other

62 Cultivating Learning Within Projects

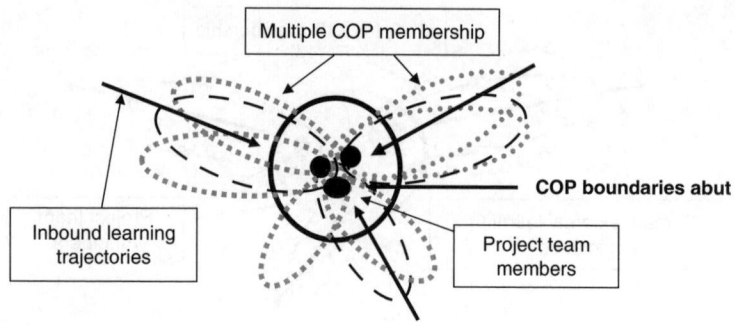

Figure 3.2 A preferred project team

in the project team, these interfaces or boundaries between individuals can become major learning and negotiation opportunities where new and unique practice can emerge.

At these points of engagement, learning across the community of practice boundaries between people (as also previously illustrated in Figure 3.1) can be either supported or inhibited by attention or non-attention to an array of sociological elements residing within the project milieu. If these elements are engaged appropriately, this presents the potential for project teams to be viewed as purposeful learning generators, rather than passive or opportunistic entities for learning. These elements constitute the findings of this study and therefore will be expanded on in detail in Chapters 4, 5 and 6.

In summary, this section provided illustrative examples of definitions for a project and project management. The constituent features of these definitions provided the broad framework with which to comprehend traditional definitions of a project team. The traditional project team definitions involve a view of project teams as implementers, mobilized around and focused on achieving a specific task. This definition conveys a limiting conception of a project team as being a separate social form that pursues a rational linear process towards achieving a tangible project outcome. Alternatively, this section also offered a conceptualization of a project team from a learning perspective. Utilizing SLT, it presented an argument that project teams should be considered an embryonic form of a new community of practice. The ontological implications of this alternate conception are quite profound. This conception does not hold a view of a project team as only a temporal, rational, output-focused and organizationally discrete entity. Instead, this conception presents project teams (and their membership) as multi-focused on both learning and project action, and intimately connected to or embedded in a complex web of social and contextual relationships external to the project team. This conception also encapsulates a notion of learning between project participants as being mediated by local sociological elements within a project setting.

3.4 The pentagon of project situated learning behaviour

This section builds on the developed conceptualization of a project team from a situated learning perspective, to illustrate a model of project situated learning behaviour. This model incorporates five sociological constraint/enabler elements that impacted the situated learning behaviour of participants within the case study project examined. Therein, it embodies the social dynamics involved in learning across project participants' COP boundary interfaces. These boundary interfaces represent important learning opportunities since they connect multiple communities of practice in which critical competencies are nurtured, and offer divergent learning opportunities by exposing participants to new perspectives and challenges (Wenger, 2003). Therefore, as argued for in forthcoming chapters in this book, understanding and attending to these sociological elements help unlock the learning potential within the social learning system of a project team environment.

These sociological constraint/enabler elements are either, intra-personal, interpersonal or infrastructural-oriented influences on participants' situated learning behaviours. They involve: the intra-personal element of cognitive style; the interpersonal elements of learning relationships and pyramid of authority; and, the infrastructural elements of knowledge management and situational context. Figure 3.3 depicts the interrelationship between these five sociological constraint/enabler elements.

As illustrated in Figure 3.3, these sociological elements are interrelated and not mutually exclusive. For example, the learning relationships that a participant has can be influenced by the pyramids of authority of individuals and their cognitive styles, or the specific situational context conditions of a project can impede or enhance the knowledge management processes and the learning relationships. Individually and collectively then, these elements impact the situated learning behaviour of project team participants. In appreciating the mutual influence one element may exert on another, the key issue here then is to recognize that ideally practitioners need to attend to all of these elements simultaneously rather than in isolation to each other, that is to take a holistic

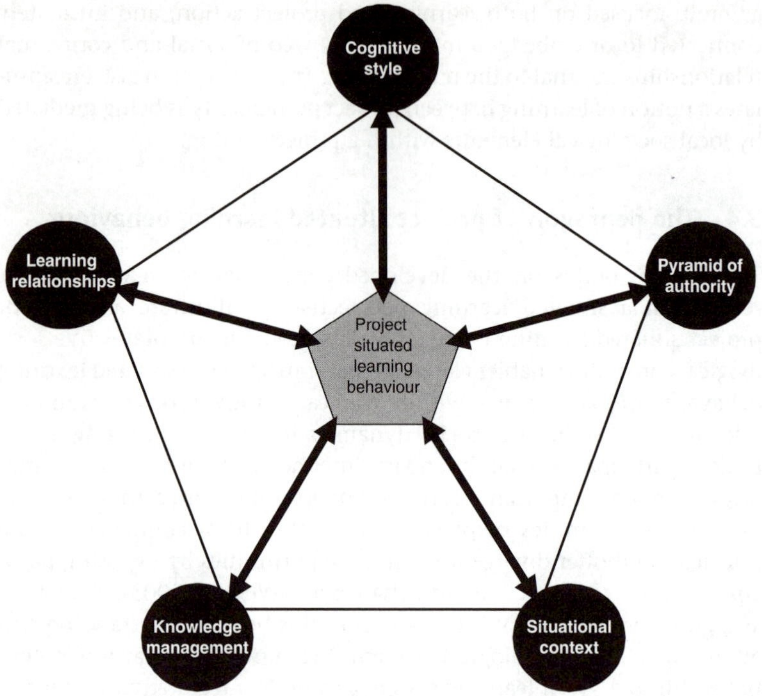

Figure 3.3 Pentagon of project situated learning behaviour

rather than a piecemeal approach towards understanding and managing these elements if they seek to stimulate project learning activity.

This model and its constituent elements constitute a form of 'conceptual architecture' (Wenger, 1998: 230) with the potential for aiding reflection on learning practices and serving as a framework for project practitioners to develop a learning practice. The purpose of a conceptual architecture is to lay down the general elements of design, thereby indicating what needs to be in place to perform a design activity (Wenger, 1998). Since learning itself cannot be designed and ultimately belongs to the realm of experience and practice, a conceptual architecture for learning provides the critical elements for learners to design social infrastructures that foster their learning (Wenger, 1998). Therein, this model (or conceptual architecture) is not intended to serve as a prescription for facilitating situated learning (although one can identify the possibility to consider it as such). Rather, it forms a framework of concepts which project participants and researchers can use as guides or heuristics in developing their own localized project learning activities (an approach entirely consistent with the contextual and social emphasis of situated learning theory), or in seeking to investigate and understand learning in projects. In that way, the identified sociological elements also serve as catalysts or 'seeding structures' (Thompson, 2005: 162) in a 'self-design' process (Mohrman and Cummings, 1989: 13) for project learning development.

4
Cognitive Style

This chapter provides an insight into how the intrapersonal constraint/enabler element of cognitive style impacts the situated learning activity of project participants. At first glance, this term seems at odds with a situated and social constructivist perspective on learning, given that cognitive implies, in one's own head. In respect to this study however, cognitive style is not considered simply an internal personalized matter for separate individuals to consider in isolation to others. It is instead a socially oriented learning issue for a project team to recognize, to understand and to manage. This comes about because in publicly and explicitly evaluating the cognitive styles of project team participants and the impacts those styles have on their learning activities within a project, the implicit style of an individual is made explicit, it is acknowledged and challenged by self and others (Hampson, 1995), and catered for in the future learning actions of the project team. Hence, in undertaking such public exposition and public reflection (Raelin, 2001), it becomes a sociological learning issue.

This learning action of developing an understanding of such cognitive style differences between people may suitably enhance situated learning opportunities within a project, and thereby provide the potential through learning, to improve project participants' collective and individual contribution to project outcomes and their own self-development. For example, during their interactions, people may model or adjust their approaches to information exchange and instruction and attend to the learning environment to accommodate an individual's style differences, and thereby also help people reach better relational understanding with others and of themselves (Sims and Sims, 1995a; Sternberg, 1997). This is akin to what Kasl *et al.* (1997) refer to as moving a team from fragmented modes of learning towards synergistic modes of learning, wherein the team mutually create new learning as opposed to individuals learning in isolation. Furthermore, as Hayes and Allinson (1996) and Sadler-Smith (1998) note, understanding individual style differences (and more pointedly, cognitive styles) also has important implications for managing human resources and for individual and team training and development initiatives.

The first section of this chapter introduces and discusses the theory of cognitive style. It provides a definition for cognitive style and describes the relationship between cognitive styles and learning styles, which serves as a point of clarification about these two constructs. In that discussion, the linkage of these constructs to personality and the learning context are also broadly described. The section that follows then theoretically and empirically expounds on four assessment methods available to assess and understand cognitive styles. Using each of those methods, it profiles the cognitive styles of the project team participants involved in this study, whilst evaluating the learning dynamics observed and experienced in their project. As part of that analysis, it also elaborates on the method of cognitive style assessment used by the project team in this study, that is the personality-based psychometric tool called the Myers-Briggs Type Indicator (Myers and McCaulley, 1985).

Following the assessment methods discussion, the next section of this chapter then details three cognitive style conditioners of project participants' learning behaviours. These include: the matching or mismatching of project information-processing demands with the cognitive styles of participants; individuals and teams selecting situations that match their cognitive style type and avoiding situations that pose alternative demands; and, the predominance of a particular style type across a team. The final section of this chapter then brings together the key themes emanating from the preceding discussions to provide a summary of the cognitive style issues affecting project situated learning activity.

4.1 The theory of cognitive styles

> My way of learning is to get involved and to challenge and to triple challenge and to pinch and to manipulate. I need to understand things and I know talking to myself ain't going to help. So, I need to talk to other people. It is a spurious way of doing it [learning]... otherwise it's no good for me.
>
> (Steve – project case study participant)

This quotation from Steve highlights two important points. First, he expressed his desired or preferred way of learning as interacting and participating with others and to be actively involved in the learning milieu (i.e. highlighting his social dependence). Second, these comments also illustrate the potential influence that the social and practical aspects of the learning context can have on this participant's learning behaviour. For example, if the learning context or environment does not facilitate him talking with others, then he is unlikely to learn as effectively as he may be capable of doing. Steve's comment on his preferred way of learning illustrates an individual's cognitive style type – which is defined as 'A person's preferred way of [or predisposition to] gathering, processing and evaluating information. It influences how people scan their environment for information, how they organize and interpret this information and how they integrate it into the mental model and subjective theories that guide their actions' (Hayes and Allinson, 1998: 849) (for similar descriptions also see Messick [1984], Jonassen and Grabowski [1993], Sternberg [1995, 1997], Sternberg and Grigorenko [1997], Sadler-Smith [1999], Sadler-Smith et al. [2000], Sadler-Smith [2001a]). Cognitive styles reflect how people make sense of their worlds, and the ways in which we interact with information is reflective of the ways in which we interact with each other through our personalities. Cognitive styles represent (relatively) stable intrapersonal traits across situations, across tasks and across cognitive abilities that learners employ in perceiving and processing information and stimuli, while interacting and learning within an environment (Coop and Sigel, 1971; Messick, 1976; Jonassen and Grabowski, 1993; Sadler-Smith, 1996, 1998; Schmeck, 1988a; Sadler-Smith et al., 2000).

Clearly, the participant's quotation presented above illustrates just one example of a cognitive style type and its effect on that participant's learning behaviour. Conflating a variety of individuals' preferred ways for learning in a task-centred and time-limited project team setting introduces more social complexity into the presenting learning opportunity. This example, therefore, also serves as a stimulus to speculate on how might situated learning in a project team be affected by individuals' preferred approaches to learning, and how might a team collectively deal with these differences to better facilitate the learning opportunity in a project? Further, it also raises the issue of the learning context and its impacts on situated learning in each project team setting – an issue that is explored in following chapters of this book.

How does cognitive style relate to learning style?

Whilst specific interest in cognitive styles dates all the way back to Jung (1923), who proposed a theory of psychological types (Sternberg and Grigorenko, 1997) (that which is still in use today through the psychometric assessment tool called the Myers-Briggs Type Indicator (Myers and McCaulley, 1985)), the volume and diversity in the measurement and descriptors of cognitive style have created some confusion in this field of study (Sadler-Smith, 1998). This suggests that there is still no clear consensus on what constitutes a style (Galotti *et al.*, 2001). For example, Riding and Cheema (1991) identified over 30 different descriptions of cognitive style and Hayes and Allinson (1994) identified 22 dimensions of cognitive styles (Sadler-Smith, 1998). The definition for cognitive style provided in this book reflects my attempt to traverse this apparent diversity. Contributing to the unresolved consensus on style is the apparent confusion between the constructs of learning styles and cognitive styles, where, for example, people may use the term of learning style interchangeably with cognitive style without necessarily appreciating the differences between the two constructs, for example the different stabilities of each construct across situations. Hence, it is appropriate here to broadly articulate the linkage between them and to conceptually position the construct of cognitive style to learning style, and to also convey a sense of my reasoning behind the focus in this study, on the cognitive style construct.

Cognitive style, learning style and personality can appear to be a messy amalgam of cognitive constructs and Figure 4.1 seeks to alleviate some of that potential confusion. With particular reference to the work of Sadler-Smith (1999), it attempts to provide a simplified pictorial representation of the relationship between learning styles and cognitive styles, and also shows the relationship of the personality construct to the styles constructs, and the learning context input to this relationship. Figure 4.1 also reinforces that cognitive styles provide bridges

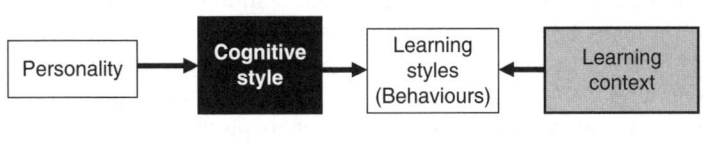

Highly stable >>>>>>>>>>>> **Highly unstable**

Figure 4.1 Cognitive style in perspective

between cognition and personalities (Sternberg, 1995, 1997; Sternberg and Grigorenko, 1997).

When people talk about differences between people, we refer to how people differ from each other in their behaviour, thoughts and perceptions in combination – these patterns of perceiving, thinking, feeling and behaviour are referred to as the personality of a person (Brunas-Wagstaff, 1998). Therefore, personality in everyday terms can be considered a social construction that can have a variety of meanings, and is thus a collective term that we tend to apply to a package of qualities that people have as we observe them (Brunas-Wagstaff, 1998). Also, as depicted on the left-hand side of Figure 4.1, this personality construct of an individual is considered by notable authors in this field to be highly stable over time, and remote from the external influences of the environment (Curry, 1983a; Sadler-Smith, 1999; Crouch, 2001). Consequently, the personality construct is too broad in definition and perception and too remote from the learning styles or learning behaviours of individuals (as indicated by this diagram) to be rationally considered a direct influence on situated learning activity in a setting. However, the cognitive processes of the personality construct are ably represented by the construct of cognitive style, which is relatively stable and mobile across situations and contexts, and does affect situated learning activity through its direct input to individuals' learning behaviours. Therefore, the most useful way to describe project participants' internal mental states for learning is to link onto their internal propensities to want to learn in certain ways, that is their cognitive styles.

The diagram also highlights that the learning behaviour manifestation or learning style of an individual project participant can be considered a socially constructed response or outcome of the conjunction of an individual's cognitive style with their (project) learning environment (Kolb, 1984; Sadler-Smith, 1999; Sadler-Smith *et al.*, 2000). Learning styles can therefore be considered highly unstable constructs that change across situations and contexts and are not the essence of the intra-personal influence on situated learning behaviour, but rather an outcome of two key inputs, that is the cognitive style of the individual and the learning environment. Like the construct of cognitive style, learning styles also seem bound in some confusion due to the range of studies proposing numerous style types (e.g. Curry [1983b] identified 21 different modes of learning styles), and by some researchers providing descriptors that seem to cross the permeable cognitive style and learning style boundaries (Sadler-Smith, 2001a). However, Kolb's (1984) and Honey and Mumford's (1992) respective works have helped practitioners to bypass this confusion in the field (Sadler-Smith, 2001a). The well-referenced and well-utilized Kolb's (1984) learning styles inventory (LSI) is based on Kolb's experiential learning cycle (Kolb, 1984; Hickcox, 1995). Honey and Mumford (1992) further developed this model, resulting in their Learning style questionnaire (LSQ), which aims to establish an individual's biases towards particular learning approaches as is defined in the LSQ (Furnham et al., 1999). These approaches include four learning style types, that is *the activist* – sensation seeking, impulsive and extravert; *the reflector* – introvert, cautious, methodical; *the theorist* – intellectual, rational, objective; *the pragmatist* – expedient, realistic and practical (Hickcox, 1995; Sadler-Smith, 1996; Furnham et al., 1999) (also see Murrell and Bishop [1995] who describe four quadrants of a learning model for managers). Whilst knowing about one's own immediate learning style may assist an individual to better grasp learning opportunities within a specific context (Sims and Sims, 1995b), at a more fundamental level, better understanding the core component inputs to the socially constructed and situation-specific learning style, that is the cognitive styles and the learning context, presents a greater potential to aid the learning of individuals *across any contextual or project situation*.

In sum, the essence of the intra-personal influence on situated learning activity across any context is the relatively stable construct of cognitive style, which, in association with the local environmental factors, then constructs or shapes a participant's demonstrable learning behaviour or learning style – relative to a specific local context.

4.2 The methods of understanding cognitive styles

Having generalized about the broad psychological framework surrounding the construct of cognitive styles, and provided a definition for it, this section moves onto a more detailed discussion of the methods/tools available to understand cognitive styles. It is valuable to expand this discussion in this way, since without such an insight, you may be left pondering what it is one can do to better engage this constraint/enabler for situated learning. This section expounds on four methods of cognitive-style assessment that may be considered equally valuable for both quantitatively and descriptively understanding and assessing cognitive styles. The fourth method described represents the method engaged by the project team in this study to understand their cognitive styles. Embedded within this discourse on the four methods are numerous empirical examples from this case study. These illustrate points raised in the theoretical conversations and establish a cognitive style profile (using the various methods outlined) of the core participants in this project case. In so doing, this section conveys a sense of how one might interpret any of these methods in helping to descriptively profile project participants' style types, and illustrate how the descriptors used in these alternative assessment methods either align or misalign with each other. In a later section of this chapter, these different descriptors are used interchangeably in generalizing about the impacts of cognitive styles on situated learning.

To begin this discussion on the methods, Sadler-Smith (1999) suggests that there are a number of assumptions or criteria relating to cognitive style. These include: it is concerned with the form rather than the content of information; it is a pervasive dimension that can be assessed using psychometric techniques; it is stable over time and bipolar; and, it may be value differentiated, that is styles describe difference rather than better thinking processes (Sadler-Smith and Badger, 1998) (also see Witkin *et al.* [1977], Messick [1984], Sadler-Smith [1998]). Sadler-Smith (1998, 1999) nominated three models of cognitive styles that satisfy these criteria whilst being complementary. They include the Intuition-Analysis dimension of Allinson and Hayes (1996), the Adaptor-Innovator dimension of Kirton (1989) and the Wholist-Analytical/Verbalizer-Imager dimensions of Riding (1991).

The Intuition-Analysis model of Allinson and Hayes (1996) defines intuition as the ability to imagine, conceive, reason or act in novel ways, and analysis as the antithesis of intuition, where it involves analysis and exhibition of the object or system's components, environment or structure (Sadler-Smith, 1998, 1999). Allinson and Hayes (1996) developed a self-report type questionnaire called the Cognitive Styles Index (CSI), which was designed to identify an individual's position on this bipolar Intuition-Analysis dimension. This questionnaire consists of 38 items with the maximum score of 76 indicating a more Analytical cognitive style and with the lower score representing an Intuitive style (Sadler-Smith, 1998, 1999). Intuition and feeling are considered right-brain activities (the more holistic/global, creative and feeling-oriented thinking processes), and sensing and thinking are considered left-brain activities (the logical and analytic thinking processes concerned with detail) – these views are also shared by Mintzberg (1976), Hurst *et al.* (1989) and Allinson and Hayes (1996), as they speculated on the hemispherical differences in the brain as a basis for cognitive style differences.

Allinson and Hayes (1996), Hayes and Allinson (1998) and Sadler-Smith *et al.* (2000) argue that Analysts prefer to pay attention to detail, focus on hard data, and are self-reliant and take a stepwise approach to learning – which may suggest they prefer learning methods that allow for opportunities for independent work with the opportunity to reflect and analyse data (Sadler-Smith, 1999). For example, one project team participant in this study called Len reflected on his own style by stating, 'I probably have a bias towards taking in information verbally with some visual reinforcement.... I often have a pencil in my hand to help me learn... If I don't have it, I feel lost, and often I'll take notes simply because that forces me to immediately reinforce the information, and to be able to check back later.' He also considers himself to be fairly verbose in getting across his concepts or ideas whilst recognizing that another project team member's style (Bill) is quite different, in that he likes precise brief points on the topic being discussed. Len stated, 'I find that often I won't have a clear understanding from just a few words and I tend to like a context to be clear and therefore I will often go to great pains to explain an issue in context. So [] I suppose at times I provide more context than people actually need. So I'm learning to judge that and learning to read the signs of whether, and when, I'm getting through to people and I suppose, because I've got quite ingrained methods [regarding communication and learning], I find it hard to change them too.' This conversation with Len was indicating his strong Analyst cognitive style and he acknowledged that attempting an adjustment to elements of his preferred style is quite challenging and difficult.

Allinson and Hayes (1996) and Hayes and Allinson (1998) argue that Intuitives are less concerned with detail, emphasize synthesis, adopt a global perspective, engage feelings in their decision-making, and take an action-oriented approach to learning and problem-solving, and they prefer to get information from direct interaction with people and things (Sadler-Smith, 1999). Therefore, Intuitives prefer learning methods that are active, participatory and gregarious rather than analytical, reflective and self-referential – highlighting their social dependence (Sadler-Smith, 1999). This separation between Intuitives and Analysts is not necessarily easily determined through only a description of how one learns – adding support perhaps to the use of psychometric assessment tools to help clarify one's biases. Illustrating this issue is the following comment by one of the study participants on his difficulty in describing his style, 'So number one, I'm a bit stuck to actually try and describe what my style is. Generally the way I gather information would be through seeing things and talking to people and experiencing things, I suppose. So, I suppose what I'm saying is that I don't read a lot of material. I think the way I process things is in a very logical form and I suppose part of that is how I evaluate things as well. Everything has to fit into place so it's always this goes with this goes with that. I don't know whether I'm doing a good job here mate – I'm trying to explain how it works.' This participant's reflections on his approaches to gathering and processing information indicate a more Intuitive than Analytical cognitive style. His ongoing demonstrable unease at performing public reflection and analysis on his own and others' learning and management activities associated with the project added further weight to classifying him in this Intuitive category.

These differences between Intuitives and Analysts affect what people pay attention to, how they interpret data and how their interpretations of experiences influence and modify their own mental models, that is a person's cognitive style influences how their mental models evolve and change (Hayes and Allinson, 1998). On a broader canvas, if individuals in an organizational or occupational group such as a project team share similar cognitive styles, they process information in similar ways which may assist a shared development of collective mental models, and therefore promote a form of organizational learning (Hayes and Allinson, 1998). This does not, however, indicate the volume or quality of the learning occurring, just that in the short term, similarities in cognitive approaches may aid some form of local organizational learning process. Conversely, over the longer term, differences in cognitive approaches may aid the development of individuals in learning-how-to-learn and also promote organizational learning activity. These issues will be assessed later in this chapter.

Sadler-Smith (1999) considers that the Allinson and Hayes Intuition-Analysis dimension of cognitive style is broadly equivalent to the Adaptor-Innovator dimension described by Kirton (1989). The primary supposition behind Kirton's (1989) Adaptation-Innovation theory is that individuals differ in their preferred ways for dealing with change, creativity, decision-making and problem-solving (Sadler-Smith, 1998). To aid classifying a person into either category, Kirton developed an Adaptation-Innovation inventory tool consisting of an inventory of 32 items. Kirton (1989) considers Adaptors as being characterized by precision, reliability, efficiency and conformity, and they solve problems in previously tried and proven ways. Therefore, they are inclined to support existing frames of reference, focus their attention on doing things better and engage in low-level learning (e.g. single-loop learning). Conversely, Innovators demonstrate undisciplined thinking, challenge existing paradigms for doing things and take tangential approaches to problems, and are unable to maintain detailed meticulous work over long periods (Hayes and Allinson, 1998; Sadler-Smith, 1998).

When Len was asked to describe what he considered to be his cognitive style in terms of the Adaptor-Innovator typology, he responded by saying, 'I suppose generally I fit more into the Adaptor style. I like to look at how things are being done. I've still got a notion of challenging things when someone starts to say that's the way I've always done it – I then think there's a good reason to change, if that's the only reason they offer. So challenging completely the existing paradigm I do find difficult. I find it difficult to visualize something that's totally divorced from the existing. I think I'm getting a bit better at it – certainly trying. I struggle with the notion of expressing a vision... certainly expressing it succinctly.' Len considered one of his co-participants, Steve, to be a strong Innovator by stating, 'Steve gets right under people's ribs and asks why things can't be different and for them to be more capable, which is one of his great strengths, as he is capable of seeing things quite differently from the way we do things now.' Steve considers that Len behaves mostly as an Adaptor style type, and himself as the Innovator among the three core project team members, but also feels that he does not push some of his ideas strongly enough, which as he states, 'may come as a surprise to the others'. Steve believes that as an Innovator he needs to see that the benefits will be a lot more than the effort required to prompt him to challenge existing paradigms. When Steve was separately asked to describe Bill's style, he recognized Bill's Innovator streak but considered him principally an Adaptor, and referred to him as the Innovator-thinker and Adaptor-operator. Len also recognized this diversity in Bill, whose style he described as, 'someone who can see things quite differently but I think is probably more the Adaptor than the Innovator and will tend to express concepts or ideas in the same language as we might use in the current system – hence his focus on the numbers. As to what style is more appropriate in this project?... Challenging the existing paradigm is really important to what we're doing. It's very easy to justify the status quo. The status quo is not going to be what's going to deliver success and I suppose if we are all Adaptors then we're not going to see the possibilities... but keeping an eye on reality – doing a reality check [from the current position] is also valuable.' Len also expressed his view that prior to the project sponsor joining the organization, none of them knew how to prompt themselves out of the current paradigm. When Steve was asked to reflect on this question of which style is more appropriate in this project, his response revolved around similar issues, that is he perceived a blend of both styles as advantageous for the project process to work and for learning. Len and Steve's reflective deliberations on this matter identify an important issue around cognitive styles in this setting. They considered that a blending of the Innovator and Adaptor styles in this project team was an important feature for their project to be successful and for their learning-how-to-learn. This expressed view being consistent with Sadler-Smith's (1999) conclusion that balancing Intuition and Analysis styles is crucial in improving an individual's learning performance. Therefore, at one level such a blending (or mismatching) of different styles may be considered as aiding the project and learning processes, but in so doing, one might expect that this blending also creates significant learning tensions between the participants, as they seek to learn from each other and the project situation.

Perhaps then at a different level, and in consideration of these learning tensions between different style types, an individual's cognitive style may actually impede the individual or collective learning processes within an event. For example, when Len was asked if he considered Steve's (the Innovator) actions impeded or assisted learning within the project team process, Len (the Adaptor) stated:

> Often it impedes rather than supports it. There are circumstances where it does support learning where he's able to throw in good challenges. However, often his actions appear to be around point scoring and not about learning... and we need to be very careful... in making assumptions about the Innovator's motives and we want to avoid missing something that's important. Steve's got some really good perspectives but I need to be on top of those. I need also to understand his challenges. Very often he comes out with a lot of bluff and bluster and people think that he's almost insecure behind it, so I have learnt to deal with his behaviour by getting straight back in his face and then you get down to a more reasonable discussion.

In this dialogue, Len has articulated his interpretation of Steve's behaviour and identified a process to stabilize his discussion (as an Adaptor) with a particular Innovator, and thereby manage the learning process mostly and perhaps perceptually on his terms. This is not a sinister development as such, but just an insight into some dynamics the project team participants demonstrated in their learning-how-to-learn. Len further suggested that Steve has actually impeded his own learning through being 'too often concerned with where he's coming from and his manipulation of the group, and not being prepared to sit back and to trust the group that he can learn from. I think that has been a real impact on his learning.' In effect, Len suggests that Steve impeded his own learning because he would not listen to others in a disciplined way and freely deposits his ideas without consideration for others' views. In this case, perhaps this was a learning-how-to-learn process issue for Steve (the Innovator) to acknowledge and redress. Consistent with Len's view, Steve himself recognized that his style may be limiting his learning although he considered his style as being aligned with the information-processing needs of the project. That being, 'I believe my cognitive style fits the fact that I probably should be out there talking to guys, getting them on board and picking things up...but I think it would be better if I was more open to learning and how I go about understanding the processes...I tend to be reactionary to the learning. If it hits me then I'll grab it rather than me going looking for them. So,...I feel inadequate sometimes [regarding his learning] and think that's something I've got to address.'

The empirical examples provided above highlight that Innovators tend to perceive the work environment as more turbulent than Adaptors and perhaps behave more turbulently within it, and therefore the two style types readily conflict regarding their views about change and how to achieve it (Hayes and Allinson, 1998). Elaborating further on the example described above, over many project team sessions Len constantly challenged Steve's style and attempted to wrestle some control of the project sessions away from that dominant participant. When Len was confronted with these observations, his response involved, 'Your observations about Steve and I having a bit of a match-up...yeah that's about trying to balance Steve's tendency to dominate by saying okay, this is what we're doing here, does everyone agree, and right, lets move on. Particularly some of the quieter people in the meetings occasionally have been letting him get away with that.' The dominating person (Steve, the Innovator) in these exchanges indicated that he enjoyed his match-ups with Len because he thinks Len tends to think differently about issues and he likes to build his knowledge on that. Steve highlights this view when he comments about working with Len, 'Len and I tend to vie for leadership and it doesn't worry me at all....If I've got a point I know that Len will honour it and play with it...show me up for the fool I am and improve it...he takes it on and that's okay, and we keep moving on from there.' To some third party observing this style interplay, these two players may seem to be simply impeding their learning through their apparent conflict. The contradiction being that whilst the participants acknowledged that sometimes they felt their styles did impede their learning and the team's learning, these two parties came to respect those differences and attempted to find ways to work with those differences to prompt their own learning on issues, and, perhaps incidentally, also prompted the collective learning in the team.

Complementary to the Intuition-Analysis and Adaptor-Innovator dimensions of cognitive style, the Wholist-Analytical dimension of cognitive style (Riding, 1991) involves describing the habitual way in which an individual learner processes and organizes information, wherein some will process it in a wholistic or global way and others break it into component parts, that is Analytics (Riding and Raynor, 1998; Sadler-Smith, 1998, 2001b; Rezaei and Katz, 2004). Schmeck (1988b) describes an Analytic style as involving field independence and focused attention on details, where an individual's thinking is more directed and controlled. Analytics are able to divorce feelings from objective facts and they are logical and critical thinkers. Schmeck (1988b) describes the Wholist or global style being field-dependent with attention directed towards scanning and forming global impressions rather than precise articulations of events or observations. Therein, the individual's thinking is more intuitive, which involves feelings in decision-making, and they are less concerned with conscious control and are more impulsive than Analytics. From his Intuitive or Wholist perspective, Steve asserts his perception of the value of learning in being its applicability to real life, that is 'Learning for learning sake has never touched me up much, there has to be some other reason and then I find I can learn heaps about something to help me understand or prove a point or whatever. The learning is a thing along the way – it's not an end in itself.' This comment is primarily reflective of Steve's context or field dependence, but also hints at his inclination towards an undisciplined, opportunistic and impulsive approach to his own learning. This opportunistic approach to his learning is further illustrated in his following comment, 'I don't go in saying I'm going to manipulate this meeting so we get the learning about whatever... if learning happens it happens, if it doesn't it doesn't... because usually I'm more focused on the outcome or something else. I'm not practiced or artful yet to get two things done at one time.'

Schmeck (1988b) argues that at the highest level of cognitive development, a person would integrate both analytic and global skills. Such integration of analytic and global skills is attuned to a person using both sides of their brain, wherein the left side is concerned with structure, logic and organization, and the right is concerned with thinking more holistically, being more artistic, and is less reliant on words and logic (Sims and Sims, 1995a). Somewhat emulating this quest for the integration of analytic and global skills, the participants in this project team attempted to pursue both rational and non-rational issues associated with the project. However, with the non-rational issues, they felt less competent and less comfortable. They referred to this activity as moving below the green line. This meant their normal attention to rational workplace issues concerning structures, patterns and processes would now incorporate an additional and significant focus on the non-rational issues of their identities, information-sharing and their relationships (Wheatley, 1999). Therefore, one might postulate they were in the formative stages of seeking to achieve a higher level of cognitive development as described by Schmeck (1988b). That is not to suggest (given their different cognitive styles) that they all wholeheartedly welcomed that exploratory journey at the start. For example, even Steve (considered a Wholist or Intuitive type) questioned the necessity of this journey into the non-rational issues in one of the early project team meeting sessions, by stating, 'I am not a non-rational person and therefore why do I need to swim in the non-rational world...I am secure about me being rational.' When asked what he was protecting, he retorted, 'My sanity!' His comments reflected his initial apprehension and insecurity in having to communally deal with such complex social issues that were not normally a deliberate focus within the traditional operation.

Coupled to the Wholist-Analytic (WA) dimension, Riding (1991) also provided what he termed the Verbal–Imagery (VI) dimension of cognitive style. This dimension describes an individual's habitual mode of representing information in memory during thinking. Therein, Verbalizers consider the information they read or listen to in words or verbal associations, and Imagers would consider the same information in fluent spontaneous pictorial mental pictures (Riding and Raynor, 1998; Sadler-Smith, 1998, 2001b; Rezaei and Katz, 2004). Like Wholists and Intuitives, Verbalizers tend to be outward-focused towards others, seeking social group activity and stimulating environments, whilst Imagers (similar to Analysts) will tend to be inwardly and individually focused and be more passive and content with a static environment (Sadler-Smith, 1998). Riding (1991) developed the computer-presented Cognitive Styles Analysis (CSA) tool to assess the WA and VI dimension of cognitive style. This tool consists of VI tests that measure the speed of response of the participants in answering true or false statements on visual appearance type questions versus semantic conceptual type questions. The tool also involves a WA test in which participants are asked to identify simple shapes from more complex ones and to judge whether two complex geometrical shapes are the same (Sadler-Smith, 1998). Like the raft of other psychometric analysis tools undergoing constant empirical evaluation and theoretical elaboration, the CSA computerized test is also open for validity and reliability challenges, since the test relies on peoples' reaction time or (latency of response) to particular questions (see Rezaei and Katz [2004]). For example, response times can be influenced by the information the respondents have about their speed in answering the questions. Riding (2003) acknowledges that the CSA test is not a perfect measure of cognitive style and that it could be improved, but in its present form is sufficiently suggestive that a particular style is more likely to exist than not. He also suggests that what is needed are robust objective methods of assessing cognitive style that probably exclude introspective self-reporting or response latencies approaches. Perhaps that constitutes a search for the holy grail of psychometric assessment? Nevertheless, these principal researchers and authors in this field of psychology have provided (and continue to develop) a means to quantitatively identify one's propensity towards a particular cognitive approach towards learning.

As a result of this relatively brief theoretical and empirical elaboration on these three cognitive style models, it appears that there is some overlap, but the idea of a consistent and complete alignment of the descriptions of Innovation-Adaptation with Intuition-Analysis, respectively, seems remote. (Note: Sadler-Smith [1999] stresses a need for validity studies on these alignment aspects.) For example, of the three core participants in the project team of this study, two of them might be considered Adaptors and one the Innovator, whilst two of them Intuitive and the other Analytic. Although noted, that misalignment issue is of little conceptual concern, since what is most important here is that regardless of the descriptor terminology used, these classifying terms help to understand relatively stable intra-personal differences between project team members and serve as one catalyst for them to both learn and work more effectively together. As the project participant Bill eloquently put it, 'This stuff helps us to work and learn together so as not to piss each other off!'

Cognitive styles assessment in the project team case study

A fourth method of cognitive styles assessment which incorporates the themes of those complementary models previously described involves the use of the assessment tool called the Myers-Briggs Type Indicator (MBTI) (Myers and McCaulley, 1985). The project team examined in this study assessed their cognitive styles with this tool, and it is essentially what Sternberg and Grigorenko (1997) refer to as a personality-centred approach to cognitive styles assessment. This approach involves Jung's (1923) theory of psychological types, which includes: functions of how one deals with oneself and others, and involves extraversion or introversion; two perceptual functions of intuition and sensing; and, two judgement or decision-making functions of thinking and feeling. An extension of Jung's theory by Myers and Myers (1980) and Myers and McCaulley (1985) extended the theory to include ways of dealing with the external world involving judgement and perception – resulting in 16 possible personality style types (Sternberg and Grigorenko, 1997) (see also, Sternberg [1995] and Sternberg [1997]). For example, a sensing person (S) is more inclined towards seeking the fullest detailed experience of what is immediate and real. An intuitive person (N) seeks the broadest view of what is possible and insightful. A thinking person (T) likes to make decisions based on rational and logical planning, and a feeling person (F) likes to make decisions based on harmony among subjective values. An extraverted person (E) seeks to actively engage the outer world of objects, people and activities, whilst the introverted person (I) prefers the inner world of concepts and ideas. A judging person (J) tends to be concerned with making decisions, seeking closure and planning and organizing activities. Conversely, a perceiving person (P) tends to be attuned to incoming information and open to new events and changes and eager to engage everything (Myers, 1993; Sternberg, 1995, 1997). As well as being the tool used to assess the cognitive styles of the project team participants in this study (and in other teams across the host organization), it has been widely used in education and business to help develop an understanding of normal personality differences between people (Myers, 1993; Sternberg and Grigorenko, 1997). Indeed, Hickcox (1995) considers personality-style inventory tools such as the MBTI as offering people excellent information for personal self-knowledge and how they may relate to different learning settings.

When Len was asked if he felt that the project participants' cognitive styles aligned readily with the information-processing demands of the project, he hypothesized that 'I suppose if you look at the group average Myers-Briggs we would have very few sensates and a whole lot of intuitives which is great, except therefore, [generally] we don't like writing anything down, we don't like getting down to detail and why worry about letting facts get in the way of a good story.' He further supported that view, by stating in a project team meeting, 'Understanding the impact on different people [of project decisions]... we still don't work on enough facts, we don't put enough value on having the sensate information to support the intuition.' Len's comments signal his personal concern about a perceived shortage of sensing type individuals in the project team mix, with potential implications for individual and collective learning, and ultimately project success. Len's MBTI score indicated him to be a fairly strong introvert (I), solid thinking (T) and Judging (J) type and based on his opinion (and those of his colleagues) he quite comfortably flips between being quite sensate (S) to being slightly intuitive (N). Whilst any direct comparison of dimensional ratings contained within the MBTI with the Intuition-Analysis criteria developed by Allinson and Hayes (1996), for example, is inconclusive, one might suggest that Len's MBTI assessment of ISTJ broadly aligns with the Analyst cognitive style described in the works of Riding (1991) and Allinson and Hayes (1996). Moreover, Len's comments may also be a reflection on his Adaptor (Kirton, 1989) orientation and his inclination to drive the change process from the existing operational paradigm, compared to those Innovators (Kirton, 1989) in the team (particularly the extraverted ones) that wanted to challenge the existing paradigm and appear undisciplined in their thinking and approaches. Whilst these sorts of dynamics were played out during the course of the project, one would regularly observe all the project team members referring to their MBTI score in their project conversations about their learning behaviours. For example, Steve readily acknowledged the perception of his style in the team by saying, 'I think people see me as somebody who will push the paradigms and stir things up and I'm happy to do that. I like thinking of different ways of doing things – just like any other ENTJ.' Steve's score on the MBTI placed him firmly in this ENTJ category, while the other core participant, Bill, was identified as an INFJ type. Hence, even between just the three core participants, one can envision the opportunity for conflict between the parties resulting from their different cognitive styles, and perhaps also the need for them to better understand their styles and the ramifications of their styles in their project workplace.

Fortunately, these project team participants undertook joint-learning activities to better understand their style differences, and their individual impacts on other people and on the collective learning within the team. The vignette below illustrates these learning activities and the richness of the personal interactions that developed around communal discussions on personal style issues. It reports on the team's reflective feedback process to Bill, involving participants' observations of Bill's project behaviour.

Steve indicated to Bill that he felt that he was very directive with his instructions to people who worked with him. Steve supported his view by making the following comment about Bill's approach, 'you imply this is what I want and this is how I want you to do it.' Steve then compared this command and control style with the future way of working, and noted the contradiction. Another team member offered a comment on Bill's ability to translate the future issues into tangible steps for people to relate to today, and on Bill's strong sense of compassion for others, and his well respected good nature. Likewise, Len also acknowledged Bill's perceived good nature and his sensitivity to others' feelings and his belief that Bill wanted to assist people to cope with the change process. Steve suggested that Bill was at risk of pandering too much to individuals, and Bill quickly reflected on that comment and agreed that was a personal risk. Steve also commented on Bill's meeting mechanics by stating, 'Once you have made up your mind to do something – you are incorrigible, although your heart is in the right place.' He also indicated to Bill that he felt that he kept some guys at arm's length (i.e. distant) – which may be a possible downside in his working relationships, but he does get things done and that commands respect from his colleagues.

Bill absorbed this feedback and then publicly reflected on these and other observations. He openly accepted that he faced a challenge in balancing his ownership of tasks with the new culture requirements (i.e. sharing that ownership). He indicated that he was progressively encouraging greater participation in decision-making with his people, and that he was conscious of trying not to just do things, without other peoples' involvement. In support of those actions, Len interjected and said, 'you really know your people and their quirks, which is a real strength' [Len indicated that he felt Bill had a strong empathy with the workforce]. Bill then summarized his reflections. These included: he felt he was perhaps too empathetic to peoples' needs; he agreed with all the feedback offered and related it to his own examples [thereby providing another learning intervention which created a further round of reflection for both Bill and the team]; he reinforced that he is a rational, practical guy and that he sometimes struggled with the philosophy [of the change program] and with the challenges and changes he personally faced, and how it all relates to his current practical world.

Clearly in this vignette, Bill was publicly confronted with other's impressions of his style and his demonstrated behaviour. He then reflected on that feedback and related the information to his own examples of his actions, which helped him to reinforce what he had heard, or to challenge the comments offered. This double-loop process helped him to understand and appreciate the impacts that his own style was having on others in the team and within the context. This process resembled what Argyris and Schön (1978) refer to as someone trying to move towards a Model II type person, wherein they challenge their mental models and basic assumptions of the world and their relationships within it, and invite confrontation of their own assumptions and test these publicly. From the vignette, one can also see the apparent strength of the F and J components of his style – as observed and offered by his colleagues. Also, the last reflective comments offered by Bill should not be treated in any dismissive manner. In the context of the project process and its goals, and from a learning-how-to-learn perspective, such public admission of one's feelings of inadequacy with core elements of the change initiative can also be considered a laudable learning action.

As evidenced in this vignette and in other empirical examples provided throughout this section, it appeared that these project participants, having developed an understanding of their own and their colleagues' cognitive styles, could better appreciate and rationalize their differences in approaches to issues. It also helped them to better interpret their observations of their colleagues' learning behaviours and to constructively converse and reflect about their differences in style, as it affected their personal and collective learning activities. Consequently, over time, this knowledge and the ensuing processes also contributed towards the building of the participants' learning relationships.

4.3 How did the cognitive styles of project participants in this project case impact their situated learning behaviours?

This section examines the pragmatic impacts of cognitive styles on situated learning activity in a project setting. It serves as a coalescence of the impacting issues raised or hinted at in the numerous empirical examples provided in the preceding section of this chapter.

To begin this discussion, I first provide a volley of some additional observations of how the cognitive styles of the core project participants seemed to influence their learning behaviours within the project. It must be acknowledged, however, that these examples are likely to have been at least partly influenced by other factors or elements in the project learning milieu. Those elements are explored later in this book. These observations included Steve (the extravert Intuitive), for example, disengaging discussions if he was saturated with detailed information and/or frustrated with a lack of forward movement on an issue, and also when his colleagues regularly confronted him with those types of observations. Conversely, when Steve felt or appeared to be in his style and experience comfort zones, he often saturated his colleagues with questions and provocative statements to stimulate what he determined to be progress within the project team. Len (the Analytic sensate type) regularly tried to coordinate and facilitate their project team meetings in a methodical and structured way. He did this in an effort to help get the team focused on the transformational project issues and away from the daily transactional ones, and thereby better utilize the project learning opportunities. He also reliably and actively engaged discussions with his colleagues and posed probing questions to them to source answers to, or to aid the exploration of difficult project issues. One surmises that the project learning space suited his style and therefore he was in his style comfort zone, where perhaps the other players were demonstrably less comfortable. Bill (the introverted, feeling intuitive type) appeared predominantly reactionary to learning opportunities presented in the project team learning spaces, particularly when the focus was specifically on him and his actions. He also appeared to strongly prefer a personalized conversational approach (Hansen et al., 1999) for his knowledge exchange and generation. Bill's behaviours culminated in a seeming reliance on the others to generate his learning for him, that is he appeared to be more prepared to be the recipient rather than the generator of new knowledge.

These observed learning behaviours of the project team participants have been shaped or influenced by cognitive style conditioners. These conditioners, which are explored below, constitute some major considerations and action points in seeking to promote situated learning activity in a project team.

The match/mismatch of cognitive style to project information-processing demands

In project environments the information-processing demands on individuals and the team are generally high and variable in content, and to some degree largely contingent on the project type and on the project phase. That being, for example, an organizational change type project in the implementation phase may present high volumes and complexity in information versus a product development project in the project completion phase, which may present quite different information-processing requirements. The volume and variability in information-processing demand in a project, over time and over type, suggest that it may be desirable to regularly appraise what are the expected information-processing demands on individuals in their project roles, and to assess whether their cognitive styles, individually and collectively, are likely to align to the perceived information-processing demands of a project (Mohrman et al., 1995; Hayes and Allinson, 1998). In the short term, where there is a match, project team participants may find it relatively easy to interpret relevant information and use it to decide how to act in order to perform effectively. Where there is a mismatch, people may not attend to, or adequately interpret important information. For example, they may become bogged down in analysis of detail when there is no time or requirement for this level of analysis, or they may ignore important detail when it is critical that they should understand it, that is highlighting the differences in the Wholist-Analytic or Intuition-Analysis dimensions of one's cognitive style. A mismatch then, as well as creating some angst for the participants, can result in team members not acquiring or correctly interpreting information that is necessary in changing their assumptions about situations and deciding how they should act (Hayes and Allinson, 1998). For example, during a major configurational change episode in the project team of this study, the project sponsor (and principal change agent) directly and repeatedly intervened in the project team. These interventions offered significant learning opportunities of a detailed and transformational nature for the project team participants. During a separate reflection session after one of these interventions, and in response to provocative questioning about their political competence to learn from these interventions, Bill (an Intuitive and Adaptor type) explicitly reflected that 'Sometimes I just don't know that I have been given a lesson.' With this comment, he reflectively acknowledged that he failed to capture the immediate learning opportunities during the event, since the detailed and transformational nature of those opportunities seemed misaligned with his Intuitive cognitive style.

Participants individually and collectively selecting situations which align with their cognitive style

A second cognitive style conditioner of participants' learning behaviours involves people individually and collectively selecting situations that allow them to utilize their identifiable cognitive styles, and to avoid those situations that pose alternative demands – thus, potentially restricting learning potential (Sternberg, 1988). That being, people are motivated to seek more certain benefits associated with their preferred approach to information-gathering and processing than take a risk in situations that are incongruent with their cognitive style, and which may require them to change their approaches (Hayes and Allinson, 1998). In these situations, when a person's cognitive style seems to be regularly in alignment with the information-processing demands of a situation, it presents a self-reinforcing cycle, which may further entrench existing information-processing routines. In the longer-term, these entrenchments may blind project team members to information that might signal a need to changes in knowledge and skills necessary to enable performance (Hayes and Allinson, 1998). This is clearly an argument in contradiction to those immediate shorter-term benefits to be realized in matching cognitive styles to the information-processing demands of a role. In a similar vein, Sadler-Smith (1999) contends that while most empirical studies of cognitive style suggest that matching an individual's cognitive style to learning methods is beneficial for learning, some authors have argued for a mismatch, to expose the learner to a wider range of learning skills. That is, to help develop their skills in learning-how-to-learn (for examples, see Entwistle [1988], Honey and Mumford [1992] and Raelin [2000]). If individuals succeed in learning-how-to-learn, then ultimately the matching of cognitive style to learning methods becomes a redundant concept (Sadler-Smith, 1999).

Tending to emulate this mismatched condition, the information-processing demands on the project team participants involved in this study were never intended, or likely to entrench pre-existing information-processing routines. That being so, the complex transformational organizational change activities of the project, juxtaposed to the immediate operational performance activities, meant that generally the information-processing demands on participants were very expansive, diverse and demanding. This situation particularly challenged the predominant Adaptor style types (Kirton, 1989) in the project team. Consequently, most participants in the team were generally and purposefully pushed outside of their cognitive comfort zones. Such a powerful mismatch between their cognitive styles with the learning demands of their situation is consistent with Sadler-Smith's (1999) comments on exposing learners to a wider range of learning skills and learning opportunities – which helped focus participant attention on their learning-how-to-learn. Indeed, the participants in this project team often reflected on each other's styles and on the benefits or drawbacks they observed in how those styles operated in response to the demands of the project environment. For example, Steve once reflected about Len's style, 'Len tends to be more active in his listening to others and I like the way he actually uses the right words to explain what he's trying to do, whereas, I tend not to do that, as I just do the tasks required without explanation.... I wish I could do that sort of thing sometime – just once would be good.'

Predominance of a particular cognitive style type across a team

A third cognitive style conditioner of participants' learning behaviours involves the predominance of a particular cognitive style type across a team of people. Therein, the general conformity of styles may tend to confine knowledge discovery and critical reflection processes to the shared cognitive comfort zone of the participants. That being so, the team misses out on new and different perspectives or ideas generated through different information-processing approaches because team processes may tend to exclude or marginalize other style types input or contribution to the project. For example, a team primarily consisting of Intuitive types may have little interest or time for considered input from Analyst-type participants. Similarly, reflection practices may only engage processes that suit the majority of participants and frustrate the other minority participants, and motivate them to minimally (or not bother to) engage in reflection practices relating to a project. For example, a majority Analyst-type team may seek to have participants independently reflect on issues and then come together and share their well-considered ideas, whereas a minority of Intuitive types in that situation would prefer to actively and participatively reflect on the issues with all of the participants together. The empirical examples of exchanges and learning tensions between project team participants provided in this chapter illustrate these participants' reactions to differing style types and also the impact on individual learning attitudes and approaches. However, perhaps as a sign of the developing maturity of the project team in this study in learning-how-to-learn, the core participants in the team considered that having a mix (or mismatch) of cognitive styles in the team was both advantageous for the successful completion of their project, and for their personal learning development.

Furthermore, in the later stages of this study, in acknowledging a distinct bias towards Intuitive types in the team and in seeking to learn-how-to-learn, the participants constructed learning actions that deliberately sought to alleviate any cognitive bias adversely affecting their learning in the team. These intended actions included: *We need to seek out the sensates to balance the information in the team* and *We need to consciously and actively recognize different styles and compensate for them.* These explicit learning actions (amongst many others) were to be enacted in the operational workplace as part of the participants' pursuit of their project goals, and then reflected on and revised as part of the participative action research process. In devising and applying themselves to these intended learning actions, the participants tended to become even more cognisant of (and could arguably better compensate for) the impacts of the dominant Intuitive style types on their collective learning activities.

This general conformity of style types across a project team can be considered a random variable input in the formation of a project team, or it can also be an outcome of the socio-cultural framework of the organization in which the project team participants operate. That is, in an organization with a long and stable history, only those employees that decide they can conform to and operate successfully within a particular socio-cultural environment stay. In that scenario, it is likely that many of those long-serving employees also share many similar aspects of their cognitive styles, and when project team participants are selected from the organization population, it is equally likely that there will be some conformity of cognitive styles in the mix. This situation was evident in the project team of this study. The organization's traditional cultural framework involved high respect for employees' technical abilities and their years of service to the organization, and fostered rational, decisive and bureaucratic decision-making processes. That being so, Steve (an ENTJ) offered the following reflection about their culture and training, and its influence on their behaviours, 'Our culture is about doing and not about reflecting, and there is not always time to reflect.' These comments and observations reflect cultural support for the thinking and judging and intuition elements of the MBTI preferences, and tacit discouragement for sensing and feeling and perceiving elements. Not surprisingly then, the majority of the project team participants in this study were grouped predominantly in the INTJ category. Therefore, this reinforcing cultural frame (Goffman, 1974) presented a significant cultural barrier to them performing personal and group reflection practices (Boud, 1991; Seibert and Daudlin, 1999) and consequently also to how they gathered, interpreted and integrated information into their individual mental models. The change programme and this project activity were directly challenging that pre-existing cultural frame by pushing project team participants into unfamiliar learning process territory, involving multiple levels of public reflection, and into unfamiliar learning topic territory on issues like cognitive styles and politics. Highlighting this difficulty in changing their past learning behaviours, Bill noted in an interview session, 'I've definitely thought about the reflection processes, and about how to improve my learning. Whether I am actually able to modify my learning behaviour every time an opportunity presents itself has not always been the case – I would suggest [to align with the new learning environment expectations]. Old habits die hard perhaps, and there're internal values probably driving some of that too.'

4.4 Summary

The essence of the intra-personal influence on situated learning activity, in any situation, is the relatively stable psychological construct of cognitive style. When cognitive styles are publicly exposed and communally reflected on, they can be considered a socially oriented learning issue. The project team involved in this study utilized the personality-centred cognitive style assessment method called the Myers-Briggs Type Indicator (Myers and McCaulley, 1985). However, whether individuals in this project team were identified as ENTJs or Intuitives, or any other classification or descriptor type from any of the assessment methods discussed is not the critical underpinning feature of the analysis presented in this chapter. Instead, the critical underpinning feature revolves around these project team participants having exposed themselves to the learning and learning development possibilities that exist, by explicitly engaging with this constraint/enabler element. In acquiring an understanding of their own and their colleagues' cognitive styles, these project participants better connected with one another. That being so, they were better able to appreciate and understand the behaviours of each other in the project and devised ways to constructively work with those differences to their mutual learning and project advantage. Therein, they progressively helped to build their learning relationships and helped develop their individual skills in learning-how-to-learn.

This chapter also presented and discussed three cognitive style conditioners of participants' learning behaviours. These included: the matching or mismatching of project information-processing demands with the cognitive styles of participants; participants individually or collectively selecting situations that aligned with their cognitive style types and avoiding situations which pose alternative demands; the predominance of a particular cognitive style type across a team. The first of those conditioners articulated the short-term value or benefits of having cognitive styles align with the information-processing demands of a project. Conversely, the second of those conditioners stressed the long-term negative learning outcomes of regularly matching cognitive styles with the information-processing demands of a situation. This contradictory position posited that, for the learning development of individuals in the longer-term, mismatching the two variables is essential. That is, through such mismatching (as was observed in the case study reported on in this book), participants are exposed to a greater range of learning opportunities and are tacitly encouraged to develop their skills in learning-how-to-learn. In progressively developing that learning skill, attempting to match these two variables ultimately becomes a non-issue for learning. The third conditioner highlighted the negative impacts on learning behaviours that a general conformity in cognitive style types across a project team might present. The core participants in the project team involved in this study concluded that having a mix or mismatch of cognitive styles in the team was advantageous for both the intended project outcomes and their learning development. Over the longer-term then, having both a mismatch of cognitive styles in a team and a mismatch of cognitive styles to the information-processing demands of a project situation can be considered quite necessary for enhancing participant learning development. Such a conclusion may be in contradiction with contemporary project management practice perspectives, since mismatching implies and likely involves some conflict, risk and additional managerial effort, and therefore something one would normally seek to minimize or avoid.

Whilst the actions described in this chapter signal that some level of situated learning activity was certainly occurring within the project, it was generally considered that throughout the study, these three core project participants appeared to be more the passengers for learning, rather than the drivers of learning. When confronted with this viewpoint, they explicitly concurred with it, which then prompted their individual and collective reflection on why that was the case, and their questioning of how they might move from one position towards the other. Steve suggested that being the passenger in this particular project was better than being the driver – with the implication that he felt safer in that role. Perhaps Len shed further light on Steve's reasoning in attempting to partly justify his passenger role, by claiming that they lack role clarity (in the project) and that they are very conscious of positional authority and the need to balance their project activities with all the other change programme activities on the site. Bill highlighted their collective dilemma by stating, 'How do we actually get out of the back seat?' In addition to the individual cognitive styles of participants constraining or supporting their learning, they seemed influenced by other socio-contextual elements as well. Those other elements constitute the focus of the next two chapters.

5
Learning Relationships and Pyramid of Authority

This chapter provides an insight into the interpersonal constraint/enabler elements for project situated learning. The first major section of this chapter explores the learning relationships element. Therein, it initially defines what a learning relationship is, and elaborates on the importance of understanding and building them in a project context. It then discusses two conditioners of project participants' learning relationships, which ultimately influence their situated learning behaviours. These conditioners include: attitudes to public exposure and public scrutiny of perceived personal matters; and, preparedness to explore one's learning relationships with others outside of the existing relationship frameworks, while viewing relationship problems as major learning opportunities. These discussions cover aspects of defensive routines impacting learning exchanges as well as issues of challenging traditional socio-cultural factors or assumptions within the presenting project relationship frameworks.

The second major section of this chapter defines and describes the pyramid of authority element for project situated learning. It articulates how politics is rife in projects, the necessity to positively engage with it and the links between learning and politics. It also describes how perceptions of the authorities that participants bring into a project setting can impact their learning behaviours. This discussion covers aspects of utilizing participant authority as something positive for situated learning activity and perceptions of participant authority as a restraint on communal debate, reflection and knowledge exchange about project issues. It also elaborates on how participants' perceptions of their authority to lead a project and their learning activity can be further conditioned by factors within and surrounding a project. Therein, three conditioners of participants' pyramids of authority within a project setting are explored. These consist of: participant ambiguity within a project revolving around the subject of learning, their roles and the process to achieve the project goals; the latent or discernable authority of the project sponsor; and, the relationship of a project to other projects that demonstrate political hegemony in an organization. The final section of this chapter then provides a summary of the key issues concerning these two interpersonal constraining/enabling elements affecting project situated learning activity.

5.1 Learning relationships

The importance of understanding the learning relationships

> I think our team isn't comfortable with silence where they can think about how things are impacting upon them or ask, 'What's my learning from this?' What actually often happens is a reflection will be made about a certain relationship dynamic and one of the guys will say, 'that happens in the other project team and you can see it in the example of blah, blah, blah.' They take the energy away from the opportunity to improve their own relationships by looking at the issue in something that's not attached to them personally. I think they can really move this project and their learning forward if they can actually spend time thinking about, 'how does that impact on me?'... 'What does that mean for me personally?' When I can actually hear their conversations using words like, 'for me', or 'in my experience', or 'honestly in my opinion'... then when that happens that will be a real milestone
>
> (Molly – frequent participant in the project team)

This reflective quotation from Molly (a junior Human Resources Facilitator in the operation and frequent participant in the project team during the early phases of this study) highlights three important points. First, she recognized defensive behaviour in the project team participants when they confronted issues about their own learning relationships. Second, these comments indicate that the project team participants were exploring some rather difficult socio-cultural issues around their learning. Third, this exploration process during the participants' team meetings included deep personal reflections on their team learning processes and on their own learning behaviours. These points serve as an illustration of the learning activities of the project team involved in this study. They also serve as a catalyst to explore and speculate on how relationship issues between those project participants might have impacted on their situated learning, and on how they might have collectively and constructively dealt with these complex issues. Such interpersonal learning relationships can be determined by broader or localized structural influences and also through personal interests. That is, a learning relationship in this study can represent a formally structured relationship between people in different departments for example, and/or informal personal relationships formed in isolation to any organizational structure. Thus, in this study, this element of learning relationships was defined as: *The relationship one has with another person/s from which one acquires or imparts knowledge or skill to increase one's capacity to take effective project action.*

Earlier, in Chapter 2, I argued that learning is a multidimensional social and contextual activity (Park, 1999; Senge and Scharmer, 2001). Seemingly implicit in the work of those authors cited in that chapter (involving situated learning theorists and some organizational learning theorists) is the notion of *having a relationship* that enables learning between people within their practice context, and enables organizational learning to develop. Project participants' multifarious interrelating within a project involves them in the situated learning processes of sensemaking (Weick, 1995), observations, conversations and dialogue whilst they develop their technical and social competencies, and ultimately their identities within the project team. Their explicit and implicit social relationships form the conduits on which these types of learning processes are enabled. For example, Baker (2002b: 166) asserts that 'At the heart of conversational learning is social, relational learning among people who each have experiences and ideas that become vital resources for new possibilities yet to be discovered.' Concomitant to those perspectives is the recognition of the importance of building relationships to facilitate learning (Bryans and Smith, 2000). These relationships between people also directly impact on organizational learning since through their interactions people are the agents for organizational action and organizational learning (Argyris and Schön, 1978; Hedberg, 1981; Senge, 1990; Kim, 1993; Probst and Buchel, 1997; Crossan *et al.*, 1999; Dixon, 1999; Andrews and Delahaye, 2000). For example, in their study into organizational learning in a biomedical consortium, Andrews and Delahaye (2000) nominated relationship issues of approachability, credibility and trustworthiness between people as mediating knowledge-importing and sharing activities, and hence also organizational learning.

A number of authors in the project management field also stress the importance of building effective working relationships for project success since people in project teams necessarily engage with multiple interested stakeholders, at multiple levels (even without formal authority), to effectively manage a project (for examples, see Frame [1995], Verma [1995], Briner *et al.* [1996], Pinto [1998a], Posner and Kouzes [1998], Frame [1999], Pinto and Millet [1999], Keeling [2000], Boddy [2002], Gido and Clements [2003]). As an example, Posner and Kouzes (1998) suggest that the most important relationships for learning in projects involve mentors, immediate supervisors and one's peers, that is stressing both the importance of having effective working relationships and the learning value gained from the more immediate and situated working relationships one has with colleagues. These networks of relationships need not necessarily be only formal in configuration. Briner *et al.* (1996) emphasize the value in consciously building informal networks to help manage the external project team image and to harness the resources and support needed to deliver a project. Some researchers have specifically identified that the establishment and fostering of these informal learning relationships significantly aid learning activity. For example, in a study of learning across projects by Keegan and Turner (2001), their respondents claimed that the informal networks within their companies were the most important conduit for transferring learning between individuals and project teams. Those respondents also posited that their informal networks required deliberate attention and nurturing to ensure and to enhance the strengthening and the speed of their learning and development processes. In a similar outcome, Lim (2002) ascertained that the Singaporean School Principals involved in his study on learning improved their workplace practices through learning from informal, unstructured learning relationships at work. These learning relationships offered a form of continuous workplace learning through providing ways to increase the sharing of information and by promoting self-management of the learning process.

Whether it is formal or informal, the interactions between people are essential in knowledge creation and diffusion, and also in providing a powerful avenue for tacit knowledge to be socialized and articulated – as espoused, for example, in the work of Nonaka and Takeuchi (1995). Smith (2001) claims that such tacit knowledge exchange is reliant on relationships which are open, friendly, unstructured, and allow for spontaneous sharing of knowledge. To achieve these types of relationships where both tacit and explicit knowledge is readily shared and new knowledge created requires, as Swan *et al.* (1999: 271–73) suggest, '...an investment in interpersonal interrelationship building, so that those involved can make sense of and envisage the broader goals of the system....' This equates to improving the conductivity of the project relationships (i.e. the links between project actors) so that their relationships then serve as more effective conduits for information flow (Brookes et al., 2006).

How did the learning relationships exhibited in this project case, impact participants' situated learning behaviours?

The learning relationships impact on the situated learning activity of project participants is best addressed through an elaboration on the two empirically derived conditioners of those relationships. These conditioners either challenged and changed, or, reinforced the participants' current learning relationships within the project and, consequently, were primal influences on the observed learning behaviours of the participants. These conditioners involved:

- attitudes to public exposure and public scrutiny of perceived personal matters;
- preparedness to explore one's learning relationships with others outside of the existing relationship frameworks, and viewing relationship problems as major learning opportunities.

As evidenced in the discussion to follow, a learning relationship conditioner that tended to constrain situated learning processes involved the project team participants' not wanting one's performances/failings/beliefs/fears/weaknesses to be exposed to one's peer group for public scrutiny, or to oneself. This conditioner resulted in the project team participants exhibiting defensive deflection onto other victims, and in shoring up their own protective veneers (i.e. applying strategies to avoid such discussions) in case of future attack. In over 36 project team meeting sessions and during semi-structured interviews, or in learning workshop activities, these actions were observed at every meeting event. That being, at those events, at least one or sometimes more of the participants would demonstrate some form of defensive behaviour.

In contrast, a learning relationship conditioner which tended to aid situated learning between the project participants involved the team's preparedness to actively explore new relationship frameworks. In so doing, participants viewed relationship problems not as problems to be quickly solved, but rather exploratory learning opportunities. Therefore, this conditioner offered challenges to, rather than reinforcement of, current relationship frameworks and encouraged different attitudes and approaches towards coaching and mentoring of colleagues.

Attitudes to public exposure and public scrutiny of perceived personal matters

At first glance, one might question the necessity to publicly expose and scrutinize aspects of one's behaviour in a project team, particularly when the usual and primary focus in a project team is on completing a major task within time constraints. However, if project participants begin to value learning and creating as much as task completion within project contexts, then they will appreciate the value in exploring the deeper dimensions of their individual and collective behaviours (Raelin, 2000). Such an appreciation and acceptance of the value of learning in projects is a fundamental catalyst for developing learning at the project team level since it provides the overarching internal stimulus for participants to want to build their learning relationships and to want to deal with the other identified learning constraint/enabler elements identified in this study. Any exploration of project participants' learning behaviours involves them in providing and accepting positive and negative feedback, dealing with internal and external politics, negotiating with others, and publicly testing individuals' espoused values and beliefs (Raelin, 2000). These processes involve confrontation with defensive routines, which has parallels at the organizational learning level.

At the organizational level, Argyris (1990) states that his Model 1 governing values (i.e. unilateral control, to win and not lose, to suppress negative feelings, and a focus on action strategies) lead to organizational routines involving deflecting or avoiding embarrassment or threat, wherein, learning opportunities are stifled. For example, a team member may deflect, disengage or fail to initiate team discussion on issues where they have failed to complete their designated project task, or when they feel less competent or confident about a project topic and do not wish to compromise perceptions of their reputation with colleagues in the organization. Organizational defensive routines are therefore anti-learning, overprotective and self-sealing. Failure to discuss these defensive routines means they will continue to proliferate, and when they are discussed, the individuals involved may get in trouble (Argyris, 1990). The result being that the defensive routines are protected and reinforced by the people who prefer they do not exist. This protection is covert and undiscussable, and these defensive routines force people to take actions to achieve political and task goals via circuitous relational routes rather than directly dealing with the issue and people concerned. This, in turn, reinforces or props up the defensive routines which caused the situation in the first place (Argyris, 1990).

Organizational defensive routines make it highly likely that individuals and groups will not detect and correct errors that are embarrassing and threatening because the fundamental rules are to bypass the errors and act as if they are not being done, and make the bypass undiscussable, and make its undiscussability, undiscussable. Argyris (1990) further suggests that attempting to engage these defensive routines for reflection and to reduce them only activates the defensive routines and strengthens them. Nevertheless, in such a situation can project participants afford to retreat from this challenge? As exemplified in this study, participants really have no choice but to systematically confront these defensive routines, otherwise they remain locked into a pattern of systemic ignorance, limited change and limited learning. In that sense, they need to be cognisant of the initial responses or challenges to reflection within such defensive routines, and continue to push the issues, wherein, they test their own endurance and perseverance in pursuit of learning. Therefore, at the level of the project team, not to deliberately confront these defensive routines only perpetuates the existing conundrum, and in the project team of this study, would have defeated the very goal of achieving significant learning and organizational change. These confrontational dilemmas are illustrated by Len when he commented,

> the things that won't be discussed in the group and yet come out in one to one encounters are real barriers, and I suppose part of the issue is developing some demonstrated behaviours that support the sort of environment, the learning environment that we're aiming for. The project sponsor often challenges us on what are the behaviours that we're exhibiting? Are they the same as the ones that we bemoan other people exhibit? So getting some of those undiscussables out is really where the barrier is, and I suppose it's been quite a deliberate exercise to get to know each other a bit better and become more confident to share, and be more confident to know how to share some of these undiscussable things.

In the project team involved in this study, confronting such difficult relationship issues and defensive routines was a fundamental activity in the project process. Learning within this project team situation was reliant on the participants' willingness to admit mistakes or deficiencies in their actions, to engage conversation about those issues, and subject themselves and their experiences to the constructive criticism of their peers. Yet, as Raelin (2001) noted, not all people in all settings have such psychological (and organizational) security to undertake such reflective practice since such public reflection would place participants in a vulnerable state. In highlighting this hesitancy to exposing one's own deficiencies or vulnerabilities during the early stages of this research, Bill stated, 'I am pushing myself outside my familiar comfort zone [to discuss my deficiencies] – and I am trying not to jump off the cliff without a parachute. Moving from my old job to my new job [with its expectations] is hard.' and, 'We seem to have, for whatever reason, shied away from actually looking at our roles and perhaps thinking about how could we do things differently.' Such an inwardly focused and communal discussion on their roles might mean the possible exposure of one's own deficiencies or perceived weaknesses – despite the opportunity for learning. To avoid that risk of exposure (later acknowledged by the participants), the participants practised a process of what I have termed – defensive deflection. This term encapsulates Argyris's (1990, 1993, 1999) extensive commentary on defensive reasoning and defensive routines, and also the observations made of these project participants, which revealed that they did more than just seek to avoid the examination of their own behaviours and the testing of their mental assumptions and conclusions drawn (Argyris, 1999). These participants also regularly deflected their discussions/reflections on difficult relational issues onto others, or other groups, when they did not wish to evaluate themselves and their own learning actions/behaviours. Therefore, this term of defensive deflection more eloquently reflects the observed defensive behaviour experiences of the participants in the project team examined in this study.

As part of their individual interview and feedback sessions, and also during the feedback sessions with the full project team, the core participants in this study were introduced to this defensive deflection term. On their reflection, they seemed to readily comprehend and accept that this was a significant issue for them in their learning activities. Len surmised that he felt defensive deflection was culturally entrenched in the organization and stated,

> Defensive deflection is a behaviour that exists fairly deeply and is probably largely unconscious, I suppose, whilst I am working within my tangible comfort zone. One general observation that has been made about the three of us and the Cokemaking Leadership Team too... is around avoiding tough discussions [particularly around non-rational issues]... one of the avoidance mechanisms is often that deflection... I suppose that's a behaviour which comes back at us

in other parts of the organization...for example, We're the best shift...its the maintenance people and the other shifts that muck us up.

At the organizational level, Argyris (1990) also noted this process where individuals learn to distance themselves from feeling responsible for creating defensive patterns – it becomes the other people who are at fault. In avoiding discussion of the project team's own relationship issues, Steve offered his observations of another project team's barriers to their learning relationships by suggesting that, 'They should be in the plywood business given the amount of veneer abundant in the Working Party process.' The implication being, that the team he observed had layers upon layers of barriers to learning within their relationships. With this comment, he momentarily deflected the attention of his peers in this project team onto another group's relationship issues, which prompted their active dialogue on what were their perceptions of that other project team within the organizational change programme. All these avoidance actions are in alignment with what Argyris (1999) describes as how professionals avoid learning, that is professionals use their criticisms of others to protect themselves from the potential embarrassment of having to admit to their responsibilities in the less-than-perfect outcomes achieved. Len noted in one of the very first learning workshop sessions, 'Defensive deflection is probably one of the strategies we will all use. As you have discovered, purposeful deflection is one of our strong points.' At that time, Len's comment strongly reflected his feeling that the team still did not have robust learning relationships in which they felt confident to freely exchange views and to publicly reflect on their difficult relationship issues.

Furthermore, the willingness and opportunities for participants to expose themselves to their peer group and to explore new relationship frameworks were also affected by their heavy involvement in, and responsibilities for activities of, the broader organizational change programme and daily operational activities. (This forecasts a link to the constraint/enabler element of situational context, which will be discussed in the next chapter.) Consequently, during the early stages of the project team, the participants' application to building their learning relationships was a more responsive and opportunistic activity rather than a systematic and planned action. As Steve noted, 'We were trying to do things differently in developing the learning relationships, but it was done by the seat of the pants rather than by a cunning plan with everything falling into place.' Some commentators might suggest that taking such an opportunistic approach to developing their learning relationships is perfectly satisfactory. However, a seat of the pants approach fails to adequately address or create the conditions necessary for optimizing learning and learning development within any specific project context – which, as suggested previously in this book, is a general deficiency in current learning approaches in project management practice. In short, opportunistic responses are useful but should be embedded within a strategic and purposeful approach to learning. Consistent with Steve's comments above, and reflecting the participants' other responsibilities, while also illustrating their defensive deflection, is a remark made by Bill during an interview session, 'I would have to say that more recently we haven't done a lot of learning together and I suppose that is probably because there's been a fair bit of transactional [operational] type stuff that we have been working on, ... therefore, we really haven't gone back and talked about ourselves, it's more been about other groups and getting things done.' In the view of these participants, particularly in the early stages of this study, attending to issues in the organizational environment seemed to take some priority over purposefully and systematically attending to the processes concerned with developing their learning relationships – despite the explicit project goal of redefining their relationships. Hence, their other organizational environment commitments helped limit their attention to their learning relationship development processes, and provided avenues or targets for individuals to more readily defensively deflect.

In contrast, however, and potentially aiding their learning relationship development was the participants' collective view that they felt this organizational environment and their project was disorderly, threatening to them professionally and personally, and difficult to analyse and plan for. Partly in response to those perceptions and coupled to other stimuli, they appeared to strongly prefer to exchange project information through personal contact rather than through codified media such as e-mails, phone calls or paperwork. Their actions seemed to mirror a proposition by Daft and Weick (1984) that if one's perceived external environment is less analysable, the greater the tendency for managers to use external information gained from personal contact with other managers. This perceived condition of the organizational environment simply encouraged these project participants to personally engage with each other, and therefore helped establish recurrent opportunities for them to collaboratively expose and scrutinize their behaviours and modify their learning relationships.

Given all the issues outlined in this section, the project team participants in this case took many project meeting sessions to progressively recognize, reflect on and move steadily away from this avoidance approach towards constantly addressing aspects of their own learning relationships. For example, half way through the project, Len expressed his concern on this matter by stating, 'I can walk around the room and still see individuals who look like there's something going on, but even when you challenge them, it is very difficult to get out what seems to be an honest and complete response...and that's probably still impeding learning progress.' Bill rationalized his actions on this issue by suggesting,

> I generally tend to operate in a very rational way. However, I think I am able to actually get into the non-rational issues more now than I used to, and we're going to have to spend a lot more time in the non-rational area talking about how people are feeling about things, and what are the individual jobs that they'd like?...I suppose I've seen the group move closer together but I can also see that we've got a fair bit more of that to do before we decide what the Cokemaking Leadership Team looks like and how it operates in the future.

The project sponsor would likely have concurred with Bill's last reflection, and in one project team session, asked the team what it would take to get them to emotionally engage with their workforce. He then expressed that he felt, 'There is a fantasy world out there about what our physical world will look like, but what is of interest to me is how people behave emotionally,...How do you build trust without the emotional connections with people?' His comments reflected his relentless crusade to motivate these project participants to focus their energies on developing their immediate peer group relationships, and also to improve their relationships with other parties throughout the broader organization. His comments also further illustrate the level and intensity of the conversations conducted between the participants in this project team around this learning relationships element.

Preparedness to explore one's learning relationships with others outside of the existing relationship frameworks

The exploration of, and challenge to, existing relational frameworks was a strategy that the project team in this study very actively pursued since they sought to develop their relationships to a new level of trust, openness and emotional engagement. Their actions mirrored Argyris and Schön's (1978) Model II type approach to organizational learning, wherein existing mental models and governing variables are challenged. In that process, double-loop learning results from individuals confronting their basic assumptions behind their views of others (often involving difficult and sensitive matters) and inviting public confrontation and exploration of their assumptions (Argyris and Schön, 1978; Schön, 1987) (also see Pawlowsky [2001]). Double-loop learning assists new knowledge creation and discovery, aids the development of skills in learning-how-to-learn and develops ways for people to behave differently within their learning contexts (Argyris and Schön, 1978). Although not explicitly referred to by participants during this study, the participants were aware of this theory-of-action perspective through their previous attendance at company run leadership development courses. During the initial stages of this project, the project sponsor had also raised this theory in his discussions with the project team, seemingly to serve as a provocative learning action. One example comment of his (of many) on this matter involved, 'When you went to leadership training...what defined a Model 1 and a Model II world...and what have you done to move toward a Model II world?'

As part of exploring their relationships during the study, Len, Steve and Bill were asked to comment on the challenges they faced in changing their traditional relationships. Their responses were multifaceted. Bill indicated that the traditional, physical and socio-cultural demarcation between different battery operations presented a difficult relationship development challenge, but stated, 'Somehow we have to change that barrier so that we start to work across the batteries, and I think that's what I'm trying to do with Steve [ ] I suppose some of the conversations that we have together in the project team are pushing us down a few different tracks, and that is making us rethink perhaps, our beliefs as to what relationships are possible.' Len emphasized the internal struggle he felt they all possessed about this relationship issue by suggesting that, 'we are all struggling around what does this change really mean? We are all struggling to come up with non-traditional, non-hierarchical responses as to how we should work and learn together' Steve articulated a list of issues which he considered were restraining people from changing their traditional relationships. These involved: the uncertainty present in the organizational, business and project environments, resulting in people persisting with the devil-you-know syndrome; a lack of courage and knowledge within the participants to pursue change of this nature; long-serving employees on the project team (most having served more than 15 years in this one organization) where their current relationships were forged by their past culture experiences, which were well-known and understood; and, not clearly seeing what's in it for them through their participation in the change process, and questioning whether their efforts would be valued. At that time, Steve subsequently concluded that changes to their relationships were dependent on the individuals being self-motivated and committed enough to drive it.

Also, at the start of this project, some learning relationships were considered more relevant than others. For example, Len commented that, 'Our learning relationship barriers involve hierarchy. The guy who sees a problem is still not prepared to share it upwards. We need to learn from the guys doing the jobs, be prepared to listen to the guys and to seek out and value the comments when we get them, even though it may not be immediately valuable [as Len might perceive it].' This comment reflected the intertwining of perceived authority with the learning relationships that these participants had with other people, and implied that their authority (or at least perceptions of it) had flavoured peoples' attitudes and approaches towards sharing information with them. Steve suggested that they (the project participants) '...only value input from the right source. We need to seek out people throughout all the hierarchy, whether it comes from the right or wrong place. In our culture we look for the answers only in certain areas. Listening to all is the key to the [learning] system working.' Steve's comment also indicated that some relationships were perceived by the project participants as more valuable for learning than others, and those other relationships were seen as more obligatory – attracting less focus or just ignored. However, all these comments also reflect that these participants increasingly and genuinely acknowledged important socio-cultural influences on how they perceived and valued their relationships, and that they considered there were positive learning outcomes to be realized through them proactively altering those existing relationships.

Immersed in this complex socio-cultural milieu, Len actively sought to reduce what were current barriers to learning in his relationships with other people external to the project team and across the traditional work silos. This primarily involved him in informal activities, consisting of conversations with people, seeking and offering advice to them, and posing questions to them about operational and change process issues. Within that context, those actions effectively constituted new approaches to coaching and mentoring of section employees. Bill and

Steve also readily acknowledged that Len was performing these many informal mentoring and coaching activities with section employees. Len indicated that during those exchanges, he was trying to talk up the notion of the CLT (the project team) since 'One of the characteristics about our traditional culture around here is a lack of trust, and that extends very much to a lack of trust of what goes on behind closed doors or assumed closed doors.' In this dialogue, Len was suggesting that he was conscious of influencing perceptions of the CLT in the rest of the organization since he considered this cultural lack of trust may have inhibited the development of the organization and of the project team activities. In performing these actions, he repeatedly confronted and challenged a governing value of cultural mistrust between different groups in the organization. Len espoused his belief in trying to work together on the basis that if they shared relevant information and a common set of principles with a team, then the team will come up with the right answers. As he indicated, 'We don't have to dictate the way that everything's to work. It's quite counter productive and maintains the old culture if we were to do that.' He suggested his own extensive informal efforts (and those of his colleagues) in reducing the relationship barriers were quite significant, given the cultural history of the site. As well as helping to build relationships between people across the organization, Len's interventions also helped to progressively chip away at the cultural authority issues for learning imposed by his own previous hierarchical position.

The following vignette provides an example of Len, Steve and Bill's informal efforts in coaching and mentoring each other. This appeared to be radically different to how they would have traditionally mentored each other prior to the project team forming, that is it would not necessarily have happened! It also illustrates them expressly grappling with their own relationship issues and those they have with other employees external to the immediate project team, but involved in the broader change process. These actions, incidentally, were in accordance with their stated project goals of redefining their relationships and practising new leadership skills.

> One morning at work, Bill sought Len and Steve's advice on an important operational and relationship problem he was having with a number of key employees in his area of responsibility (i.e. the coke batteries). This problem involved the employees' current work behaviours not being seen as aligning with the needs of the current or future operation, and Bill aggressively seeking to change those

employees' work behaviours. Bill, Len, and Steve talked expansively through what exactly were the issues that Bill needed to address and how he might keep attacking the assumptions that sat behind the employees' demonstrated behaviours. As a team, they appeared to both try to help solve the problem Bill presented, but also, to challenge and explore what were the critical underpinning aspects of Bill's relational conflict with the employee group – thereby, not simply focus on the exhibited behaviours of the employees and the presenting problem. Notably too, their dialogue included much about Bill's own behaviour with the group. After the event, Steve reflected positively on this mentoring episode, by stating, 'So that event was good as a joint learning experience... we actually sat down and said how do we actually break the psychological barrier exhibited in the issue and better understand how we reward people, and, we questioned how we get into peoples heads to better understand them. This activity was an attempt to draw upon our collective experiences and to learn from each other... It was a comforting thing for Bill to try, and for us to be the sounding boards.'

While at the time of this one particular event it may not have been readily apparent to the participants, through their actions on that occasion, they were also developing their ability in learning-how-to-learn. Through helping to reduce their fear of sharing information and their concerns with each other, and through exposing and sharing their tacit knowledge, these types of occasions provided further opportunities for the participants to jointly challenge, better understand and steadily build their own learning relationship frameworks. This example (amongst others) of project participants conducting an operational-focused discussion first, which then led onto critical reflections about their learning behaviours, was a general circumstance shaped by a number of issues pertaining to the situational context of the project – which will be discussed further in Chapter 6.

As a brief example of treating a perceived relationship problem as a learning opportunity, during the middle of this study Len reflectively noted that

> One of the things that can create learning barriers is where you get individuals not actively participating [in team meetings]... whether they are taking it in and reflecting internally or whether they are just switched off and thinking about something else... The internalising creates a barrier where the collective wisdom is not getting shared.

Often guys who are sitting there internalising have got a good point of view, a valid point of view [in his opinion], one that will carry a discussion somewhere else and to someplace valuable, and, they're not sharing it and the group is being denied some wisdom.

These comments may reflect a cognitive style issue, but also reflect that Len perceived there were learning difficulties between project team participants which may be rooted in their relationships. That being, people did not seem to freely and actively participate in the meeting sessions. When asked if he felt that situation was happening a lot in the team, he replied, 'Oh yes. At any time we've probably got 50 per cent active participation.' When challenged on what he does to change that situation, he responded by saying,

I have no easy answer on that. I'm starting to challenge them more. If somebody is disengaged I'll sometimes try a question that asks how they are feeling? Where they are up to? Or, whatever seems appropriate in the context. So I'm probably doing those more... doing them enough is another thing and if I'm going flat out [actively participating himself] then I'm not taking notice of that anyway.

Rather than ignore or reject these disengagement or non-participation situations, Len demonstrated his preparedness to challenge and change these situations by pursuing the other participants for their opinions and ideas. In doing so, across multiple events, he undertook many actions that frequently energized participants to interact more, and through their new interactions (both verbal and reflective in character) they learnt and better contributed to the learning of the team.

5.2 Pyramid of authority

What is a pyramid of authority?

In all aspects of life, as people participate in their various communities of practice, they develop and temporarily possess different levels and different kinds of authority or power, which can also include assigned authority from others to achieve particular sets of goals or activities. As described by Frame (1994) and Pinto (1998a, 2000), for example, these authorities can include technical authority, formal authority, bureaucratic authority, crisis authority and charismatic authority. Possessing these accumulated authorities represents 'the potential ability to influence behaviour [] and to get people to do things that they would not otherwise do' (Pfeffer, 1992: 30). The exercise of these accumulated authorities represents political action or the exercise of that influence, and therefore, represents power in action (Pfeffer, 1992; Buchanan and Badham, 1999). These authorities can be applied to any situation or task or topic (e.g. project leadership), but what is of concern here is how a member of a project team might positively and legitimately apply or not apply their accumulated authorities to pursue situated learning while participating in a project. This section therefore presents a discussion on the interpersonal learning constraint/enabler element termed 'pyramid of authority', which involves the application or non-application of one's own power or authority to support or constrain situated learning in a project team.

Different project team participants will bring a varying combination of authorities to a project team. The term 'pyramid' tends to capture the notion that a person arranges or incrementally builds up their authorities over time, from some base level, and through that incremental building process there is some value to be realized. Importantly, these authorities can be real or perceived – meaning, for example, that a person may think they possess a certain authority like technical or charismatic authority and yet, in reality, the project team and the organization may consider that they do not and vice versa. At the level of the project team, the consolidation of individuals' various authorities around the project team activity also constitutes an incremental building process, with the collective base consisting of the base level authorities of all the participants. The term 'pyramid' also captures the notion that building up authorities is a dynamic and positive construction process, as opposed to the negative connotation sometimes attached to power and politics in organizations (Note: Block [1983], Frame [1994], Buchanan and Badham [1999] and Pinto [1998a,b, 2000] also take this positive position on the management of politics).

To support the theoretical and empirical discussion contained within this section, and relevant to the case study, an individual and collective definition for this constraint/enabler element of pyramid of authority is now provided.

Individual pyramid of authority – an individual's perceived or real accumulated authority level within a project, affecting their own political approach to their learning. This accumulated authority may consist of an individual's own perceptions of their authority, others' perceptions of their authority and the organization's assigned authority to assist them to successfully deliver a project.

Collective pyramid of authority – a project team's collective authority within the organization, influencing the team's political approach to their collective learning. This collective authority can be either a summation of the real individual authorities of the participants in the project and/or can be authority assigned to the entire project team by the organization to aid project success.

Why mention the individual and the collective variants? The individual pyramid of authority can clearly have impacts on situated learning in the dyadic interactions and exchanges between individuals. Collectively, a project team may have an accumulated and/or assigned authority which affords them the freedom to activate or provide multiple and varied learning opportunities, to experiment with ideas, and to share and seek information and resources. While an individual may also possess and enact this potential, if the collective does not possess such authority, then situated learning activity in the team may be significantly constrained. That is not to suggest that the individual within such a broader constraint situation cannot seek to improve their learning – merely, that the broader, more enveloping organizational context may constrain or hinder that potential learning development. Or, as Buchanan and Badham (1999: 11) assert, 'the power one has [to exercise on issues] thus depends upon the organizational context as well as the skill, will and other resources (funds, position, credibility) of the individual.'

This element requires project team participants to identify and appreciate the political issues impacting their project and their learning potential, and to recognize the individual and collective authorities that they bring to, and think they can exercise, within that project political context. The public exposure and collective reflection on those accumulated authorities within the project team represent a positive and systematic learning action, which aids an individual or team in deciding its political approach towards their project learning opportunities (Sense, 2003a; Sense and Antoni, 2003).

The importance of managing politics for learning in projects

Why politics is rife in projects

The situated learning theorists Lave and Wenger (1991) support a position that politics is a part of any community or group by expressing that a community of practice is neither a haven of togetherness nor an island of intimacy insulated from social and political relations. As a result, communities of practice exhibit multiple and diverse forms of participation. In a later work, Wenger (1998) referred to the politics of such participation within a community of practice as involving issues of influence, nepotism, discrimination, charisma, friendship and ambition – which also signals the potential range of positive or negative political behaviours an individual in a situation might choose to pursue. In her discussion of change management and managerial teams, Kanter (1994) also reflected these themes of differential interest groups facilitating political behaviour by suggesting that a philosophy of participation (as in project teams) does not mean the departure of politics in a group since people have different perspectives, needs, expectations of the group, and the organizational structures of segmentation into specialties encourage divisiveness and non-cooperation across areas. Project teams typically consist of members that normally would belong to, identify with, and be influenced by other multiple communities of practice (or specialisms) within an organization and beyond it (Sense, 2003b). This commingling of participants around a project opportunity suggests there are unavoidable and varied political interests present, which influence the political actions of individuals within the project team. Therefore, since projects involve change and uncertainty (Buchanan and Badham, 1999), and since project teams exist as temporal specialist subgroups within a matrix of multiple specialisms or organizational groupings, projects therefore tend to greatly accentuate this political dynamic – and consequently, the learning-political linkage as well (Sense and Antoni, 2003). Beyond individualist orientations towards different communities of practice (or specialisms) being fundamental in causing political activity, if historic tensions between team members exist and have not been resolved, then they will also manifest themselves as political behaviour within the team (Kanter, 1994).

In addition to those arguments, Pinto (2000) (also see Boddy [2002]) offers three further reasons (stemming from an epistemological project characteristic of separation) why such political processes are so stimulated into action within projects. These revolve around: projects needing to negotiate for resources because of their separateness to the traditional functional structures; project managers not normally having a stable, functional base of power to do that negotiation for those resources, and hence, needing to learn to cultivate many methods of influence to obtain resources for a project (also see Frame [1999]); project managers do not normally have the formal authority to conduct performance reviews on their project team subordinates, and therefore, they are denied a source of hierarchical power. With all these combined and significant stimulants in place, little wonder then that politics is usually rife in project settings and is an issue one is unable to, nor should seek to, avoid. Indeed, Buchanan and Badham (1999), Pinto (2000) and Pinto and Millet (1999) posit that there is no escape from politics in any organizational setting, and therefore, organizational politics can be considered a naturally occurring phenomenon and one which participants need to engage with if they intend to be successful within any practice. Bourne and Walker (2004) liken a project practitioner's engagement with politics in projects as to tapping into the power lines to aid a project's success, and argue that project managers need to develop an understanding of those power lines and become skilled in using them – particularly in large organizations. A number of other notable researchers in the project management field have also argued the need to better understand this phenomenon in projects, and also offered pragmatic guidance on how to engage it (for examples, see Block [1983], Frame [1994], Briner et al. [1996], Pinto [1998a,b, 2000]).

Any engagement with politics in projects essentially involves two themes. Frame (1994) offers a definition for politics that encompasses both of these. That being, 'Politics is the process whereby attempts are made to achieve goals through accommodation and the exercise of influence' (Frame, 1994: 127). In that process, the ability to influence or shape the actions of others requires a project team member to have developed or accumulated several bases of authority (Frame, 1994), particularly when the influencer has no formal ability to force another person to perform an activity. The exercise of influence may create conditions which discourage the active participation of recipients during political exchanges since such displays of power can 'intimidate many into tacit acquiescence' (Buchanan and Badham, 1999: 55). Accommodation, on the other hand, involves the adaptation of oneself to a purpose or meaning different from one's original position and its character invites the more active participation of all participants in specific political exchanges. This theme of accommodating others' perspectives to reach consensus between parties on a common outcome also appears in some other authors' definitions and comments on managing politics (for example, see Briner et al. [1996] and Buchanan and Badham [1999]). How much influence and how much accommodation a project participant employs in an interpersonal political exchange depend on their intentions and the situational context surrounding the specific issue at hand. Nevertheless, while the exercise of influence (i.e. to get your own way) is important in any organizational endeavour, reaching a compromise and mutual agreement on issues, that is the alignment of disparate perspectives, can be seen as equally important in achieving project success. In essence then, to engage politics in projects requires participants to be both purposeful about achieving one's goal, but at the same time, to be flexible in aligning oneself to a purpose that may differ from one's original starting point.

Politics and learning

An appropriate engagement with politics is essential to get a myriad of things done in projects. But how is learning in projects specifically associated with politics? At the personal level, the political choices of either taking an influential or accommodative political approach towards learning (or the prevention of learning) for oneself or others during a project present significant impacts for learning activity. For example, project participants may exhibit behaviours that limit participative exchanges and knowledge flow between people during their interactions. That is, they may be too influential or, alternatively, they are so accommodative that they fail to create conditions that afford them the opportunity to explore a situation in a way that helps them to learn. These personal political choices available to project participants also signal that an individual's learning is not only subject to the broader external political issues surrounding a project. People, individually, have a direct political impact on their personal learning activities. According to Sense (2003a) in his study on project leader learning, this political dialectic involving influence and accommodation, as applied to either formal or informal information sources, can result in four potential personal approaches a project participant may pursue towards their own learning activity. Those learning approaches are broadly defined as purposeful learning, adaptive learning, opportunistic learning and networked learning. Those personal approaches are determined by how the participant perceives their own actions relative to the learning opportunity, and are not a measure of how the recipient or other observers perceive the participant's actions, nor is it a measure of the tactics or strategies that the participant may employ to achieve their learning goals (for more discussion on these four learning approaches, refer to Sense [2003a]).

In highlighting the interrelatedness of learning and politics at the project team level, project teams can provide sites for the expression of power where dominant individuals form oligarchies and dictate the course of team actions, which may potentially stifle diversity in learning approaches and learning activity. Furthermore, if learning becomes an explicit project action, it may itself be considered a highly political endeavour. So, rather than politics impacting learning, learning actions may further fuel the political activity of individuals in and around a project. This may come about because a focus on learning may be in contradiction with the traditional convergent and technical task-focused view of projects. Exploration of the learning opportunity in projects emphasizes divergent themes or objectives of searching, experimentation, discovery and innovation (Arthur *et al.*, 2001), which can generate changes within the project process itself. Because of that additional learning focus and the subsequent actions that may be pursued in that regard, learning activities within a project may become highly political events. For example, learning actions involving a project team undertaking public reflection (Raelin, 2001) about their project activity and their learning could, arguably, be very political. Therein, individual knowledge generated during a project may be shared amongst project participants and the broader organization, and the interactions and conversations generated in the process provide the crucial channel for tacit knowledge to become articulated (Nonaka and Takeuchi, 1995). To deliberately enact such public reflection practices and establish conditions to expose what might be considered exclusive knowledge held by participants in a project may therefore be considered a highly controversial move to generate learning. Moreover, opening the opportunity in a project to explore and experiment with different ideas and different approaches to the technical aspects of a project, or the conduct of the project process, may be equally controversial in terms of traditional project measures, or perhaps threatening to various project stakeholder interests. Nonetheless, to promote systematic rather than opportunistic learning in a project requires deliberate project learning actions which are likely to stimulate further project political activity and perhaps the more controversial it is, the greater the learning generated.

At the organizational level, and consistent with the individualist orientations towards different communities of practices, Salaman and Butler (1994) refer to one of the key factors in managerial resistance to learning being that organizations are irredeemably political structures because they are differentiated into a hierarchy of specialisms, departments and sub-groups where power, resources and rewards are differentially distributed. They consider that 'These specialisms breed differences of perspective, priority interest [] [which] may generate conceptions of interest and in-group loyalty, out-group resistance, which seriously gets in the way of managers willingness to learn' (Salaman and Butler, 1994: 38–41). Coopey and Burgoyne (2000) and Argote (1999) submit that in these specialisms information is often hoarded and exchanged and that certain groups possess superior bargaining power and will not relinquish their knowledge freely to other groups such as, for example, project teams. This political condition also leads to distortion and suppression of information, and people then follow less informed paths in their decision-making processes. To avoid this situation, Easterby-Smith (1997) suggests that these issues can be addressed through reflection and mutual inquiry and open dialogue. He logically suggests that such free and open exchanges are difficult to achieve since players are dealing with conflicts between short and long-term agendas, and difficulties in their preparedness to discard old knowledge and embrace new knowledge. Hence, it becomes crucially important for knowledge-sharing and learning to recognize and address the various interests of different organizational units and sub-groups (i.e. to accommodate their interests), particularly in major restructuring initiatives (Buchanan and Badham, 1999) – such as seen in the project case reported on in this book.

One might reasonably conclude that any project can be considered a hotbed of political activity involving the deliberate or accidental exercise (or not) of participants' accumulated authorities. Ultimately, in an effort to capitalize on the learning opportunities in such circumstances, an important recognition for participants in project teams is to understand that they are not simply victims to any (external to the project team) organizational or sub-group political interests or forces. Instead, they individually (and armed with their own levels of authority) can have a political impact on their own and their team's learning activities within the life of a project – while also helping to develop their skills in learning-how-to-learn. Recognizing that learning can be impacted positively by one's own political actions, or negatively through one's own inaction or lack of understanding of the political condition, may assist the political processes in projects to become a significant source of creative energy leading to greater learning endeavours (Buchanan and Badham, 1999).

How did the pyramids of authority of project participants in this project case impact their situated learning behaviours?

The presentation in this section involves two parts. The first part involves a discussion concerning the authority that the core participants imported into the project environment, and how perceptions of that authority impacted their situated learning behaviours. The second part of this section then explores how the core participants' perceptions of their authority to lead their project and pursue learning activities when in the project setting were conditioned by factors within and surrounding the project.

The authority that the core project participants imported into the project setting

Given their historical and high-level Superintendent positions in the traditional organization, the core project team participants in this study (Len, Steve and Bill) each possessed, and brought into the project setting, culturally entrenched technical, bureaucratic and referent authorities, and expectantly people from across the organization frequently referred to them for advice and decision-making. Collectively, these authorities can be considered their prior organizational authority, and it emerged as an influential factor on their project learning behaviours in two ways. First, Len, Steve and Bill strongly perceived the need to reduce perceptions of their prior organizational authority, so as to aid the team in building their relationships and in learning. This focus tended to exclude them seeing their prior organizational authority as a positive tool to aid their collective project learning activity and, alternatively, encouraged them to see that authority as a bad thing to be expunged. This focus on authority being considered negative and to be removed or avoided, as opposed to something positive, that could be utilized in pursuit of their project learning, in part, stems from the past organizational culture being strongly aligned to bureaucratic and hierarchical control, compared to the new, democratic and shared ownership model of the organizational change programme. Second, as particularly observed during the first half of this study, the other participants in the team held back from open exchanges with the core participants. Emphasizing this blockage and some of the efforts made in overcoming it, at one point in a project team meeting, a Senior Supervisor made direct reference to the latent authority of the core participants and questioned whether their authority was still intimidating them (the Senior Supervisors) in that meeting. Another Senior Supervisor participant then asked the others, 'Who in this group feels that this is alive in the Coke-making Leadership Team?' In accordance with their past hierarchical dependency structures, it seemed that the traditional higher authority members (Len, Steve and Bill) were perceived by the other team members (the Senior Supervisors) as being the providers of their learning as opposed to being co-recipients of learning. In this project, however, all participants were exploring previously un-chartered territory and all were potential developers and recipients of new knowledge. Hence, this project situation presented a major challenge for Len, Steve and Bill.

That is, for them to access and apply their prior organizational authority to promote the team's situated learning activity (e.g. to encourage and engage dialogue and participation and provide opportunities for collaboration and exchanges between individuals) but also to minimize other participants' negative perceptions of their authorities so as to enable their better engagement with those others in the team.

In the first learning workshop towards the end of this study, some of the learning actions devised by these core participants expressly involved reducing this perception of their authority. For example, one such action included: *Deal with the perceived authority differences between people by being active about putting our views on the table at a common level.* Len commented further on this intended action and stated, 'We need to be active in putting our views on the table because there is an assumption that if we are not putting them on the table we are playing some political game where the outcome will be whatever we want to come about... at the same time those views need to be put in a way where they will be treated no better or no worse than if they came from another person.' This intended learning action presented a tough application dilemma for these participants. That being, they had to express their views honestly, but, at the same time, attempt to do so in ways that did not portray their views as emanating from their previous hierarchical authority positions. If handled well, such actions would promote their building of their learning relationships with others in the team and help to steadily reduce perceptions of their traditional authority. Some other intended learning actions included: *Devolve responsibility/authority to others and support them in that process* – a sharing of the requisite authority; *Build interrelationships based on business objectives not hierarchical imperatives;* and, *Listen to all persons involved to support input and challenge to traditional authority perceptions.* Hence, in the constructive learning process pursued within the learning workshops, the core participants devised some learning actions that were intended to progressively reduce perceptions of their traditional authority and help reduce traditional hierarchy dependence. In pursuing those actions, they sought to open up the possibility for people to better engage with them and each other and build their relationships to aid their mutual learning.

At around the mid-point of this study, Len recognized that perceptions of his prior organizational authority also depended on the subject under focus, that is 'If it's something that's perceived to be in my area of expertise then my latent authority is probably pretty high, almost worryingly so... because I'd actually value people challenging me on things to make sure that we really are getting the best result.' These reflective comments also illustrate an impact of Len's latent authority on the other members of the project team. That is, their trust of him in his recognized authority area tended to minimize debate on specific issues and in doing so, limited the exchanges between people and the learning for the group. At this time, Steve also acknowledged that the project team participants were relying on Len more and not challenging him and his ideas enough. These outcomes were possibly also a result of Len building his relationships with other team members, and by default developing a new referent authority in the team, which in the eyes of some of the participants did not need to be challenged. Away from his recognized areas of expertise, Len generalized that his influence was far less. He suggested that, 'Sometimes it'll [my authority] have an impact, other times it won't [ ] I suppose I'll often test ideas by throwing them out for the team to consider and seeing what response I get. The thing I value is getting a response rather than throwing the bait in the water and having no bites.' Len indicated that these interventions of his were executed from an objective position, which sought to assist their team learning and build their relationships. As observed, such actions by him in the team meetings stimulated conversations, debate and reflection on issues between team members, which consequently provided opportunities for individual and team learning. In that way, his actions over time actively promoted situated learning amongst the participants while helping to reduce traditional perceptions of his authority.

Steve also acknowledged that the core participants' prior organizational authority was still perceived to be ever present by people in the organization, and that it impacted the learning processes within the project team. He illustrated this point by referring to an e-mail that he and Bill had jointly issued to colleagues during the mid-phase of this study. It concerned a declaration of a new organization structure involving one Cokemaking division – an action intended by them to only make fun of their own predicament. However, their e-mail had recipients in the organization apparently believing that Steve and Bill had just decreed the new structure, and it drew an angry or greatly concerned response from many of those who received it and, consequently, did not prompt rational dialogue and reflection between participants on the content of the e-mail. This generated response spoke volumes about how those recipients still viewed Bill and Steve as possessing the positional authority of the roles that they previously occupied. As Steve noted after this event, 'So I'm learning about people as well. There are still people out there who are not reading me the same way I'm not reading other people. That's either one of those things we'll get better at or just cope with.'

Steve also considered that he had not deliberately used any of his prior organizational authority with peers or others in the project team to promote his own personal learning. Throughout the project cycle, none of the project team participants unless asked would have considered using their prior organizational authority to promote their learning. Steve actually felt his prior organizational authority had helped inhibit his own learning, because when he was abrupt and overpowering in getting his points across in team meetings (also a cognitive style issue), it caused the recipients in those exchanges to consider that he was just exercising his power. His actions tended to shut down the development of dialogue between those participants and himself, rather than encourage it. Subsequently, he also recognized the possible negative impact his perceived authority may have had on the other project team participants' relational learning during project meetings, that is through inhibiting their free speech and challenge to his views within the team. Ironically, Steve indicated quite passionately that he needed people to argue with him to enable him to extend his own knowledge and perspectives.

On occasions, in the meeting sessions of this project team, a number of project team participants (other than Steve, Bill or Len) also observed that the respect conveyed towards an individual's bureaucratic and technical authority level and trust of a colleague within the group was tending to minimize debate and exchanges on specific issues. These situations resembled what Coopey and Burgoyne (2000) refer to as the normalizing pressures within an organization that work against the creation of a space for learning. The implication being that learning and knowledge exchange between the project participants was limited. Hence, not to engage in debate or discussion because of authority perceptions was considered to restrict learning and simply reinforced the culture of deference to authority figures. Steve, for example, acknowledged this authority impact on learning associated with technical experts in the organization, and suggested that to improve knowledge transfer between people in all the projects of the organizational change programme, they needed to 'Breakdown the barriers...get the specialists to communicate...do not have privileged information. Actually attacking that demarcation on privileged information is one way of doing it [improving learning].' In articulating this somewhat idealistic goal, he was recognizing a desire to remove the informal rankings applied to knowledge from perceived expert sources, and also to remove the barriers to who should have access to it, through getting the experts to communicate with others. As such, Steve perhaps naively proposed a broader sharing of what was considered privileged information through the technical experts sharing their knowledge and expertise. Although commendable, such dramatic action did not appear to readily occur during the course of the project meetings. The different experts in this team may have considered that to readily relinquish aspects of one's power or expertise at that time may have been rather foolhardy at the individual level – unless instructed to do so by a higher authority. That is not to suggest for one minute that this project team did not share knowledge or expertise, or engage multiple discussions and debates on the issues associated with the project. It simply emphasizes that, as one might suspect, full disclosure and completely uninhibited sharing of expert knowledge was more likely an idealized goal that they aspired too, rather than a practical reality within the project milieu at that time.

The conditioning of the core participants' authority to learn within the project setting

It would seem that based on their prior hierarchical positions and generally perceived operational competencies, the three core participants possessed high levels of prior organizational authority, which one might reasonably expect to translate into the effective leadership of the project activities. In addition, once the team formed, the project sponsor also assigned these participants substantial freedom or authority in decision-making in regard to their conduct of their project. One participant expressed her view on this matter by stating, 'I think that he [the project sponsor] has enough faith and he puts a lot of trust in them [the core participants] that they will actually do the right thing.' Yet, despite these substantial authority inputs to the project setting and in relation to the project goals, they seemed to lack authority, or at least the application of any authority, to effectively self-drive their learning and project processes. Bill, in particular, repeatedly expressed that he felt he lacked authority on issues concerning this project, and as a consequence attested to feeling that he was the dumb bunny of the three core participants in the project. This situation suggested that the core participants' authority within the project seemed to be conditioned by other factors from within the project milieu. This situation is explored below, through elaborating on three empirically derived conditioners of the participants' pyramids of authority – which ultimately and significantly influenced their exhibited learning behaviours.

Ambiguity within the project

Despite their project goals expressly including a learning focus and the project sponsor broadly and publicly supporting learning activity as being critical for the organization to move forward, these project participants still did not appear to have gained enough clarity about the topic of learning or the means to competently and confidently pursue it. As such, they lacked a working and detailed knowledge about this project goal and they were expected to aggressively pursue it through their own minimally informed approaches. This subject of learning was not their usual topic of discussion within their normal operational duties associated with the plant, and was perceived by them to be ambiguous and outside their normal latitude of control. Early in the project, when prompted to reflect on and explain how they generally sourced new knowledge, how they reflected and how they intervened in the learning situations they participated in, their responses often reflected this unease with the topic. This was evident in their pensive thought, delayed responses and digression from responding to the actual questions asked, or in defensive deflection (as previously discussed). Expectantly, this unease with this topic was generally more evident in their behaviour in early project team meetings during the first half of the project. However, even later in the project, during one of the learning workshop sessions, Len still acknowledged that 'learning is still a difficult issue for us and self-design of the learning space was particularly so'. With these comments, Len acknowledged that learning and actions targeted towards advancing their learning activity were still perceived by them to be difficult to deal with. This topic ambiguity condition could have been perceived by them as an opportunity to stimulate their personal growth, and to some degree it was perceived that way. However, for them, this ambiguity on the topic of learning was in contradiction with their cultural norms of dealing with assigned and clearly defined rational issues that they usually understood and could directly exercise their authority on, to reach some form of tangible outcome. Perhaps, if they had more clarity about the topic of learning they would have more confidently exercised greater authority in pursuing it, and thereby promoted their situated learning activity. This ambiguity on the topic of learning in this project facilitated these project participants referral to perceived higher authorities to gain their guidance or permission on how they should, or might, proceed to pursue their learning activities – thereby also demonstrating and helping to perpetuate another cultural norm of behaviour in this organization.

As articulated in Chapter 1, the Superintendents established the project goals as: first, to redefine their roles and their relationships and responsibilities in accordance with the new vision and values of the organization; secondly, to practise new leadership skills; thirdly, to learn through this project team process. These broad project goals were open to all sorts of interpretation (henceforth, further aiding ambiguity within the project) – which incidentally is what the project sponsor wanted. He sought to have the project participants passionately engage with these goals and to spur debate amongst them around defining the specifics of the goals and their roles in meeting with the newly espoused vision and values of the organization. In that way, the project sponsor felt they might develop deep ownership of the project, its goals and its processes and embed the notion of a constantly learning and changing organization in all levels of the hierarchy. However, the participants were emerging from an organizational cultural milieu consisting of a highly structured and predominantly rational operational environment which was low in role ambiguity and where they were collectively viewed as quite competent operators. This conflict between their 'personal foundations of experience' (Boud, 1991: 13–14) in this organization and the quite different project operational challenges presented by the project sponsor's approach meant that they faced uncertainty and risk in how they should proceed to construct their project roles. Highlighting this conflictual situation towards the middle of the project, Steve commented that the project sponsor and the Human Resources Manager had a teacher–student relationship between them. He implied that those persons should be teaching them (the core participants) as students and provide them direct instruction on issues, rather than simply dumping such ambiguous expectations on them. This initial role ambiguity in the project, as created by the project sponsor, was intended to help extend the participants beyond their current cultural conditioning, but conversely seemed to contribute to their insecurity or powerlessness they felt about moving forward on the goals of the project. It would seem that despite the unfettered authority assigned to them by the project sponsor to establish their own roles and to pursue the project activities, they stalled in these project processes to seek guidance or direction or approval from some form of authority figure, because they felt they lacked authority to make those decisions competently by themselves.

Further illustrating this ambiguity about their project roles and its impact on their perceived authority to progress their learning activity, Len reflectively noted, we are tending to be passengers for learning because probably all three of us are struggling with where is our role? That's to say that the carriage is outside and the pumpkin is starting to re-emerge... The question then, is to what extent should we be in there [the carriage]? We need to be careful we are equal participants with other people and not dominating the situation. At the same time we've got strongly held views and we've got an obligation to put that into the ring in the same way as anyone else.

Len's comments illustrate how he felt they lacked role clarity and that he was conscious of his positional authority and of the need to balance his actions in the project team with other project objectives. These comments also highlight another key dilemma for these three core participants. That being, their shift from being in-charge and being the primary decision-makers, to moving towards more co-operative and democratic forms of work. At that time also, Bill acknowledged that his fear for his own personal career and a lack of clarity surrounding his current and future role was a factor in his reluctance to fully embrace the project process as designated to them, and thus also affected his learning efforts.

Towards the final stages of the research process (after the project sponsor had imposed a new organizational structure on the project participants), these participants still lacked clarity about their current project roles and about what their future organizational roles were meant to be. Steve, for example, considered that the role clarity he had about his newly assigned organizational role was not sufficient in providing a greater impetus for him to action more project issues – compared to the role clarity he really wanted to have. In his actions at that time, the project sponsor had re-framed the project environment in quite a dramatic fashion. As he indicated to the project team at the time, 'the time for talking about changing things has gone!', and he also indicated that he would be the bulldozer on that issue. This exhibited behaviour of the project sponsor, in this instance, seemed to perpetuate the old culture of command and control, which he so passionately and publicly desired to change. He also appeared incapable or reluctant to attempt to offer his views on their newly assigned organizational roles, or on their future reporting relationships in the new organizational structure. Those inactions led to some considerable confusion and further ambiguity in the minds of the participants about exactly what the sponsor wanted them to now do.

At that time, one might have conjectured that perhaps this new imposed organizational/innovation structure would, over time, provide enough of a framework for the participants to feel they had greater authority to explore and progress their learning in a bounded manner – given the structure provided a hint of detail about their future roles, and that it had been sanctioned and indeed implemented by the higher authority. Such speculation also being consistent with Adler and Borys's (1996) commentary that organizations can have high levels of formalization that actually help reduce role conflict and ambiguity and personal feelings of alienation, which then consequently increases work satisfaction and commitment. Alternatively, however, the project sponsor's actions at that time were so decisive that it may have helped shut down any deep exploratory learning between participants after the event – thereby perpetuating the presenting conundrum. Ultimately too, increased and persisting anxiety levels regarding their future roles may have led to longer term avoidance or retreat from learning opportunities. Hence, the seeming lack of clarity about their roles within the project and about their intended roles after it, as facilitated by the project sponsor's actions, seemed to constrain their enthusiasm to embrace the change process independently of that authority figure, and thereby also constrained their self-driven exploration of learning.

Particularly towards the start of the project, and coupled to a lack of clarity about their roles and some trepidation about the topic of learning, the participants also seemed to lack clarity about how exactly to conduct their activities to achieve the goals of the project. Consequently, this also helped facilitate their deference to higher authorities to obtain guidance on how they should proceed. This involved them not being sure about what they precisely needed to do (or were expected to do) to explore their relationship issues and their learning, and in demonstrating new leadership approaches. Possessing substantial freedom in decision-making concerning the project meant participants confronted multiple options in deciding how they might act, which perhaps only exacerbated their situation through providing them too much flexibility in choice in addressing the challenges presented by the project situation. Furthermore, there were no formal or normative processes for them to apply to assist their achievement of their challenging project tasks. Perhaps in acknowledgement of their dilemma, a junior Human Resources Facilitator regularly sat in on early project meetings to help stimulate the team members to find their own way through the opportunity – but not to direct them. The team came to affectionately refer to that person's regular participation and interventions as

'Molly's manipulation'. This assigned tag reflected that her actions were openly considered by the project participants as a means for the project sponsor to have an indirect input or influence on the activities of their project and also served as a conduit for the participants to send messages indirectly back to the sponsor. However, while these actions of interested others in the project, from time to time, did stimulate reflection and conversations, it did not provide the details or directions to the participants on exactly how they should conduct their activities. Therefore, they were effectively asked to navigate their own way through the project – a situation in stark contrast to their past cultural conditioning. In the later stages of this research, as a simple micro example of one participant's desire for clarity in how to conduct their learning processes, and his preparedness to yield to the perceived authority of the researcher in a learning workshop, Len offered the following remark about their reflection activity: 'The format set out more clearly, telling me what to reflect on before the next meeting, would help.' One suspects then, if the project participants had more information or more process guidance at the start of the project (e.g. some specific processes or actions to apply to their project tasks), they may have felt they had greater authority to enact the project activities and be able to become more independent of the project sponsor. Such improved independence through less ambiguity in the project process may have also helped to build the participants' authority (and confidence) to extend their exploration of the project learning opportunity.

In this project case, the issues concerning the levels of ambiguity about the topic of learning, about participant project roles and about the processes to pursue to achieve the project goals, culminated in a degree of powerlessness, or a perceived lack of authority, that participants in this project team seemed to possess to influence their situated learning activity and their project outcomes. This situation being consistent with Baumard's (1999) observation that unintentional ambiguity leads organizations (even temporary ones) to inaction. These ambiguity issues, coupled to other conditioners of the pyramids of authority which are elaborated on below, resulted in the project team participants deferring to, and being highly dependent on, the sponsor or higher authority figure for decisions or guidance – which tended to inhibit (but not eliminate) their situated learning activity.

Latent or discernable authority of the project sponsor

In concert with those ambiguity issues evidenced within this project setting, the project sponsor's discernable political actions and latent (not presently active or evident) authority also impacted the perceived authority that project participants felt they had to pursue learning activity in the project. In this project setting, the project sponsor's charismatic and traditional bureaucratic authority tended to encourage the project participants into constant deference to him, thereby further promoting hierarchy dependence. Highlighting the latent impact of the project sponsor's authority on this project team's learning activity and also their hierarchy dependence during one of the earlier project team meetings, Steve remarked, 'X [the project sponsor] will dictate what the milestones are and how the milestones will fall out.' At that time, both Bill and Len quickly responded to this comment from Steve and explored why he felt that way. They indicated that Steve's perception of their situation presented a challenge to them and their leadership of the project. In a different project team meeting session, Len made a similar observation about this dependency view, and stated, 'From the actual discussion yesterday we didn't need to do that and we should trust those things to the leader and get on with it... I am sure X [the project sponsor] has the answer for that.' Even much later in the project cycle, Steve reflected that 'we still want to be told what to do', and suggested that 'I don't believe we've yet mastered the management of X's [the project sponsor] expectations. There's always an un-stated question of what does he want out of this, and it's almost a dependence on the hierarchical interactions in that case.' In Steve's view, the unclear expectations or second-guessing of the project sponsor's desires, by default, created their hierarchy dependence, with the further implication being that it constrained the participants' preparedness to explore issues and to learn, and to action the project with increasing confidence independently of the sponsor. Steve recognized, however, that they needed to pursue improving the clarity on this issue by suggesting, 'That's something I feel we need to get around and be more confident about.' Further reflective commentary from Len, which illustrates this hierarchy dependence condition as culturally embedded, was his statement that 'Dependency on the leader is built into our psychological contract.' This cultural aspect also included a view that it was unacceptable to challenge perceived authority. As Steve noted, 'We only listen to authority – is the culture in here! The authority saying you can't challenge me and when someone has an issue with a topic/situation no-one listens to him unless he is the authority.' Hence, the project team participants' own pursuit of learning (concerning the volume, the scope and the pace of learning), as desired by the project sponsor, was constrained since they would generally not progress on major project issues until the project sponsor (or key authority figure) directly or indirectly provided permission, guidance or advice to do so. In turn, that emergent approach frustrated the project sponsor since he expressed his goal was for them to explore the project issues and grow professionally and independently of him.

A specific example of the impact of the project sponsor's discernable actions on project participants' authority, and ultimately on their learning activity, was the decision he made to expand the membership of the project team to include lower level managers, and to directly and regularly participate in project team meetings. This action was his response to his apparent frustration with this project team's perceived limited progress, as previously outlined. His decision to proceed in this manner resulted in the core project team members explicitly welcoming the news. For example, Bill stated,

> I think that X [the project sponsor] is able to see more of the road forward and perhaps the three of us keep looking very close to home...I suppose that his latest intervention will assist our learning...occasionally it's difficult to see the light at the end of the tunnel, whereas, I think he can see that light and then help others to see it.

These comments also represented a lack of personal authority Bill felt he had with the change processes, and a cultural readiness to follow the leader and deflect responsibilities onto those higher authorities. At this time, all three core participants appeared to abdicate their responsibility for their project process and their learning activity to the project sponsor, that is he let them off the hook through his participation in the team meetings. As one participant reflected, 'I acquiesce to X [the project sponsor] and Y [the Human Resource Manager] probably far too much...I probably gave up to protect myself before they turned up.' This abdication of responsibility to a higher authority meant that during team meeting sessions, when the project sponsor was present, the whole team visibly awaited his commentary on issues, frequently directed gazes at him (rather than others) to see if he agreed with their comments, and avoided topics which may have placed them in conflict with the project sponsor (e.g. such as their efforts in changing their own relationships). Perhaps noting their avoidance of the difficult topics like their relationships (or simply his frustration with them), on many occasions the project sponsor repeatedly focused the discussion of the team precisely on their efforts in building their relationships and what fears they possessed about the new opportunities. Notably, however, when the project sponsor was absent from the team meeting sessions, the team became less directed and often seemed adrift, meandered readily onto rational operational issues rather than wallow around in the non-rational change issues, and made more explicit reference to the political alignment of their roles and their actions, while also questioning their learning processes. For example, one participant commented, 'Does this group feel that we fit the role that the sponsor wants? Do the Supervisors feel they fit the role that the Leadership Team wants?' When asked if he felt that all the participants came to this team equally (in status), Len responded by noting this difference in the team dialogue when the project sponsor was present, by stating, 'X [the project sponsor] still carries a lot of authority in the team and in X's absence the discussion is quite different. I think similarly Y [the Human Resources Manager] carries a lot of authority because of her expertise in facilitation.' Therefore, learning may have been assisted by the project sponsor being there and in offering his perceived informed views and ideas and provocative questioning, but in doing so, he narrowed the degree of the learning challenge for the participants. That being, his recurrent interventions served as both a catalyst to help activate some situated learning (thereby advancing some exchanges between team members that may have occurred at a future point in time), but at the same time, limited and constrained participant exchanges to what participants perceived was necessary to comply with what the project sponsor wanted to hear or wanted to see them do.

Towards the middle of the research process, a rather heated and important meeting session occurred between the project team and the sponsor, where major frustrations felt by participants and the sponsor concerning project progress, their relationships and their accountabilities were aired. Steve, who was particularly animated in this meeting, was asked what he thought of the project sponsor's actions in initiating and participating in that session, to which he replied, 'He made a surgical strike and I am sure he will do it again as that is the way they go about their business.' He went on to say that 'My feelings on the intervention?...Shit happens!...I am happy that it happened...but what am I going to do about it?' His cavalier approach managing to leave the question hanging and unresolved in the team. While there is a cognitive style issue involved in this exchange, Steve's views tended to suggest that he saw himself as a victim to the whims of the higher authority and also stressed his preparedness to perpetuate the traditional blame culture, so evident in the organization. When asked if he was happy to have those types of interventions happen again, and after much pensive thought, Steve responded by saying, 'It really comes and goes – it's the flavour of the month.' He then proceeded to expand on his views of management fads and how they come and go – indicating, perhaps, that maybe they will outlast this one till something else becomes the new focal flavour. At that time, one suspects that the project sponsor's direct interventions with the team failed to assist Steve's situated learning, through discouraging him from openly exploring issues with others consistent with his cognitive style, and tending to minimize his input – until the project sponsor otherwise guided or instructed him. Indeed, later in the project cycle, Steve expressed his belief that knowledge and information sharing was impeded in the project team because of the lack of depth in their relationships and the authority exerted by some in the group. When Steve was further asked if he felt that the project sponsor regularly sitting in on the project team was hindering his learning, he stated, '...I feel deeply about how he is actually inhibiting his desire for us to do things, by being around [ ] he has got to piss off so we can have a conversation around here. It's certainly something I need to talk to him about.' While Steve's comments indicated that he felt the project sponsor's authority in the project team was hindering his learning, it may also reflect a clash of cognitive styles, where Steve would prefer to lead the process – as he often did assume such leadership in the absence of the project sponsor in team meetings. This is not a sinister development on the authority issue, but it does highlight the active interaction of cognitive styles with the learning relationships and pyramid of authority constraint/enabler elements in affecting situated learning for this participant. From an observer's perspective then, the project sponsor's participation in the project seemed to perpetuate the traditional cultural authority structure that he so vehemently wanted to change and yet he felt compelled to proceed in that manner. Therefore, despite the assigned freedom in decision-making provided to the project participants by the sponsor (coupled to the inability of the participants to engage most effectively with the challenges provided to them in the project), the sponsor's interventions during these project events contributed towards them perceiving that they had a low level of both individual and collective authority concerning this project.

Overall, the project sponsor's authority, whether latent or active across events in this project, conditioned the perceived levels of authority the core participants felt they had to conduct their project. Accordingly, this condition affected the team's learning activity. For example, pending the sponsor's influence or actions, participants delayed or avoided making decisions on their project activities which otherwise may have enabled them to explore issues more broadly, more deeply and more freely. In addition, their dialogue was often biased or framed only by what the issue or topic might mean to the authority figure (i.e. whether or not it aligned with his expectations or decrees). The chief irony in this project case being, that those very things the project sponsor sought the project team participants to achieve (i.e. building their relationships, learning and becoming better leaders in the organization) appeared to be hampered by his own latent and discernable authority in the organization. Incidentally, this also tended to reinforce the embedded cultural feature of hierarchy dependence.

The relationship of this project to other projects in the change programme which were perceived to be more politically important

Early in this study, the perceived relationship of this project to another interrelated project of the overall organizational change programme also affected the core participants' perceptions of their authority to conduct this project and their learning activities. That being, the core participants frequently deferred to another project that they felt was the priority or lead project of the change programme, in advance of pursuing their own project actions. At times, this resulted in the core participants' actions in project meetings being completely reactive to, or dependent on, inputs from the perceived priority project, and those issues consumed much of the available meeting time. Whilst one can easily accept that occasional influential inputs from external projects or other sources to a project team process can constitute valuable process and learning aids, a form of hierarchical dependency on another project or input source can actually stifle learning activity as participants await that influential and, perhaps, confining input. In this project case, this informal hegemony of projects resulted in the project team refraining from being more independently proactive about their own project processes. This situation became apparent in one of the first project team meeting sessions when Bill was asked what he thought this project team was fundamentally about. He responded by saying, 'The drive behind the project is the integration of the three silos which involves the Batteries 4-5-6, Battery 7 and Coke Handling and, Technology Support.' He also stated that 'This project's activities are required to move in parallel with the Working Party activities.' At that early stage in the project process, Bill's last comment illustrated his perception that the Working Party (a perceived higher priority project team) was the primary influence on the activities in each of the other project teams or forums involved in the change programme. When Len was asked the same question, he sketched out his view of the entire change programme with all the forums (project teams) shown. His pictorial indicated a hierarchy of projects where the job design and cultural change process of the Working Party was again the primary focal point of the diagram, and of his explanation. Interestingly, he placed the project team involved in this study (at that time, referred to as Coke Inc.) at the end of the hierarchy in both position and size – seemingly indicating its subservience or lower priority to the other project groups and activities on the site (Figure 5.1). Similarly, in one of the project team's earlier meeting sessions, Steve stated, 'Our time [in this project forum] has to be focused on the things that will get us a success at the end of the Working Party.' At that time, the implication being, that Steve saw this project team purely as an extension of the Working Party where they might jointly discuss issues from that forum.

This perceived dominance of the higher profile Working Party project affected the case study participants' learning activities in insidious ways. That being: it impinged on the learning space of the project

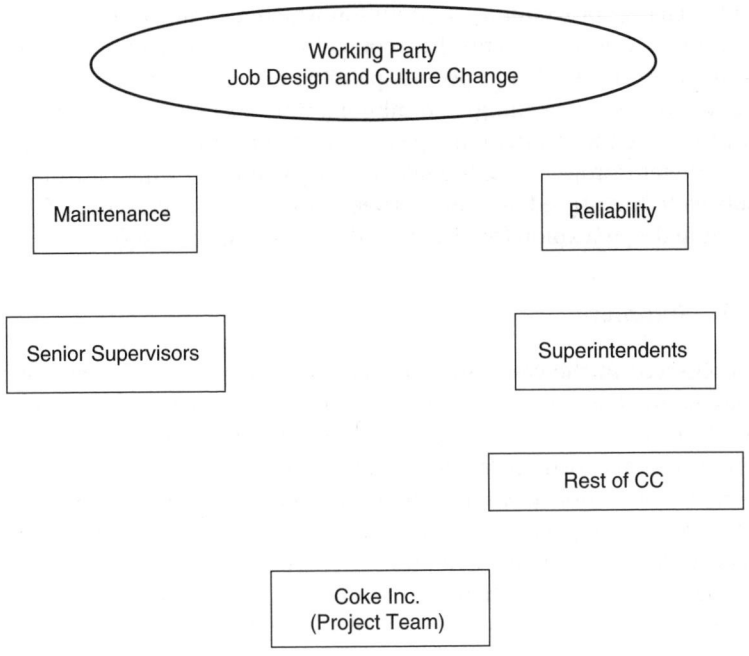

Figure 5.1 Len's view of the project team hierarchy

team involved in this study and distracted the participants' attention and energy away from their project goals; it also provided avenues or conduits for participants to defensively deflect and avoid difficult project discussions; and, it provided opportunities and excuses for participants to avoid meeting commitments on their agreed project tasks – including their learning activities. Importantly, all three participants indicated that prior to this project team formation, they each had a vested interest (and active participation) in the success of the Working Party, and therefore it demanded and attracted their ongoing attention.

Although none of this project hierarchy was formalized, the ownership of and/or participation in the Working Party project team activities by all members of the project team of this study signalled that this higher profile project might dominate their attention more than others. Sense and Antoni (2003) found a similar situation with learning between projects, where in their study, projects with informally perceived higher profiles gained more attention and participant effort than those considered lower in status, and the former attracted more effort on learning activity. Further compounding this situation in this project team was the core participants' multi-membership of other project teams in the change programme – a condition which resembled a competitive multi-project environment where competition for resources (in this case, human effort) resulted in people spending only that time necessary to get the project happening, and minimal time on reflection and deeper learning. In those situations, people chop their time into little slices for different projects (i.e. the salami time syndrome) where learning is subject to high-speed hopping between projects and such actions fail to nurture deeper exploratory learning (Sense and Antoni, 2003).

5.3 Summary

As observed in the case study project, and as potentially difficult as it may be for practitioners to engage with at a personal or professional level, achieving a better understanding and engagement with these interpersonal constraint/enabler elements of learning relationships and pyramid of authority is fundamentally important for project learning. This can be progressed through participants' collaborative and critical reflection on them while in a project setting.

The section of this chapter that explored and argued the importance of understanding the learning relationships element elaborated on two empirically derived conditioners of the participants' learning relationships, which ultimately influenced their learning behaviours. These conditioners included: attitudes to public exposure and public scrutiny of perceived personal matters; and, preparedness to explore one's learning relationships with others outside of the existing relationship frameworks, while viewing relationship problems as major learning opportunities. In this study, the first of those conditioners involved the participants demonstrating defensive routines in order to avoid discussion on their own relationship issues, which in turn only tended to stifle relational learning activity and knowledge exchange between participants. However, in concurrence with the second conditioner, the participants in this study were prepared to, and did explore, alternative learning relationships and came to view existing relationship issues as significant learning opportunities. Their learning actions in this regard found them challenging traditional socio-cultural factors that had previously forged the development of the presenting relationship frameworks. It also resulted in them altering their approaches to mentoring and coaching of each other and people external to the immediate project team. Over time, as the project participants explored the functioning of these new relationship possibilities, they reduced their defensive routines and repeatedly confronted their assumptions behind what relationships were possible, and learnt about and from each other.

The section of this chapter that explored the pyramid of authority element described why politics is rife in projects and argued that it must be embraced (and not avoided) as a normal part of the project management process. This section also articulated how learning was implicated with politics in projects and concluded that participants in a project team are not simply victims to the political forces enveloping them and their project, but that they, as individuals (armed with their own authorities and making choices to be either influential or accommodative in their political exchanges), can have a political impact on their own and their team's learning activity within a project. For example, being more accommodative to other peoples' requirements or desires generally opens up opportunities for the more active participation of those people involved, which may foster learning activity during and after the event. On the other hand, being too influential (e.g. forthright and aggressive) in getting one's own way may discourage the active participation of people (and limit their dialogue and knowledge exchanges) during a political exchange. However, being influential in an event may generate downstream conditions or situations that stimulate multiple knowledge exchanges and encourage dialogue between people. As demonstrated by the political actions of the players involved in this study, this political dialectic necessitates project participants to play both ends of that spectrum and be both purposeful and flexible in their political approaches towards their learning.

This section also examined how the pyramids of authority exhibited in this case study impacted the participants' situated learning activity. Therein, the core participants' perceptions of their prior organizational authority influenced how they chose to pursue their learning activities within the project, that is they felt the need to reduce others' perceptions of their authority and generally failed to see or utilize this authority as something positive to accelerate their project and learning processes. Consequently, in acknowledgement of this and in responding to other influences, their behaviours generally reflected a more discreet, fluid and reticent approach towards encouraging learning activity amongst team members – in contrast, perhaps, to a more overt and authority initiated or executed series of learning actions. Moreover, as observed in this study, the perceptions that the other participants held of the prior organizational authority of the core participants, at times, constrained open communal debate and reflection on issues, which only served to reinforce the traditional deference to higher authority figures. These perceptions of the prior organizational authority of individuals in this project team culminated in a hesitancy towards maximizing their potential engagement with the learning opportunities.

This section also presented and discussed three conditioners of the participants' authority within the project setting. These conditioners included: participants' ambiguity within the project revolving around the subject of learning, their roles and the process to achieve the project goals; the latent or discernable authority of the project sponsor influencing the project learning activity; and, the relationship of the project to other projects in the change programme which were perceived to be more politically important. These conditioners contributed to the project team participants' feeling they lacked authority (or felt powerless) to lead the project and to confidently lead their own learning activity. This condition tended to suppress (but not eliminate) situated learning activities within the setting until the perceived higher authority, that is the project sponsor, provided direct or implicit guidance or instruction on project matters. As such, participants generally deferred to this higher authority for guidance and decision-making rather than operate in a more self-driven and independent fashion. These project actions also tended to mirror and help perpetuate a cultural norm within the case study organization involving hierarchy dependence.

This story is still incomplete. The discussion presented within this chapter has hinted towards yet other socio-cultural factors that might also help shape the attitudes and approaches of project participants towards situated learning activity. For example, intimately associated with (and not in isolation to) these interpersonal elements is the milieu within which political behaviour operates and relationships develop. If the milieu is conducive to supporting learning relationship development, through providing time and resources to encourage people to engage with each other, or alternatively perhaps fosters aggressive and shark-like political behaviour (Pinto and Millet, 1999), then the project milieu itself may also cast distinctive imprints on situated learning activity. Furthermore, if the participants' conversations and knowledge-sharing activities or approaches can manage to help change perceptions about their traditional hierarchical authority (an issue these participants felt strongly about), or simply better align with the individual cognitive styles of participants, then one might suspect that a better understanding of how one shares knowledge in the project team might also significantly impact situated learning activity. These speculations again highlight the mutual relatedness of the various constraints/enablers to situated learning observed in this study. These other socio-cultural constraint/enabler elements are the subject of the next chapter to follow, and since they are not strictly intra or interpersonal, but more enveloping in character, they can be considered the infrastructural constraints/enablers to situated learning.

6
Knowledge Management and Situational Context

This chapter provides an insight into the infrastructural constraint/enabler elements for project situated learning. These consist of knowledge management and situational context. Infrastructural, in this discussion context, includes those aspects from within and around the project environs which influence how knowledge is shared and created within a project team, and which help establish and facilitate a project learning environment. These elements present a more conspicuous character than perhaps the intra and interpersonal elements elaborated on in earlier chapters.

The first major section of this chapter explores the knowledge management element. It initially provides a definition for knowledge management as relevant to this study, and discusses the relative merits of matching or mismatching cognitive styles to the knowledge management processes applied in a project. This section then articulates numerous considerations for facilitating knowledge flow in projects and elaborates on two generalized forms for knowledge management: codification and personalization. Therein, it describes how the personalization approach (involving individuals interacting and communicating directly with each other) is essential in exposing and sharing tacit knowledge held by team participants, and how codification processes, whilst supportive, are inherently deficient for situated learning. In consideration of its criticality for situated learning, the section then focuses exclusively on a discussion concerning the dynamics of pursuing a personalized knowledge management approach within a project, and explores how that approach can positively stimulate the situated learning activity of project team participants.

The second major section of this chapter defines and describes the element of situational context. It first discusses the importance of establishing and organizing the project setting to help create and facilitate a project learning environment. It then articulates how a situational context can influence participants' situated learning behaviours through three categories of support. These include: a project learning intention or strategy to learn; the establishment of a set of infrastructural supports for learning within a project setting, for example spaces and time to learn; and a local organizational environment engulfing a project that stimulates participants to learn. These categories of support resonate strongly with the dominant organizational design literature on managing change – that which asserts the establishment of conditions devoid of fear and the participative and mutually cooperative engagement of people. Hence, they do not subscribe to the alternative view of managing change as involving top-down, fear-driven and directive control processes. In that light, the issues raised within this discussion support the development of trust and cooperative participation to change people and motivate them into action and into learning – a proposition also broadly consistent with SLT. Project participants' systematic attention to these categories of support can provide the stimulant conditions for them to practise learning within a project setting, and to progressively develop their skills in learning-how-to-learn.

The final section of this chapter provides a summary of the key issues concerning these two infrastructural elements affecting project situated learning activity. Our immediate attention now turns towards exploring the issues of managing knowledge flow in projects.

6.1 Knowledge management

Managing knowledge flow in projects

In recent times, it appears that knowledge management as an orientation has received substantial exposure and marketing across many management and organizational change literatures. As a result of these exposures and perceived value-creating processes, there has been a popular development of the notion of knowledge management as a key to competitive advantage (Easterby-Smith et al., 2000). However, the achievement of competitive advantage, through a focus on knowledge management processes, may be an elusive organizational goal if either of the primal dimensions of knowledge management, that is the human and technical dimensions, are not clearly understood nor equally and appropriately addressed.

When Scarbrough *et al.* (1999) did a review on knowledge management literature they found a significant gap within this literature revolving around the people management issues and a bias of focus towards developing and implementing databases, tools and techniques to codify knowledge and information. Therein, knowledge management was frequently reduced to only the implementation of new information technology systems for knowledge transfer (Swan *et al.*, 1999). Swan *et al.* (1999) report that where an organization (one of their case studies) attended to both the technical and the social dimensions of knowledge management, then exploitation of existing knowledge and exploration for new knowledge were actively embraced. In contrast, their other case study, by being focused only on the technical and infrastructural issues, failed to engage the social and cultural aspects of the change process and exploration was not pursued, and even exploitation was limited (Swan *et al.*, 1999). Similarly, other evaluations of knowledge management processes (Davenport and Prusak, 1998; Ruggles, 1998) have shown that a lack of attention to these social factors has impaired the effectiveness of information technology implementations, and hence there is renewed interest in how the social aspects of organizational learning might be combined with the more technological views of knowledge management (Easterby-Smith *et al.*, 2000).

More recent literature in this field is now spotlighting this human-focussed, or social and cultural, dimension of knowledge management. For example, Wenger *et al.* (2002), Mårtensson (2000) and Baumard (1999) emphasize knowledge as being an eclectic mix of information that is coupled to individuals and their experiences within their practice contexts. Similarly, Brown and Duguid (2000) also posit that resources for learning lie not simply in the information, but in the practice that allows people (within a practice) to make sense of and use the information available. In those circumstances, knowledge travels with remarkable ease. In that same vein, Fernie *et al.* (2003) claim there have been various attempts to carve up and typify knowledge and all of them share a theme that the creation and usage of knowledge is undoubtedly a human endeavour, and therefore knowledge can only be of practical use through the interaction of individuals.

Organizational theorists such as Nonaka and Takeuchi (1995) also highlight this necessity to view knowledge as embedded in and constructed from and through social relationships and interactions in a community or network of people (Swan *et al.*, 1999). Or, as Calhoun and Starbuck (2003) posit, knowledge always reflects social construction and people acquire information through social networks. In accordance with this social constructivist perspective, knowledge cannot be processed, it must be 'continuously re-created and re-constituted through dynamic, interactive and social networking activity' (Swan et al., 1999: 272). This then necessitates the people involved to engage in activities such as dialogue, negotiation and sensemaking (Weick, 1995). This view of knowledge as being complex and multidimensional and in constant interactive social development within and between humans, is also shared by Choo (1998) and Davenport and Prusak (1998), and also resounds in the work of Lundin and Söderholm (1998) and Andrews and Delahaye (2000).

The adoption and promotion of a socio-cultural perspective of knowledge creation and management, and the demotion of the alternate technical perspective in this study, is primarily a result of the technical processes being inherently deficient for situated learning through their inability to expose and share tacit knowledge held by participants. In that way, information technology focused assumptions about knowledge being codifiable and explicit and able to be captured, stored and retrieved in isolation from the conditions which created it only address the smallest part of the knowledge iceberg (Fernie et al., 2003). Hence, the technical dimension of knowledge management only assumes a supporting role in the knowledge creation and management process. In unison with the views of Leonard-Barton (1995), Nonaka and Takeuchi (1995) and Choo (1998), it then follows that purposefully providing and maintaining conditions within a setting that nurture and enhance both tacit and explicit knowledge exchanges, and knowledge creation between people, is critical for enhancing individual and organizational learning development. Part of those conditions concerns the processes of managing knowledge flow within a setting, as those processes can directly and dramatically either facilitate or impede individual and collective knowledge-gathering and knowledge-sharing activities.

How people actually attempt to manage knowledge flow largely depends on how they understand and define it, since 'knowledge is multifaceted and complex, being both situated and abstract, implicit and explicit, distributed and individual, physical and mental, developing and static, verbal and encoded (Blackler, 1995)' (Story and Barnett, 2000: 147). Or, as Fernie et al. (2003: 184) concluded in their project team study, 'knowledge should not be considered unidimensional and accumulative' but be considered highly individualistic and shaped by and enacted in the project contexts in which it is created (Fernie et al., 2003). To support the further discussions contained in this chapter, a definition, which incorporates this multidimensional and constructivist view of knowledge, is provided for this element of knowledge management. That being, *the way a project team actually goes about acquiring, creating, exchanging and assimilating knowledge in and around a project team setting.* This definition is an adaptation of a definition for knowledge management provided by Swan *et al.* (1999).

One might note the similarities in the wording used in this definition with the definition provided for the element of cognitive style, that is gathering and processing and interpreting information or knowledge. However, cognitive style specifically refers to the preferred way an individual likes to gather and process and interpret information. Whereas, knowledge management differentiates from cognitive style, in that it refers to the way a project team actually goes about managing their project knowledge between project participants and other interested parties. During the middle of the project, when Len, for example, was asked if he considered the knowledge management process in the project team was appropriate, he responded by saying, 'We talk about concepts, we talk about issues, and we're still not good at identifying and agreeing on a resolution. Having said that, I think there are some things, which we've done far better recently. Things like agreeing on a vision statement, which is a fairly painful and long process and yet it was also a good learning process – thinking about what does it mean? Thinking and talking about the impact of those fairly innocuous terms and yet thinking through what they mean, what's the impact on different people? [ ] However, we're not writing down enough about what it is we've done and what it is we've agreed to do. In some ways I think it's sometimes an avoidance strategy, so that you then don't have a list of things that you have to do before the next meeting. That I think is an area that will change. So, that's an issue and sharing the knowledge and information both within and outside the team is also an issue because of that.' While Len's latter comments may be a reflection of his predisposition to want to capture information in a rational and ordered way (consistent with his strong Analytic cognitive style type), his full comments also identify two important issues for his learning. First, he considered that at that time, the personal interactions and knowledge exchanges he had with others assisted their learning in the project and, second, that he felt more written recording of particular events or commitments might further aid knowledge-sharing within and external to the team. It appears that the situation Len described represented some degree of matching, but mostly a mismatching of his style type with the way knowledge was managed in the project situation – with implications for his learning activity at that time.

What are the overarching facilitative considerations for knowledge flow?

Von Krogh (2003) suggests there are at least three considerations associated with managing knowledge-sharing or flow in a community. These involve having the opportunity structures to share knowledge in a form of community, the care to or incentive to share that knowledge, and the authenticity or legitimacy of knowledge such that it is considered genuine, accurate, valid and reliable (von Krogh, 2003). These three factors combined impact knowledge-sharing activities where participants' interests are diverse and distributed (von Krogh, 2003) – such as in a project team environment, which resembles an embryonic form of a new community of practice (Sense, 2003b). Project teams represent significant 'opportunity structures' (Saint-Onge and Wallace, 2002: 50) for both tacit and explicit knowledge to be exposed and exchanged.

These considerations for knowledge-sharing or flow in project settings are underpinned by two generalized forms for how knowledge is managed. Hansen et al. (1999) and Kasvi et al. (2003) define these two general forms as codification and personalization.

> *Codification* – refers to the ways in which explicit knowledge is codified, stored and then reused independently of its source and its context (Hansen et al., 1999). Bresnen et al. (2003) refer to this approach as the cognitive model of knowledge management. Examples of codified knowledge can be artefacts such as intranets, documents, databases, manuals, guidelines and reports. The aim of codification is to put organizational knowledge into a form that makes it accessible to those who need it, and the difficulty in doing so involves how not to loose the knowledge-distinctive properties and turn it into less vibrant information or data (Davenport and Prusak, 1998). Codification approaches typically engage many information technology solutions. However, this approach is inherently deficient in exposing and sharing tacit knowledge held by participants. Many people, particularly in the information technology industry, may still consider that knowledge management is only about this codification process, that is the storage and retrieval of information, and yet for others it is about discovering and developing processes that value and cultivate a process of learning that is collectively shared and irreducible to information – since the ability

to change knowledge, that is to learn, is the real source of power (Willmott, 2000).

Personalization – focuses on dialogue between individuals and not on knowledge objects in a database (Hansen *et al.*, 1999). This approach is dependent on the individual as the means of transferring experiences to others, and thus enables tacit knowledge (e.g. such as values, norms of behaviour and personal competencies and inadequacies) to be exposed and shared amongst others. As Davenport and Prusak (1998) and Linde (2001) logically claim, it is impossible to codify tacit knowledge, but they consider narratives to be a powerful means to achieve the exposure and capture of it. Or, as Davenport and Prusak (1998: 81–3) state, 'a good story is often the best way to convey meaningful knowledge'. Personalization approaches require space and time to enable the getting together of people to perform such personal exchanges and to develop interpersonal networks – something that may be particularly problematic where people are dispersed over large geographical distances. Nonetheless, Hansen *et al.* (1999: 9) suggest that in the personalization approach what is most important is to 'have a system that allows people to find other people.' When that is achieved, public exposition and sharing of tacit (and explicit) knowledge becomes more probable.

Illustrating that last point, Bresnen *et al.* (2003) studied a construction industry project case, wherein the company was attempting to develop explicit social mechanisms to encourage knowledge-sharing and learning across projects. The project involved the introduction of new management practices in a construction firm (including the re-organization of the engineering expertise in the firm). They concluded that in addition to illustrating the difficulties and limitations of adopting only an information technology codification approach to learning in projects, processes of knowledge capture, transfer and learning relied very heavily on social patterns, practices and processes, in ways which emphasized the value and importance of adopting a community-based approach (Bresnen *et al.*, 2003). They further concluded that because projects are spatially, temporally and culturally differentiated, knowledge is not as readily diffused as it might be in a well-established community of practice (Bresnen *et al.*, 2003). In addition, Fernie *et al.* (2003) performed a study into the challenges of knowledge-sharing across business sectors (i.e. a construction company and BAE aerospace), and their conclusions also revolve around knowledge not being able to be separated from the knower, and therefore not readily captured and transferred across contexts. In effect, they posed a people-centric view, where knowledge is essentially personal and any attempt at sharing it must engage the individual, and that it must be facilitated in a socialized setting which aids dialectic debate (Fernie *et al.*, 2003) – which also alludes to establishing the situational context to aid such situated learning activity.

How did the project participants' knowledge management approaches impact their situated learning behaviours in this case study project team?

The approach pursued by this project team to acquire and exchange knowledge within their project involved a dominant preference for the personalization approach over codification type approaches. This dominant approach appeared to very positively impact the quantum and quality of knowledge exchanges between participants. This acknowledgment of the dominance of the personalization approach does not suggest that codification approaches were not used for explicit information exchange, since the recording of minutes of meetings, sending e-mails and the sharing of reports and memos were also observed in this case. However, those processes assumed a relatively very minor status in how knowledge flowed across the project team. This preference for personalized knowledge flow reflected a link to the project being a complex 'process innovation' type project (Bresnen *et al.*, 2003: 163) which also involved a specific project goal of redefining participant relationships. These types of projects tend to require and encourage such personal contact because they involve changes in work practices, roles, responsibilities, attitudes and values (Bresnen *et al.*, 2003). This preference also reflects other issues from the project milieu such as topic and role ambiguity – as elaborated on in the previous chapter. The following lengthy and reflective comment from Bill tends to indirectly summarize the learning value he believed this dominant personalization approach to managing knowledge flow generated in their project team activities:

> We have been having a meeting once a week, for at least two hours, and some of the conversations that we have together are making us rethink perhaps our beliefs as to what is possible. I also see that when we go out in the work place, where we talk about change and those sorts of things, then there's pressure coming back on us saying 'well, what are you guys doing differently that supports a better future for Cokemaking?' There are things that are happening differently. I think

in a number of different ways the three of us are working across our boundaries that we have previously had and actively going to other people's plants and talking to those people in those plants. Even from the point of view of our discussions around the future, it's really about saying well, Cokemaking is one department, and then how does it work together, and we then keep challenging ourselves and others about what possibilities does that then throw up. [] I think the relationship between the three of us is now closer than it was before. With that brings a willingness to do things differently and take a few risks here and there.

From Bill's comments, one can readily appreciate the positive community learning and practical relationship-building impacts realized through pursuing a personalization approach to managing knowledge flow within his project setting. The discussions that now follow elaborate on the situated learning impacts experienced by the case study project team as they engaged this personalization approach in managing their knowledge flows.

Tacit knowledge-sharing

In undertaking such personalized processes as multiple face-to-face meetings, personal feedback to colleagues, and communal reflection activities across multiple project events, tacit knowledge held by participants (including their fears about their futures and the expectations of them) was frequently exposed and shared. In sharing their tacit knowledge participants helped to progressively develop their learning relationships, which enabled them to better respond to their collective challenges and share and generate more knowledge. For some participants too, this personalization process aligned closely with their cognitive style type. As Steve noted, 'the process of reflection for me is a verbal one, so that if I didn't have someone to listen to... or someone else to capture my thoughts... then some of my reflections would be lost. I don't like writing in journals. I am not good at that, and its quite handy for me to have people like X and Y who aren't necessarily judgemental in the process... they take on board what is happening and what I say and then they offer their reflections on my reflections.' When Bill was asked to comment on his own reflection activity he stated, 'I don't generally tend to write a lot of stuff down about reflections. I don't keep a diary or any of those sorts of things [] For me, I spend a fair bit of time talking to groups of people.' Both these comments illustrate the potential value of communal reflection in helping develop the learning relationships and the criticality of a personalization approach to generate and share tacit and explicit knowledge when undertaking collective and reflective enquiry.

Len also illustrated his preference towards personalization approaches to knowledge management in this project by stating, 'I probably have a bias towards taking in information orally with some visual reinforcement.' He indicated that he deliberately and predominantly sought to harvest new knowledge about technical, operational or change management issues directly from the major political influences associated with the project, and also through his many informal conversations with a network of colleagues across the broader organization. In performing those actions, Len tended to build his tacit knowledge through multiple and diverse personalized channels.

Knowledge flows affected by team parameters

In this study, the personalization approach to managing knowledge flow appeared to be moderated over time and project phases by the variable size and mix of the project team. When this project team consisted only of the three core participants, the formal and informal personalized exchanges between them appeared to be (by my observation) high in quantity and quality. Conversely, Len acknowledged that an increase in group size hindered their knowledge-sharing by stating, 'The biggest issue in the bigger group versus the one on one, or the small group, is sharing the issues and sharing the concerns. Sometimes I like to bounce an idea off somebody to see whether it's valid. I'm more comfortable doing that in a small group and yet you need to share the ideas with a bigger group.' When the team expanded in size to include 16 members, it reduced the volume of these formal exchanges between the three core participants, but opened up avenues for increased formal (and possibly more superficial) exchanges with others, while the three core participants' exchanges became more informal and more opportunistic. Steve also noted the differences in their learning exchanges and learning relationships when this team size changed by stating,

> when we had Coke Inc. – the three headed monster and all the rest of it, we spent time talking to one another and reflected more [ ] the power, for want of a better word has been diluted, especially in the learning front, probably more so than anything else, [ ] that learning that we had with each other, that openness that appeared every now and again in the small meeting has changed.

Argote (1999) considers that this group size issue affects the sharing of knowledge because larger groups rather than smaller groups are likely to focus only on shared information, that is information that is commonly held, and this mediating influence tends to increase with group size.

When this project team increased in size, information sharing appeared to be more concentrated on those things the larger group had in common (such as immediate plant operational issues), and it was therefore more difficult to cross this barrier to get the larger group to broach the difficult project issues than it was for the smaller group to do so. That is not to suggest that getting the smaller group to deal with these project issues was easy – just that the larger group made that process even harder to achieve. When Steve, for example, was asked if he felt there was anything they could do to support learning in the expanded project team, he felt that providing the opportunity to the expanded team to engage in introspection, just like they had done when the team consisted only of the three core members, would help. Then, as he stated, 'we should actually share things and get people to share things about the anxiety they've gone through, so that we can actually understand that yes, everybody's been through this [ ] to have them articulate the issues that we face on an emotional level is a learning for all of us.' These comments also reflected a desire for increasing the opportunity for collective and reflective enquiry and thereby the opportunity to further stimulate situated learning activity.

Coupled to this issue of group size orchestrating a general propensity to share commonly held information and thereby affect knowledge flow between participants is ignorance or avoidance of sharing ideas or alternate information that is unique to individual members (Argote, 1999). This situation tends to shut out the opportunity for generative tacit knowledge flow because the commonly held information dominates group discussion and somewhat fills the conversation void (Argote, 1999). In the expanded project team of this study, the team members demonstrated a strong propensity to regularly discuss and share information on operational matters associated with the plant (i.e. their issues in common), which helped discourage individual participants' preparedness and their opportunities to express unique ideas on issues involving the project goals. This focus on the shorter-term operational matters rather than the longer-term developmental project activities was also assisted by the participants' lack of project role clarity and uncertainty about their activities in pursuing the goals of the project (as described in Chapter 5) – a situation also consistent with Bresnen *et al.*'s (2003) observations of knowledge management activities in a construction industry project case.

Therefore, in this study, the domination of these operational discussions constrained the volume and potential scope of conversations and learning on issues involving the project goals. The paradox being that, on one hand, the common issues focus, prompted interaction and discussion that helped some form of situated learning, but conversely, whether it was learning which actively related to and progressed the activity of the project, is somewhat contentious – and from any traditional project leadership perspective, potentially quite frustrating. Nevertheless, one suspects that incrementally these situations (particularly during the formative stages of this project case) served as a catalyst or relationship-builder to enable the participants to progressively, over time, get involved in the difficult project issues and to better share some of their tacit knowledge through their personal contact. That being so, it would seem important to tolerate such seemingly divergent discourse within a personalization approach to knowledge management and to provide the conditions for it to occur – particularly in a 'process innovation' type project (Bresnen et al., 2003: 163) if one seeks to support situated learning activity over time. Alternatively, a non-incremental shock and pressure process, where participants are bluntly forced to confront such difficult project issues may achieve some immediate and limited sharing of explicit and tacit knowledge (and likely to be accompanied with fear), but may fail to assist the ongoing participative development of participants' project learning relationships. In that condition, situated learning would ultimately be severely constrained.

Formal and informal channels for knowledge flow

The personalization approach pursued to attain, create and disperse knowledge in this project case involved both formal and informal channels, including, for example, formal project team meetings and all-day workshop sessions, plus impromptu network discussions. Steve commented that with some of the guys in the project team, 'I don't interact daily with much at all [ ] I tend to have philosophical discussions with them in the corner or in the corridor or somewhere for a while rather than in any planned daily interaction.... [when I meet with them] I try to inoculate my ideas into their thinking and they do the same to me. Then it's a question of how's it picked up and what's learned.' Expectantly, Steve's comment may reflect his Intuitive cognitive style, but also reflects his personalized approach in use to informally gather and impart knowledge.

As the three core project participants steadily built their learning relationships throughout the project life cycle, and linked to this personalization dynamic, there appeared to be a greater bias towards informal activities and meetings to exchange knowledge. Towards the middle of the project cycle, for example, in responding to a question about their seeming propensity to source knowledge informally, Bill remarked, 'I suppose the time where you go and sit in someone else's office and have a chat about things in general, that then adds to your knowledge or understanding of where the other person's coming from and perhaps where the direction [of the project] needs to be going. There's a fair bit of that happening now that didn't happen before. An example of that is last night, Steve came and sat in here for half an hour and we just talked about things around Working Party issues and perhaps how we look at the shift supervisor role and the shift operator role... and some of that was also a result of a casual conversation I had with X earlier, about the same things as well.' Bill's comments highlighted the value he perceived in less formal interactions assisting the development of their relationships and, in this case, achievement of some project activities.

Len also recognized that project team knowledge flowed around the team through both formal and informal channels and that he increasingly utilized the informal channels to discuss things with others and to learn. As he stated, 'I think it's both [ ] But because of the totality of the activities we've had together, the informal is working far better. [ ] Certainly in terms of my learning about what's going on in maintenance, the formal sessions have made a big difference, but also now, I spend more time stopping and chatting in the corridor [informally with colleagues from that area] than would have been the case previously.'

Unofficial rankings applied to knowledge sources

During the course of the project, and tending to complicate the opportunities to improve knowledge flow within the setting, were the unofficial rankings sometimes applied to knowledge from particular authority sources. This illustrates a direct interrelationship between the constraint/enabler elements of pyramid of authority and knowledge management and, as previously introduced in Chapter 5, suggests that certain knowledge exchanges were more sought after and listened to than others. Commonly held knowledge of how expertise is distributed among group participants affects how team members retrieve and integrate information, that is such awareness increases the likelihood that unshared knowledge uniquely held by certain team members will be shared, since expert roles in the group validate the credibility of this information (Argote, 1999). This sharing presumes that people will want to seek out the information from the source as it were and that the source is prepared to relinquish control of the information and share it with others. If that holds, then knowledge provided by a recognized expert or authority figure (i.e. they are perceived to be in leadership roles either through their intelligence or through bureaucratic and other forms of hierarchy/authority) 'receives more weight in determining the group output than information provided by someone not perceived as having special expertise' (Argote, 1999: 108).

From a learning perspective (and in addition to the expertise or bureaucratic authorities of select individuals in a group tending to minimize other group members' debate and discussion on project issues), the awareness of prior established expertise or authority within the project team of this study, at times, narrowed the participants' knowledge capture and enquiry activities to that which they felt were the more important priority sources, for example the project sponsor. These actions helped limit the full learning potential to be realized from more fully interacting and exchanging with others in the project process. Therefore, a paradox exists: while the presence of authority or expertise sources might help stimulate some enquiry and unique information flow within a group, it can also concurrently serve as a broader restraint to knowledge generation and flow across the group. Len acknowledged this hierarchy on information flow by stating that 'what we need to do is to focus on avoiding the negatives of impeding information flow and failing to provide feedback because of hierarchical interactions'. Similar reflections from these participants, concerning their hierarchical dependence, were also provided in the pyramid of authority discussion in Chapter 5. Recognizing this barrier to knowledge exchange and flow within a project team posed by sources of privileged information and espousing ways to better include others from the team constituted positive steps in broadening the knowledge capture and creation possibilities in this project setting.

6.2 Situational context

Situational context and situated learning

In every project case, workplace conditions have the potential to restrict as well as enhance any possibilities for learning (Müllern and Östergren, 1998; Matthews, 1999). How participation in learning activities is invited, and how the unrestricted sharing and use of knowledge can be encouraged through shaping a workplace environment, is a central concern for learning in any setting (Billet, 2001a; Smith, 2001). Smith (2001) particularly emphasizes the provision of opportunities for tacit knowledge to be made explicit and shared (Also see Polanyi [1966], Nonaka and Takeuchi [1995] and Baumard [1999]) so that valuable human and knowledge resources are not wasted. Such tacit knowledge-sharing is crucial in situated learning activity and the source of real competitive advantage in projects. Moreover, one of five factors Bain (1998) considered was significant in aiding organizational learning included the provision of spaces for reflection and learning, since such spaces helped decrease social defences to organizational learning. Therefore, consistent with Senge's (1990) perspective that leaders (in their designer roles) need to build into their organizational structures (even temporal ones like projects) antecedents for effective learning, implicit and fundamental in promoting situated learning processes, is the organization of the project setting to create and facilitate a learning environment. Any deliberate attention to designing and implementing project conditions that invite, encourage and support individuals and teams to come together to dialogue, to critically reflect and to expose and exchange tacit and explicit knowledge clearly also represents a dominant bias towards aiding the personalization approach to knowledge management.

This constraining/enabling element of situational context involves two intimately connected workplace domains, that is the workplace of a project team and the organizational workplace immediately surrounding a project team. This combination forms the situational context of a project, since any attempt to organize the project setting to affect learning activity can be initiated or influenced or halted either by the actions of project stakeholders in the organizational workplace surrounding a project team or by the actions of participants within a project team. Reflecting this combination, an appropriate definition for this element of situational context is: *The way a project setting is organized to help establish and to facilitate a project learning environment.*

Expectantly, this infrastructural element has a very direct influence on all the other constraint/enabler elements identified in this study. For example, if the situational context conditions of a project do not support the development of learning relationships, nor permit traditional authority to be challenged and cognitive style to be assessed and understood, then situated learning is quite likely to be impeded. Of course, the converse situation applies and may assist the handling of other constraint/enabler elements even if the project participants find

Knowledge Management and Situational Context 151

those individually difficult to deal with. For example, if dealing with the defensive reasoning of participants was difficult to overcome and they were reluctant to challenge their current relationships, establishing a situational condition that encourages them to meet and converse may provide the initial impetus to them to progressively engage with those issues, whereas not providing such a motivating condition may only lock the participants into a cycle of ignorance and denial and excuses.

Consequently then, deliberate attention to creating the overarching situational context in a project setting – where those issues that drive our learning behaviours can be exposed, challenged and reflected on and where tacit knowledge can be shared and participants can practice being reflective practitioners (Schön, 1987) – would seem not only to be an interesting focus to help facilitate learning, but essential for it.

How did the situational context of this project case impact the situated learning behaviours of project participants?

The situational context of this project generally supported the situated learning activity of this team, and in some ways that support was extraordinary – which is partially why this project became such a valuable case in which to study learning. The following discussion highlights three empirically derived categories of that support. These include an organizational and participant intention to learn, the provision and operation of physical infrastructures at the project team level to support that intention, and the project setting providing a further stimulus for situated learning activity. Missing any one of these categories of support in a project setting may inhibit the development of learning activity. For example, having the commitment (intention) and the infrastructure establishes the conditions to initiate and encourage learning activity, but without the stimulus or incentives from the workplace itself, that is the reasons to do it, learning may be more readily avoided or overlooked, or remain opportunistic. Alternatively, if there is no commitment or infrastructure and yet there is some form of situational stimulus to learn, then the engine of learning may not really get started.

Provided an explicit organizational and participant commitment to learn (the intention to learn)

As part of the broader organizational change programme, the local organization immediately enveloping the project team of this study was attempting to construct an environment for learning that involved a culture of sharing and experimentation which emphasized broad and diverse participation and interactions throughout the organization and which motivated participants to change from their current condition, while reducing traditional control and fear (Englehardt and Simmons, 2002). Consequently, these efforts formed part of the background (or strategic) inertia supporting and energizing the learning activities associated with this project. In that way, there was an explicit local organizational commitment to the project team to learn and to take the time to learn and build their relationships. In contrast to this developing local organizational attitude towards learning as a premium operational concern, the broader corporate culture, external to the CC operation, did not appear to be in such alignment. At the corporate level, there was neither an explicit nor an implicit commitment provided to the broader organization and its business units to place a premium on learning. The corporate focus was primarily concerned with more immediate and tangible business unit performance and cost-reduction activities. Indeed, given this corporate focus, the Plant Manager of the CC operation did well to gain the support of his higher authorities to pursue the change programme on the CC site. In that corporate consciousness, the CC change programme might be considered an organizational design experiment with the Plant Manager accepting multiple career risks. Having gained the corporate level support for his experiment, the Plant Manager set out to change the local environment quite radically to that which predated it and to that in which it corporately resided. This meant that under his stewardship, the local environment intentionally became one of high turbulence, uncertainty and constant change. In line with Fiol and Lyles' (1985) call for organizations to establish a corporate culture conducive to learning, and with Davenport and Prusak's (1998) observation of senior management support as highly beneficial for transformational knowledge projects, this local organization (through the project sponsor's expressed ideals, behaviours and exerted authority) provided an explicit and enthusiastic commitment to pursue learning as one of the key goals of this project and of the broader change programme on the site.

Throughout this study, the participants in the project team readily acknowledged this explicit organizational commitment for them to pursue learning and also that they were empowered to enact leadership changes. For example, Bill acknowledged that this local organizational level support had opened up opportunities for him and others to personally grow and change and that the project sponsor had demonstrated his commitment to that on a number of occasions by simply being involved. At the participant commitment level within this project team, Steve also recognized support for his learning from his peer group, which wasn't there before the project team commenced. Towards the middle of the project, he suggested that because of that peer group support '...the Cokemaking Leadership Team in its own way should be trying all the leadership type things and I believe that the whole group is willing to get in now and do that'. At that time, the implication of this comment was that he felt they now had both the permission (from key stakeholders in the project) and the personal inclinations and greater confidence to experiment with their leadership and learning approaches. Len expressed that 'Now there's much more sharing, and certainly I'm feeling more readiness to accept that I'm allowed to learn. So yes, I think I've got support to learn.' These (and other) explicit recognitions of the organizational and participant commitments to learn in this project do not at all mitigate the perceived ambiguity issues concerning participants' pyramids of authority that were alluded to in the previous chapter. While possessing the commitments or intentions to learn within a project setting is critical, it is simply not enough to initiate learning activity. Those factors which drive ambiguity in participants' understanding of their situation also need deliberate managerial attention.

Provided the physical and social infrastructure to learn at the project team level

In the project case examined in this study, some multifaceted infrastructural supports were engaged to stimulate learning and relationship-building. These included: meeting rooms and offices and a myriad of other physical facilities being made available for participants to use; consultative input and support from human resource management staff and the project sponsor when sought after by participants; funding provided for process and leadership benchmarking visits to other organizations (such as regional coal-mining operations); time being made available for participants to pursue learning activities and conduct regular and discretionary weekly or full-day meetings; time being made available for participants to attend formal workshops run by in-house and external consultants and university researchers, for example the learning workshops conducted in the final stages of this study. This infrastructure assisted the project participants to meet, to explore issues and to reflect and converse in a rational way on a topic of learning that they perceived to be so ambiguous to possibly be irrational. Furthermore, for these participants, the personalized sharing of individual reflections and the articulation of their tacit knowledge and concerns may have been a much more difficult task without some facilitating framework causing and/or supporting their interactions and these learning activities. During the final stages of this study, in one of the workshop sessions, for example, Steve noted, 'We need to value learning and take the time from the day-to-day to recognize the value. Following through on commitments and reflecting on actions is a novel focus in this forum.' His comment, as well as acknowledging the value he now placed on learning, also highlighted the indirect value he placed on those workshop forums or learning spaces in aiding his learning process.

The meeting sessions that were part of this infrastructure for learning were both formal and informal. They included: the formal, regular weekly project team meetings; formal, all-day or three-day forums; learning workshop sessions; informal sessions such as private meetings in offices or in other workplace locations; mentoring and coaching activities with people in the organization; and, formal or informal reflective discussion sessions with the researcher on issues involving the project. Len and Steve freely acknowledged that many formal forums were instrumental in developing the informal working relationships, which particularly helped some people like Steve to pursue their relationship development and learning activity in a manner which better suited their preferred cognitive style. That is, the formal forums opened the door for him to pursue many learning relationships in an informal manner during the project life cycle. The structuring conditions provided in this case also resembled those conditions that, Davenport and Prusak (1998) suggest, allow for spontaneous, unstructured knowledge-transfer opportunities to occur. Those being, to allow time for informal and personal discussions in informal places so people can share and develop creative ideas to address problems, and holding open forums or knowledge fairs which facilitate both structured forms of knowledge transfer and knowledge transfer through face-to-face meetings and narratives. Likewise, Shani and Docherty (2003), when discussing the characteristics of learning mechanisms in a knowledge-based work environment, claim that informal discussions and conversations are very important to learning at work, since it is not only what is being learnt that is important but also the learning capability that is being developed in the process of learning. That being, the immediate product of learning is the ability to learn more, or participants learn-how-to-learn. These social interactions, be they formal or informal, are therefore opportunities for people to enquire, reflect and interpret their experiences (Seibert and Daudelin, 1999), and in this project case (and likely in others) having the opportunities for both personal reflection and reflection through interaction with other participants was an important part of the team learning and development process (Baker, 2002a). Moreover, these formal and informal meeting sessions appeared to successfully create the spaces or provide the occasions for reflection that were closely linked to the dynamics of the project work (Boud, 2006).

In this study, those formal project team meetings, workshops and the researcher–participant interview sessions constituted the principal learning spaces for the participants in the project. This theme of learning spaces for learning was advanced by Nonaka and Konno (1998) and consists of a space for interactions between individuals, between individuals and their environment, and between individuals and information (Shani and Docherty, 2003). Such spaces can include a physical space, a temporal space or making emotional space through receptive listening. The paradox being that creating a space means setting boundaries which initially may be interpreted as inhibiting or blocking conversation and learning, but through establishing these boundaries a space is established that is safe and open enough to explore with conversation about differences. As such, boundaries are shape-givers which provide a space to grow (Phillips, 1994; Kolb *et al.*, 2002; Shani and Docherty, 2003). Rifkin and Fulop (1997) further define a learning space as a space opened up by a release of control and privileges by management, which represents a rather disorganized and disaggregated concept of learning. This resonates with Coopey and Burgoyne's (2000) view that learning spaces that are free from fear and allow people to express their views openly are a critical condition for ideal speech situations that facilitate learning. Providing such a learning space helps nurture ideal speech opportunities through reducing moral and social risks and therefore increasing participants' willingness to experiment in their communicative actions (Coopey and Burgoyne, 2000).

Organizing these learning spaces within a project to be receptive to listening, silence and speaking, and to aid exploitative and exploratory learning activity (March, 1991) and knowledge creation and exchanges between people, is important (Baker *et al.*, 1997). Baker (2002a), for example, suggests five ways to create and support a receptive conversational space for learning. These involve: opening a space for conversations to freely flow where the participants feel safe to explore issues with others; encouraging partnership and imagination to develop trust between participants, which then fuels the conversation process; allowing for differences between the parties involved, which stimulates diversity of thought and approaches and expressions of ideas and values; taking time for reflection at both a personal and a group level, as this practice is core to learning and the stimulus for conversation;

and providing a space for humility to aid collaboration and the exploration of difficult issues and to challenge existing norms and behaviours (Baker, 2002a).

Learning activity can be difficult and challenging, and establishing and supporting such participative learning spaces ultimately provides significant opportunities for both tacit and explicit knowledge to flow more readily amongst project team participants. In contrast to this approach, some observers might suggest that creating conditions that foster some fear and anxiety or trepidation in the participants about the project issues may be viewed as a good accompaniment for their learning, in that it can act as a stimulant for learning activity. However, (while acknowledging the potential to provoke people into some immediate and limited learning activity) such fear and anxiety amongst participants in a team generally tends to restrict the quantum and quality of their learning exchanges and their communal reflection activities. This happens because these conditions of fear and anxiety reinforce other barriers to situated learning such as poor learning relationships, misunderstood personal differences, restrictive political and authoritarian cultures, and entrenched or inadequate knowledge management practices.

Illustrating both the depth of some self-reflective activity and the value that these learning spaces created for the participants' relationship development, early on in the project, Len offered, 'That general sharing of personal information about ourselves [in our project meeting sessions] has helped to give us all a much better appreciation of each other and open up the work relationships.' He also noted (while still acknowledging the extraordinary influence of the project sponsor), 'Everybody comes to the meetings bringing different skills and attributes, but there's been some quite open discussion that would not have occurred if the circumstances were one of a strong hierarchy and the need to protect yourself from the more powerful in the team, and there have been some significant initiatives that have come from right around the table as a result.' Steve indicated that the weekly meeting forum provided the opportunities for in-depth discussions that challenged their existing relationship models, which may not otherwise have happened. Towards the middle of the project, Steve commented, '...the fact that we meet on a regular basis and have some desire to change supports the learning objective', and 'We generally rely on the project meeting forum to guide our learning within the project [ ] I don't tend to have those in-depth discussions that happen in the project meetings outside [of it].' Furthermore, while acknowledging the negative impact on the degree of project tacit knowledge flow resulting from increasing group size (as previously discussed in this chapter), these project team learning spaces still provided a supportive environment for tacit knowledge to become articulated and shared. As the project progressed, for example, participants appeared to freely and frequently offer personally held views about their own roles and their concerns for their futures when the project sponsor asked questions like, 'We all have a story... are we prepared to share our stories?' These types of provocative questions and the accompanying reflections and conversations would not normally eventuate external to the project learning spaces. In effect, the regular project meetings and workshop learning spaces provided the participants a zone of opportunity (away from the daily challenges of their operational responsibilities) for them to either fully or partially engage with their learning activities associated with the project, and to exercise free speech in a perceived relatively safe environment.

Whether it is critical reflection or conversational processes for learning which one seeks to engage or promote, it takes time, and in projects (including this case), time is considered a premium resource to be closely managed. When Keegan and Turner (2001) investigated learning between projects within project-based firms, they concluded that one key impediment to project-based learning was this issue of time pressures. That is, participants in their study indicated en masse that they did not have time to reflect and operate effective feedback processes in projects. They further concluded that the overwhelming trend appeared to be a focus on short-term pressures, which drove out space for reflecting, conversing, experimenting and team-based learning (Keegan and Turner, 2001). While these concerns about a focus on short-term pressures were also evident in the project case examined in this study, fortunately in this project case however, space and time for learning activities were supported and actioned because learning was such an explicit project and organizational goal. Perhaps in contrast to those actual practices identified by Keegan and Turner (2001), and to encourage conversations, dialogue and reflection activities, Kasl *et al.* (1997) and Mårtensson (2000) suggest that the role of making time available to learn and explore is fundamental in team learning. That being, 'Time is an ingredient of learning when members take time to explore ideas for which relevance is not immediately apparent' (Kasl *et al.*, 1997: 242–3). Taking time to explore and learn provides opportunities for relationship development and generative thinking that is typical of synergistic learning activity. Time also serves as an incubator, wherein tacit knowledge can find its way into the situated learning milieu.

For the major part of the project process, and further structurally aiding situated learning in this case study, the core participants were co-located together and also with some other managers who later joined the project team during the middle of the research process. Their separate offices were located in the same small Operations building amongst the heavy engineering plant and equipment associated with the CC operation. Eskerod and Skiver (2001) consider such co-location to be a vital condition for enhancing informal knowledge transfer between participants – as indeed it appeared to do in this project team, particularly between the three core participants. In the later stages of this project, however, the three core participants relocated themselves (along with other Superintendents from the CC operation) to one large office in the CC Administration building, approximately one-half kilometre away from the Operations building and those other project team members. When these three core participants were discussing their learning environment, they were challenged on their decision to co-locate down in that Administration building and away from many other participants in the change programme. Their replies firmly rebuffed my concerns regarding the impact on their learning, and they then proceeded to justify their move as being about helping to actualize the project sponsor's new operational/innovation structure. That being, these newly designated team leaders of a recently imposed and radically different organizational structure needed to work together more closely, and those lower level managers (the Senior Supervisors) needed to assume greater daily leadership and decision-making over plant operations. Hence, at that time, their relocation action tended to physically isolate them from the plant and other operational personnel. Whether their action was simply about appeasing the Plant Manager and about being physically located closer to him as some form of self-preservation, or it provided some relief (through physical separation) from the daily dramas of managing the plant operation is debatable, given they still frequently visited the plant and still worked with many other people in their new roles and in various project activities. Nevertheless, their decision to relocate into one large office with the other CC Superintendents was observed to help their informal dialogue and sharing of knowledge and ideas at that level, but it worked against the same happening with a myriad of other operational people in the plant. Therefore, part of the infrastructural support for their learning involved them having the ability to make physical location decisions – which in the instance observed and cited seemed to be made on the basis of more immediate pragmatic and political concerns, rather than learning issues.

Interestingly, after a few weeks in this new location, the large shared office that the core participants occupied became affectionately known as the departure lounge for CC – a good-natured jibe directed at the Superintendents by the plant personnel, but which may have also been representative of some of the Superintendents' tacit job security fears and the plant employees' latest disconnection with them.

Overall, the comprehensive infrastructural arrangements engaged (as illustrated in the discussion above) suggested that situated learning was quite well supported in this particular project case.

Provided environmental stimulus to the participants to learn

In addition to the infrastructural learning support provided to the project team, the change activity in the local organizational setting (i.e. the environment was unstable and evolving) provided an ongoing stimulus to the participants to learn. It helped encourage them to confront and re-evaluate their traditional authority and cultural norms of behaviour, their relationships, their learning competencies and fears associated with the overall change programme, and their future operating scenario.

The genesis of much of this stimulus came from the actions or interventions of the project sponsor. As such, the project sponsor was also an integral part of the environmental stimulus for the project participants to learn, even though there were authority implications negatively affecting participant learning as a result of his actions – as explored previously in Chapter 5. In that sense, his involvement demonstrated a mixed influence on the participants' situated learning activity – which serves to only reinforce the need to be aware of and to understand the learning impacts resulting from a sponsor's involvement. An example of the project sponsor's interventions which affected the team's situated learning activity was when two-thirds of the way through the research process, he announced his imposition of a new organizational structure. This decisive action could be interpreted by some as a demotivating factor for learning, but equally by others as a positive learning intervention. In alignment with the latter response, Len stated, 'I think overall the changes will be positive. Positive because they will force us to work a new way and force some new learnings, and they are positive because it simply breaks the excuse of not making a decision and delaying... which is a response that we probably do with a high degree of unconscious competence around here.' Len viewed the emergent organizational environment as promoting them into new learning situations rather than perhaps avoiding them as they had done through their past indecision and deference to higher authority in their project. Len may also have felt relieved that there was now some reduced ambiguity about their future roles in the organization, given the sponsor had now provided them a rational organizational structure on which to move forward. These actions may have also satisfied his desire for some specific rational detail on those complex matters, in accordance with his Analyst cognitive style type.

A further significant example of how the project sponsor's actions in the organizational environment stimulated participants to learn involved his approach to learning from mistakes. As a prelude to describing how that occurred, early in the project, Steve indicated that he felt they needed to identify a formal process of learning from mistakes, and that they needed to throw out a challenge to other team members to pursue their own learning. As he stated, 'Challenging people to learn... we need to put more thought into how that actually works. [ ] The thing about learning from mistakes is that we haven't got the processes – so there is no fear of making mistakes at this level.' The last part of his comment implied that the mistakes they made were more than likely to be hidden rather than exposed and reflected on for learning. In that scenario, they did not fear making mistakes since no one would find out about them anyway. Those conditions resembled Schindler and Eppler's (2003) finding that project amnesia (and one might also argue, learning ignorance) results from high time pressures to complete a project and an insufficient willingness of participants to learn from mistakes and to share those experiences due to modesty or fear. However, during a learning workshop, much later in the project, another participant in the project team offered a positive observation about the project sponsor's interventions changing the organization's approach to the handling of mistakes. As he described it, 'Since X [the project sponsor] has come along he has certainly changed the approach to that [learning from mistakes]. I can't remember too many one-on-one's that X has had around mistakes. He tends to turn them around into opportunities... instead of playing the person he plays the ball, and turns that back into a larger forum so that we can learn from that discussion. You might leave that discussion feeling a bit weak personally about it, but that is certainly not done in a way that is meant to do that. That was the intention in some of the forums, unfortunately it doesn't always go that way and many of the attendees don't see the benefit in actually sharing the learning [ ] then we don't apply the learning... that is something we are not real strong on. X intuitively expects it to happen and then a week later on, down at the plant, he talks to someone about it and finds that nothing has been done...' Given the previous discussion in this chapter, one might readily appreciate that this approach to learning from mistakes during team meetings created the opportunity for participants to collaboratively and critically reflect on important events, and for a raft of tacit to explicit knowledge exchanges to occur.

Other examples of how the project sponsor's actions in the organizational environment stimulated project participants to expose and share tacit knowledge, involved his interjections in project meetings. Therein, he constantly prompted participants to think beyond their past rational experiences. A very brief, but typical example of such an intervention in a project team meeting, early in the project life cycle, involved:

> Sponsor: 'What behaviours do you three model as the leadership team of Coke Inc? What do you need to do to move the place somewhere else?'
> Bill: 'Can you give us some examples so that I can see where you are coming from?'
> Sponsor: 'I suspect you guys are insecure... and that needs to be made explicit.'

With those types of enquiring or provocative comments and questions, the project sponsor repeatedly kept on encouraging the participants to reveal their tacit knowledge and fears, and to deal with the non-rational issues they seemed initially reluctant to embrace. In other team meeting sessions, during the middle of this study, and with the active presence and forthright encouragement of the sponsor, the project participants purposefully explored a number of undiscussable issues, such as: Who is the leader of the CLT? Who is Spartacus? Therein, they collectively challenged the status quo of the sponsor currently leading the team. Two other example undiscussables that were explored, included: We are afraid to challenge each other – wherein, their current relationships and behaviours were again examined; and, A CLT manager's role is to add value to the business by creating an environment where people want to contribute and feel secure to participate – wherein, they explored their concerns and fears about not possessing the skills necessary to achieve that intention. Over a number of team meeting sessions, these undiscussable topics created opportunities for participants to express their tacit knowledge and their fears about these and other matters, and to collaboratively explore ways to alleviate these conditions and build their learning and working relationships.

Further stimuli for learning were provided through having rather fluid interpersonal and organizational dynamics between managers, and between factory employees. For example, managers were moving into different roles that stretched their competence in task achievement and their confidence in their own abilities, particularly with the pressures in the workplace to achieve results. A specific example is of one Superintendent being moved from a line-management role in one part of the plant, to being the Human Resources Leader for the entire plant. This change in role shifted his relationships with others onto a different level, and challenged his personal approaches to how he normally managed people and also his competency to perform in the newly assigned role. Similarly, Senior Supervisors and Supervisors were progressively assuming more conventional daily operational responsibilities in managing the plant, which also challenged and changed their working relationships with subordinates and peer groups. Indeed, at varying points in the project timeline, all the managers in the organization were undergoing some form of either dramatic or subtle role change. As a result of these types of ongoing operational/relationship changes, participants were somewhat forced, through necessity, to interact more and differently, to converse, to reflect and hence to learn with others if they intended to be successful in the new emergent organization.

In contrast to those stimulating effects of the local organizational environment in promoting project situated learning, the environment also served to constrain the conversations and reflections about the project goals. This came about because it was a very busy and disruptive operational situation (coupled to a challenging project change agenda) where immediate business objectives seemed to demand the participants' attention. There were also considerable external company pressures to get results soon, that is deliver some productivity improvements and get returns on the investment in the change process. Subsequently, and consistent with a view on impediments to project learning offered by Keegan and Turner (2001), this demanding work situation helped to limit the time available to reflect and converse about project issues and to learn. In the project sessions, this situation also assisted the participants' opportunism in exhibiting defensive behaviour when difficult issues of their relationships were under focus – a conundrum which persisted to varying degrees throughout the full project timeframe.

This business environment of the local organization required the participants to deliver on improved plant operational performance and to achieve outcomes on specific business tasks. For example, this involved a number of productivity improvements in Coking process time, and the delivery of a Workplace Labour Agreement (with supporting documentation) which required extensive negotiation with, and input from, many employees. Len commented on the difficulties of having this dual responsibility for those business issues and the project goals, and stated, 'One issue around the [project] meeting schedule is the conflict between, we've got to get this done, so let's just pump the resources in and get this done, and then walking out of there and finding that there's some other alligator biting at your heels... You've got to pay it some attention to get it to go away for a while. So, say we are all going to spend the whole day together... then that means it's a day that you're not doing other [operational type] things.' Len noted also that, for him, 'Sourcing new knowledge is something that ends up suffering in terms of time availability because you're pressured on doing other things...' Len's comments reflected how the daily operational matters concerning the plant demanded their attention and distracted them from their project and their learning activity. Whether this was always necessary is of some debate. For example, the project sponsor privately expressed that he considered the participants sought to be focused on the business issues, in preference to the longer-term project issues, because they did not wish to relinquish their traditional authority and control, or confront personally difficult project activities. Perhaps echoing the project sponsor's concerns on this issue, Steve's following comments hint at some underlying participant preferences, that is 'We retreat into comfort rather than push into learning.' Also, as he checked-in during a project learning workshop session, he stated, 'I am physically not there, nor mentally not there at the moment. We have started a new job but have continued on in the old way. We haven't actually stopped doing the old job.' In effect, the sponsor interpreted their actions as a form of avoidance strategy and yet he expected them to also perform and deliver on numerous and diverse business objectives. He also seemed quite prepared to regularly confront the participants on those matters if he felt that they were not adequately attending to them. So, it would appear that the project sponsor also helped contribute to this conundrum for the core participants – that being, the conflict between the transitional necessity to apply themselves to and deliver on immediate business issues, and also to have a focus and deliver on the longer-term and more personally challenging project goals.

In the later stages of the project, Steve noted the impact of these competing pressures on the quality and quantity of their reflection activities and their learning behaviours. During one learning workshop, he stated, 'This [situation] is exacerbated by having half the team tied up with outside issues – such as the new coal mine, the Coke Guide, coal preparation issues and contract maintenance issues, meaning that nearly all of us have had significant issues on our minds rather than concentrating on learning and the job of this change process....' Len also acknowledged such a context, by stating, 'We're all seeing more need for urgency. X [the project sponsor] has reinforced it in a number of different situations, in a few different ways, but it's clear that the business urgency is there. The steel business performance is very ordinary. We're being impacted by very poor export steel prices, having to accept orders and prices not much above the cost of production...and with that, it's driving the urgency up to turn around this business quickly. We don't have a lot more time. The maintenance outsourcing issue is being brought to a head and we will need to drive that. The Working Party output is there and we need to drive getting the acceptance [of it], so we can start going through the implementation process.' Len's comments provided a likely indicator of where his immediate attention was to be directed and reinforce his observation that 'Our culture is about doing and not about reflecting, and there is not always time to reflect and to share.'

Despite this dampening influence of the short-term business issues on the situated learning activity associated with the project, overall the stimulus provided by the organizational environment was a source of significant and ongoing motivation for the project participants to learn. This, indirectly, also aided the steady development of their capabilities in learning-how-to-learn.

6.3 Summary

The infrastructural constraint/enabler elements of knowledge management and situational context are critical antecedents for effective learning in projects since they provide the supporting frameworks on which learning opportunities and learning actions unfold.

The section of this chapter that explored the element of knowledge management articulated numerous considerations for managing knowledge flow in projects, and described how those considerations are underpinned by two generalized forms for knowledge management, that is codification and personalization. The personalization approach is particularly important in situated learning since it is the agency through which tacit knowledge is exposed and shared. The project team in this study predominantly pursued a personalization approach in managing their knowledge flows. That choice was influenced by the type of project, the specific project goals and other issues from the project environment such as role ambiguity. This personalization approach involved many formal and informal dyadic or team meeting sessions, the provision of group and personal feedback to participants, and critical reflection activities in the team. These activities placed the participants in multiple interactive situations which encouraged their exposure, reflection on, and sharing of their valuable tacit knowledge. These actions also significantly aided the building of participants' learning relationships and prompted confrontation with and critical reflection on participants' own learning behaviours. A personalization approach also illuminated other issues that affected situated learning activity. For example, as seen in this study, the awareness of the distribution of expertise or knowledge authorities in the team sometimes limited the scope of knowledge capture or enquiry activities by participants to certain individual members or perceived priority sources. This condition limited the access to and engagement of other team members in knowledge exchange activities across the team. Also, at times, the project team seemed preoccupied with sharing common operational information as opposed to project information, which helped suppress tacit knowledge flow on project-related issues. Although a focus on such common issues between participants presented an immediate constraint on the volume of learning exchanges and tacit knowledge flow relating to project goals, it did however prompt their interactive conversations on significant issues. These conversations served as an initial relationship-builder from which participants could collaboratively broach more difficult project issues and then establish conditions where generative tacit knowledge on project issues could better flow. In sum, the personalization approach dominating knowledge flow processes in this project setting very aptly facilitated situated learning for these project team participants. Moreover, in seeking to support and stimulate situated learning, the experiences or observations from this study connote a necessity for project participants in any project setting to better understand how selected knowledge management processes can impact learning activity.

In the section of this chapter that examined the element of situational context, it was argued that the establishment and management of a project setting that invites people to dialogue, converse, reflect and to share tacit knowledge is vitally important for individual learning, organizational learning and competitive project advantage. This section also detailed how the situational context of the project examined in this study mostly positively impacted situated learning for the project participants. This was achieved through three categories of support. These included: the explicit organizational and participant commitment to learning and building their relationships in the project; the provision or construction and operation of physical and social infrastructures for learning at the project team level, where knowledge exposure and sharing between the participants could be nurtured and enhanced; the local organizational environment mostly providing a stimulus to the participants to learn and to reassess their place and behaviours in the organization.

These positive local organizational environment stimuli included a myriad of interventions or actions often initiated by the project sponsor, and fluid interpersonal and organizational dynamics resulting from people moving into different roles with new functional responsibilities. In contrast, the external pressures on the local organization to achieve results in the change programme, coupled with immediate and compounding business commitments, tended to limit the time and the inclination participants had to pursue conversations and reflection on longer-term project goals. This presented a contradiction – on one hand the infrastructure provided the time and the resources for participants to pursue the learning goals of the project, but on the other, the shorter-term business commitments tended to invade that space. Nevertheless, all these categories of support combined largely served to promote situated learning activity through increasing and encouraging the opportunities for interactions, conversations and reflections between participants, and through focusing their individual and collective attention onto learning.

7
The Project Learning Opportunity: Where to Now?

This chapter initially provides a summary of the key issues for project learning raised throughout the preceding chapters of this book. Therein, it recaps the central conceptual findings from this study and reinforces the practical and personal implications for project participants in either systematically addressing or not addressing the five sociological elements that impact their situated learning behaviours. Also included in this chapter is a brief reflective account of some key methodological issues confronted in conducting this study since they too constitute important pragmatic and conceptual insights for researchers involved in the project management field. Building on those important summative discussions, this chapter then comments on the limitations of this study and makes recommendations concerning future research in this area. It then provides a set of questions relating to each of the five elements for situated learning. These questions are intended to provide some further encouragement to you to reflectively assess your current attitudes and approaches to project learning activities. This complete chapter is intended to cement an understanding of project participant learning as primarily a sociological activity whilst they are on the job – a process which necessarily requires participants' deliberate commitment, understanding and ongoing attention.

7.1 A summary of the key issues for project learning

The prime purpose of this study was to make a contribution to understanding how one can better cultivate intra-project learning activity. As an early outcome of initial empirical explorations and theoretical deliberations, this purpose was then refined to a proposition that the most poignant and encompassing affect on learning activity in the project case study, was the situated rather than the cognitive dimension of learning. Consequently, this study became focused on seeking to identify and explain the influencing or detracting socio-cultural elements of the project environment that were primal in shaping the observed learning behaviours of the project team participants. Therefore, this study became an exploration of the dynamics of situated learning – applied to the selected case study of an active project team. From a further review of the literature, it then also became apparent that the outcomes from this study would help address a major gap in the project management and organizational learning literatures about how to cultivate learning in a project context. Moreover, this study would also make contributions to situated learning and knowledge management literatures, through highlighting and affirming the significance of the social dimension of learning and the necessity to engage effectively with it. Additionally, it also became evident that this study would provide an insightful view into the complexities of conducting a participative action research process in a project environment, where presently, there is a dearth of any such examples.

The conceptual issues

As an outcome of the cross-disciplinary literature review and the consideration of field data, the first core finding and subsequent argument of this book is that project teams are dynamic constructors (and not just passive recipients) of learning processes within their specific contexts. In their project practice, participants construct, maintain and reproduce learning as they seek to make sense of their world and to operate successfully within it. In that way, project knowledge is socially constructed and conjoined to the project practice (Brown and Duguid, 1991). As is argued by SLT, and confirmed in this study, the social context is therefore crucially important in affecting learning activities. Consequently, a better understanding of, and attention to, the sociological components that moderate learning within a project practice is also of central importance in assisting the complete individual and team learning processes.

The second core finding and argument of this book is that situated learning within a project, as observed in this one 'process innovation' type project (Bresnen et al., 2003: 163), is influenced by five interrelated sociological constraint/enabler elements. These sociological elements impact situated learning across the boundaries or intersection points between project individuals' multiple COPs (Sense, 2003b). The model of project situated learning behaviour presented in this book, and which comprises these five elements, constitutes a 'conceptual architecture'

(Wenger, 1998: 230) that is capable of aiding reflection on project learning activities. It forms a framework of themes for project practitioners to self-design and cultivate a localized learning practice – an approach entirely consistent with SLT.

As observed in the activities of project participants in this study, one way to locally develop effective and purposeful strategies to stimulate and promote situated learning in project workplaces, involves a project team publicly exposing and communally reflecting on these sociological elements. Notably also, this approach aligns strongly with Boud's *et al.* (2006) perspectives on engaging productive reflection at work as a means to change work practices to enhance both productivity and the personal engagement of participants. In practice, this communal reflection process requires practitioners to simultaneously embrace multiple perspectives on issues of concern, while also building a strong sense of accountability, transparency and self-reflection (Cicmil, 2005). Consequently, such actions may be personally and professionally threatening and challenging to practitioners, as their credibility and project identity might be affected, their personal and political relationships changed, and knowledge management practices and the project working environment may be altered. In so doing, however, practitioner learning and learning competency are significantly enhanced. The data illustrated throughout this book is one testament to the value to be gained in pursuing such learning actions. In this study, the pursuit of those learning actions was assisted by the employment of a participative action research process. In other project settings, without that research stimulus, it may be more difficult to enact these learning actions. Yet, it appears important to do so if one seeks to devise conditions that promote situated learning within projects, and to help to develop the skills of project practitioners to practice learning.

The first of these five sociological elements is the intra-personal constraint/enabler element of cognitive style. This involves a participant's predisposition towards or preferred way to gather, process and interpret information. Through publicly exposing, communally evaluating and reflecting on their cognitive style, project participants in this study developed an understanding of their styles and the impact of those intermeshed styles on learning activity in the team. Collectively, participants' critical comments on this matter indicated that they better appreciated their cognitive style differences and were better able to interpret and understand the behaviours of each other in the project and in their workplace. They also acknowledged the generally positive contribution those differences in cognitive style made to their collective learning and project processes, and described how they devised ways to constructively work with those differences to their mutual learning and project advantage. Consequently, they better connected with one another, which helped them to progressively build their relationships and their skills in learning-how-to-learn.

The second sociological element is the interpersonal constraint/enabler element of learning relationships. The learning relationships element concerns the relationships that exist between participants and how they affect the creation and sharing of knowledge in a project team. Initially in the case study project, the participants demonstrated a regressive attitude towards the public exposure and scrutiny of their personal concerns regarding project matters, or on matters concerning their project performance. This was revealed in their deployment of defensive routines to avoid discussion of their difficult relationship and project issues. These defensive processes tended to restrict knowledge exchanges and learning activity between participants, and it took many meeting sessions for participants to openly acknowledge their defensive actions and to re-direct their attention onto issues regarding the building of their own learning relationships. Over time however, since learning and building their relationships were established as core aspects of the project team activity, and through their open and communal reflection on these issues, the participants were increasingly prepared to, and did, positively explore and implement alternative relationships. They came to view existing relationship issues as significant learning opportunities – a situation punctuated by a comment from Len, when he stated, 'our task is to make these things explicit and build our relationships and to understand what our relationships need to be, and to manage the egos around it'. Over the full project cycle, their communal learning actions in addressing this element reduced their defensive behaviours and altered their approaches to the mentoring and coaching of each other and other people external to the immediate project team. These relationship-building outcomes were evident, when, for example, the core participants collaboratively analysed operational and relationship problems that individuals were experiencing, and when they took deliberate actions to energize the collective input from colleagues during meetings – where previously, perceived relationship barriers to eliciting and expressing that input existed.

The third sociological element is the interpersonal constraint/enabler element of pyramid of authority. This involves the application or non-application of a participant's accumulated layers of power or authority to support or constrain situated learning within a project. In this study, the core participants' perceptions of the prior organizational authority that they and others imported into the project setting (including the formal authority they had assigned to them to learn and operate their project) significantly influenced their learning behaviours. Conscious of not wanting to build up or maintain barriers to achieving the learning and relationship-building goals of their project, the three core participants held back from exercising their prior organizational authorities within the project, and their learning behaviours were generally more reticent, discreet and incidental, rather than deliberate and forthright. Ultimately, they failed to acknowledge and use those prior authorities as something positive to be exercised in pursuing the goals of their project. Emphasizing this situation, for example, was when, during a learning workshop late in the project cycle, the core participants developed specific learning activities that pointedly sought to reduce perceptions of their prior organizational authority. Furthermore, as observed during the middle of the project in particular, these perceptions of participants' prior organizational authorities also constrained open debate, critical reflection and knowledge exchanges on project issues. This came about because other participants seemed reluctant to offend or challenge expertise or recognized prior formal authority held by individuals in the project team. This condition contributed to all the participants generally appearing hesitant to fully engage with the substantial learning opportunities available.

When in the project setting, the participants' perceptions of their authority to lead their project and learning activity were further conditioned by factors from the project and organizational environments (e.g. project role ambiguity and the latent or discernible authority of the project sponsor), which contributed to them generally appearing to lack authority (or feeling powerless) to confidently lead their project and their own learning activity. This resulted in them deferring to higher authorities for guidance and decision-making, rather than operate in a more self-driven fashion independently of the project sponsor. Consequently, their learning and project actions were hesitant and restrained while also being slow to emerge, until the higher authority had expressed some input to their process. These project actions also tended to reflect and uphold a cultural characteristic of hierarchy dependence in the case study organization.

The fourth sociological element is the infrastructural constraint/ enabler element of knowledge management. This element is concerned with the way a project team actually goes about handling the flow of project knowledge in and around a project setting. The flow of project knowledge takes two different but general forms – codification and personalization. Influenced by factors from the project environment, the project team of this study predominantly pursued a personalization approach in managing their knowledge flows in the team – that which involved many formal and informal meeting sessions, personal and group observation and feedback, and critical, communal reflection activities. These activities placed the participants in interactive situations which: encouraged their exposure, reflection on, and sharing of their tacit knowledge; stimulated the building of their learning relationships; prompted communal reflection on their learning behaviours; and, illuminated other issues that constrained their situated learning activity, for example the participants' awareness of the distribution of expertise knowledge in the team, and their preoccupation with sharing commonly held operational knowledge over project knowledge. As well as reinforcing the significance of a personalized knowledge management approach in promoting project situated learning, all these issues emphasize a necessity for participants in any project setting to give scrupulous consideration to how they might organize their project knowledge flows.

The fifth sociological element is the infrastructural constraint/enabler element of situational context. This element is concerned with how a project setting is organized (physically and socially) to help establish and facilitate a project learning environment. It involves issues of the organizational and participant commitment or intention to learn, the provision or construction and operation of physical and social infrastructures to learn (e.g. the time and spaces for conversation and reflection), and the ongoing environmental stimulus encouraging learning throughout the project life cycle (e.g. the project sponsor's interventions in the project). The situational context of this project case study was significantly supportive of increasing the opportunities for, and the quality of, the interactions, conversations and reflections between participants on project issues. Therefore, it was largely a very positive influence on situated learning in this setting. In contrast to this positive comment, however, more immediate and compounding business commitments and external pressures on the organization to achieve tangible business results tended to limit the time and the inclination participants had to pursue issues relating to the project goals. Therefore, at times, through distracting participants' attention and energy away from project activities, the organizational environment unwittingly impeded rather than supported project situated learning activity.

The methodological issues

The core findings presented in this book were the outcome of a case study analysis undertaken as a participative action research exercise. A key feature of the research process employed in this study involved the use of a single revelatory case. Using a single case as the object of study provided a very pragmatic and supportive research context for the researcher to longitudinally and intimately explore the social practices of learning in a project setting, and to iteratively develop and refine theory – and in this study, the case also had a specific project goal of learning. Coupled to using a case was the employment of an emancipatory form of action research – participative action research (PAR). Since learning and participation are integral parts of the PAR process, this methodology provided the means to broadly, deeply and longitudinally investigate the social practice of learning in the project case. Additionally, this methodology was well equipped to deal with the complex and often unstable operating environments of projects, and provided the opportunities for participants to safely (relative to the organizational context) explore the learning phenomenon. From participants' numerous comments and their observed project actions, it was concluded that the methodology seemed to foster participants' very honest engagement in the research process. Furthermore, it was a methodology that appealed to the client organization involved in this study. This primarily came about because it assisted the project participants in engaging with their problem of conceiving and developing themselves as learners and leaders – commensurate with the demands of the new and emergent organizational environment. In that sense, the research process was capable of and was expected to deliver tangible project-related outputs for the client organization.

A key dilemma confronted by this researcher (and likely by other PAR researchers in different PAR and project settings) involved the issue of researcher control versus participation within the research setting. A situation the author equates to, 'driving the bus from the rear passenger seat' (Sense, 2006b: 1). This concerned how much control to exert on the research proceedings and when to exert it in the process, so as to stimulate action and maintain the overall research momentum, but still encourage participant co-ownership and co-conduct of the research process (consistent with the participative ideals of PAR). This methodological practice dilemma is highlighted by the researcher's following notation in his reflective diary during the last major action research cycle, 'Do I take the passenger position on this bus, or do I take the driver seat and be a little more provocative to energize the [workshop] session [] I am trying not to chip away at my belief in a participative process [] At a broader research perspective, this dilemma is based around how much action should I have, what form should it take, should it be inquisitive or should it be more provocative? The same dilemma I have faced throughout this research project'. The often competing dual client demands of a PAR process are such that a researcher might be drawn into inadvertently controlling a process, where alternatively, their contributory participation might be a more appropriate strategy in exploring the phenomenon under study. Conversely, a researcher focus mainly on fostering participation may allow the PAR process, from both client and researcher outcome perspectives, to meander aimlessly, to momentarily stall or to seemingly waste time and resources, and contribute little to the research or client goals. Therefore, throughout this study, in attempting to achieve an appropriate application of control and participation in the research setting, the researcher's actions became more or less an outcome of an intentional consideration process, rather than an outcome of an opportunistic or normative response process that might have been governed by personal biases for action.

Was every participation or control decision the researcher executed in this study correct in each circumstance? No one can answer that question with full confidence, but one can acknowledge the real strength of the PAR process being the opportunity to work intimately with client participants over time, wherein, numerous cycles of interventions and learning are initiated as the client group undergoes change. In that process, the researcher confronts multiple opportunities requiring decisions on control or participation, while seeking to successfully complete a PAR project. Ultimately then, within any PAR context (as in this study), the flexibility and the resourcefulness of the PAR researcher to execute appropriate research actions with regard to their control and participation, and their selection of specific research activities, are put to the test. Hence, while emancipation and the full participation of the participants was always the guiding intention in this study, the degrees of emancipation experienced by participants to co-conduct the research activities was subject to the researcher's decisions on being more participative, or more in control of the research activities. His decisions in this regard reflected his interpretations of the changing project context conditions and participant learning development. Clearly, this situation also meant that the researcher frequently altered his mode of engagement with the participants while still seeking to continue to engage their skills and knowledge in the process. In the light of these critical reflections on the methodological process pursued in this study, it is argued that in any form of emancipatory action research, the PAR researcher needs to be considered as a 'skilled bricoleur' (Weick, 2001: 63), since they release degrees of control of the research activities to their co-researchers and the vagaries of the context. Faced with such practical complexities, they become accommodative of multifarious inputs to the research process. Therein, they flexibly and creatively engage with those inputs to develop and construct research actions that remain relevant to the organizational client in aiding their change processes, and that meet the needs of academia in terms of theory generation and knowledge development (Badham and Sense, 2001).

7.2 Limitations of this study and recommendations for future research

There are four notable limitations associated with this study. The first of these included the quite obvious issue that this research involved one case study, in one division of one company, in one type of cultural setting. As previously mentioned, a single case study presented a powerful opportunity to gain an intimate insight into project learning, in what is an organizationally determined case study structure, that is the bounded and temporal entity called a project team. As a consequence of pursuing that opportunity, the findings of this study are generalizable to theoretical propositions rather than representing universal predictive cause and effect relationships across all project settings (Gummesson, 1991; Yin, 1994; Flyvbjerg, 2001). These theoretical propositions (e.g. the sociological constraint/enabler elements for situated learning) are now available to be further iteratively tested or explored in other project settings, or to be used as embarkation points by researchers seeking to delve more deeply into learning within those contexts. Therefore, whilst accepting a case study as a limitation surrounding the scale of the research work performed, it provided the avenue to pursue the intended depth of investigation into the learning phenomenon, whilst accounting for the pragmatic resource limitations on there being one sole researcher. In sum, it was a limitation but a very appropriate and positive one in respect to the intentions and process of this particular study.

Coupled to this positive structural arrangement was the project type being an organizational change project, with one of the core project goals being learning. This actually represents a further limitation of this study, since this project team represented only a 'process innovation' type project (Bresnen *et al.*, 2003: 163). What has not been evaluated in this study then, is whether different project types, such as product innovation or civil construction type projects for example, may present other sociological elements (or derivations of the elements identified in this study) that affect situated learning in those contexts. Also, in a similar vein to different project types, this study could not take account of different organizational settings in which projects may be embedded. In this study for example, and as reported on in this book, the rather fluid, but broadly supportive organizational change setting immediately surrounding the project contained major influences on the learning behaviour of the project participants. It may be, however, that a project embedded in a more stable or even less stable organizational setting could confront different types of organizational stimulants or constraints on learning activity. Such desirable, but additional, research pursuits were well beyond the resource capacity and scope of this study, and are clearly logical extensions to this original work.

A further limitation throughout the study involved the selected focus on the three core project participants, consisting of Len, Steve and Bill, in preference to attempting to perform the same level of data collection and participative research with all the project team participants. This decision, to primarily focus the participative interventions on a limited number of key participants, facilitated the deep exploration of the learning phenomenon – which was consistent with the intended research aims. Despite the high quantum and quality of data attained in this study, one should however acknowledge that this decision perhaps limited the potential volume and diversity of data received. Future studies of this nature may have the opportunities and resources to actively involve a larger number of participants, thereby sourcing additional data from more input sources involved in the research process.

In addition, this study involved a further limitation of primarily observing these core participants' learning behaviours (with others) in project team meeting forums. Hence, they were not generally observed by the researcher across events external to those team meetings. That being so, their learning behaviours external to the team meetings were assessed through other data collection processes, including interviews, their reflective observations and reporting of their own and others' behaviours, and feedback from other team members. This observation limitation arose because the various meeting forums served as the substantive project activity in pursuing the project goals and required extensive research focus and effort. Hence, those meeting forums were the primary source of observable research data, which was then supplemented by data derived from other research activities.

In conclusion, the limitations involved with this study direct our attention towards broadening future research initiatives concerning project learning to include different types of projects with different project goals, within different organizational settings – which would be a valuable adjunct to this highly original work. At the least, the findings from this study serve as embarkation points for researchers to pursue those opportunities and aid their theorizing on how best to understand and promote learning activity within localized project contexts.

7.3 Some questions to further stimulate your thinking on this topic

The questions presented in this section have been derived from a set of statements in a project learning survey tool. This survey tool, which has been developed by the author, is built on the findings generated from this study and seeks to assist project teams to better understand and to profile their propensity and their application towards stimulating situated learning within their projects. In that way, it can help project practitioners to locally and cooperatively explore and develop their learning competency within their project activities.

In the context of this book, the 20 sample questions presented below simply serve to further stimulate your reflection (and possible actions) on your own or others' project learning attitudes and activities.

- Is a team's understanding of each participant's cognitive style important for the successful functioning of a project team?
- Is it important to have a good understanding of one's own cognitive style?
- Do participants in my project team exhibit diversity in their cognitive styles?
- Do I feel challenged in respect to gathering and processing information in my current project?
- Do I know how the learning relationships in my project team impact my learning activities?
- Do I frequently undertake actions to develop the learning relationships between myself and other participants?
- Am I quite comfortable in subjecting myself to peer-group scrutiny about my defensive behaviour?
- Do I frequently approach the development of my relationships from a learning perspective?

- Is a team's understanding of each participant's pyramid of authority important for the successful functioning of a project team?
- Do I know all team members' levels of authority which are imported into the project?
- Do I have clarity about the processes I need to pursue to achieve the project goals?
- What influence does the project sponsor have on my decisions relating to my project learning actions?
- Do I know how effective my project team's knowledge management practices are in aiding participants' learning?
- When knowledge management processes appear ineffective in assisting knowledge flow in the project team, do I investigate those situations?
- Do I diligently pursue actions to become aware of the distribution of expertise knowledge in the project team?
- Do I actively source project knowledge from all project team participants?
- Do I know how the team's learning in this project is affected by the situational context?
- Do I regularly pursue actions to improve the project situational context for learning?
- Does my project generate a great need for me to personally get together with other team members to discuss project matters?
- Does my project environment constantly stimulate me to learn new things outside of my normal comfort zone of activities?

7.4 Summary

To varying degrees, situated learning will undoubtedly and opportunistically occur in any setting and across different socio-cultural conditions. However, one key issue raised in this book is whether such an opportunistic approach to such learning may indeed limit the quality and the quantity of learning activity situated within a context. That being the case, it would seem that organizations have a responsibility to provide or construct stimulant conditions which deliberately and actively encourage the social learning exchanges and interactions between people. Indeed, Ellström (2006) and Shani and Docherty (2003), for example, posit that learning at work is a matter of organizing the workplace for learning, while Wenger (1998) notes that it is vital to design social infrastructures to foster learning. In the case of project teams in particular, their formative conditions present very difficult circumstances for situated learning between participants to germinate, since the membership of the 'embryonic form of a new community of practice' (Sense, 2003b: 9) may not have previously interacted and formed any direct working and social relationships. This situation resembling what Eskerod and Skriver (2007) refer to as lonely cowboys operating within their separate knowledge silos. Hence, in such a condition, it would seem that deliberate actions and activities directed towards enabling and promoting situated learning activity would be considered rather essential, and certainly not considered optional, or simply as something nice to do. Nevertheless, in the traditional project management model, learning (other than formal external training and professional certification, or, post project completion reviews) is not normally represented as a deliberate or organized action within the project management process. One core argument presented in this book, however, is clearly that it should be a more prominent and more deliberate project action, and that the unitary assumption that participants' interests and goals will seamlessly align to the organizational project interests, whereby they will freely surrender their knowledge and learning to the project team, is blatantly naive (Field, 2002). In undertaking such deliberate project learning activity, the emphasis should also be directed towards the sociological (or social and practical) dimension of learning within each project context, rather than be confined to the narrow consideration of learning as only a cognitive process. Furthermore, as a major outcome of this study and as illustrated in this book, there are five sociological elements within a project setting that can either constrain or assist situated learning activity. The public exposition and communal reflection on these elements provides a practical, locally relevant and participant-oriented approach to better understanding and addressing them. Ignorance of their influence or applied preferences seeking to avoid this additional management complexity within a project setting, in effect, only continues to consign intra-project learning and pragmatic individual competency development to a peripheral and opportunistic project activity.

Therefore, just as a farmer ploughs the field, fertilizes the ground, sows the seeds and prays for rain, situated learning also requires cultivation. The farmer does not ignore or leave the growth and success of the crop solely to the mercy of the random variables within the context. He/she actively engages and works with the prevailing conditions (or variables) of a specific situation, accepts the risks in the setting and purposefully monitors and adjusts those conditions where they can, to ultimately maximize the quantity and the quality of the crop at harvest. Over time,

180 *Cultivating Learning Within Projects*

the farmer learns, develops his/her competency and expands his/her potential influence on the performance and success of the farming operation. Just like a farmer participating in and working intimately with his/her context, project participants seeking to reap their learning harvest, must actively participate in, and work with the sociological context of a project. Since project practitioners operate within temporary fields of situated learning potential and their professional development ultimately depends on learning, they are more or less compelled to consider cultivating a situated learning practice as an active constituent of their project management practice.

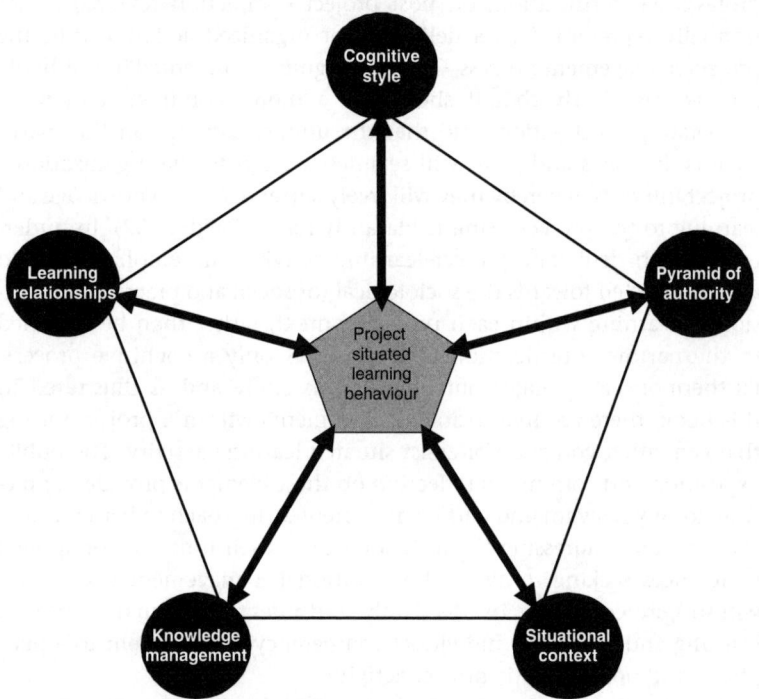

References

Adams, P. with Mylander, M. (1993) *Gesundheit!: Bringing Good Health to You, the Medical System, and Society through Physician Service, Complementary Therapies, Humour, and Joy*, USA: Healing Arts Press.
Adler, P.S. and Borys, B. (1996) 'Two types of bureaucracy: Enabling and coercive', *Administrative Science Quarterly*, Vol. 41(1), pp. 61–89.
Agashae, Z. and Bratton, J. (2001) 'Leader-follower dynamics: Developing a learning environment', *Journal of Workplace Learning*, Vol. 13(3), pp. 89–103.
Allinson, C.W. and Hayes, J. (1996) 'The cognitive styles index: A measure of intuition-analysis for organizational research', *Journal of Management Studies*, Vol. 33(1), pp. 119–35.
Alrichter, H., Kemmis, S., McTaggart, R. and Zuber-Skerritt, O. (2002) 'The concept of action research', *The Learning Organization*, Vol. 9(3), pp. 125–31.
Amit, R. and Schoemaker, P.J.H. (1993) 'Strategic assets and organizational rent', *Strategic Management Journal*, Vol. 14, pp. 33–46.
Andrews, K.M. and Delahaye, B.L. (2000) 'Influences on knowledge processes in organizational learning: The psychosocial filter', *Journal of Management Studies*, Vol. 37(6), pp. 797–810.
Anell, B. (1998) 'Patterns of success and failure in renewal projects: A study of eight projects for developing a learning organisation', in R.A. Lundin and C. Midler (Eds.), *Projects as Arenas for Renewal and Learning Processes* (pp. 99–113), USA: Kluwer Academic Publishers.
Antonacopoulou, E. (1997) 'Towards the learning manager: An empirical investigation of managerial learning in the context of changing organizations', in Proceedings of the 13th European Group for Organizational Studies (EGOS) Colloquium, July, Budapest, Hungary.
Antoni, M. (2000) *Inter-Project Learning – A Quality Perspective*, Licentiate thesis No. 44 from the International Graduate School of Management and Industrial Engineering, Institute of Technology, Linköpings Universitet, Linköping, Sweden.
Antoni, M. and Sense, A.J. (2001) 'Learning within and across projects: A comparison of frames', *Journal of Work, Human Environment and Nordic Ergonomics*, Vol. 2(2), pp. 84–93.
Argote, L. (1999) *Organizational Learning: Creating, Retaining and Transferring Knowledge*, USA: Kluwer Academic Publishers.
Argyris, C. (1990) *Overcoming Organizational Defenses: Facilitating Organizational Learning*, USA: Allyn and Bacon.
Argyris, C. (1993) *Knowledge for Action: A Guide to Overcoming Barriers to Organizational Change*, San Francisco: Jossey-Bass Publishers.
Argyris, C. (1999) 2nd edition, *On Organizational Learning*, Oxford: Blackwell Publishers Ltd.
Argyris, C. and Schön, D.A. (1978) *Organizational Learning: A Theory of Action Perspective*, USA: Addison-Wesley Publishing Company.

Argyris, C. and Schön, D.A. (1991) 'Participatory action research and action science compared: A commentary', in W.F. Whyte (Ed.), *Participatory Action Research* (pp. 85–96), USA: Sage Publications Inc.
Arthur, M.B., DeFillippi, R.J. and Jones, C. (2001) 'Project based learning as the interplay of career and company non-financial capital', *Management Learning*, Vol. 32(1), pp. 99–117.
Ayas, K. (1996) 'Professional project management: A shift towards learning and a knowledge creating structure', *International Journal of Project Management*, Vol. 14(3), pp. 131–6.
Ayas, K. (1998) 'Learning through projects: Meeting the implementation challenge', in R.A. Lundin and C. Midler (Eds.), *Projects as Arenas for Renewal and Learning Processes* (pp. 89–98), USA: Kluwer Academic Publishers.
Ayas, K. and Zeniuk, N. (2001) 'Project based learning: Building communities of reflective practitioners', *Management Learning*, Vol. 32(1), pp. 61–76.
Badham, R. (1999) 'Significance in learning to change: Development and testing of a Learning Forum model for managing organisational change', W. Rifkin, R. Badham, D. Buchanan and R. Tenkasi (Eds.), Australian Research Council Collaborative Grants Scheme – Proposal.
Badham, R.J. and Sense, A.J. (2001) 'You are the rats: Action research, academic forums and the reflective practice of professional bricoleurs', in Proceedings of the European Group for Organizational Studies (EGOS) conference, July, Lyon, France.
Bain, A. (1998) 'Social defenses against organizational learning', *Human Relations*, Vol. 51(3), pp. 413–29.
Baker, A.C. (2002a) 'Receptive spaces for conversational learning', in A.C. Baker, P.J. Jensen and D.A. Kolb (Eds.), *Conversational Learning: An Experiential Approach to Knowledge Creation* (pp. 101–23), USA: Quorum books.
Baker, A.C. (2002b) 'Extending the conversation into cyberspace', in A.C. Baker, P.J. Jensen and D.A. Kolb (Eds.), *Conversational Learning: An Experiential Approach to Knowledge Creation* (pp. 165–83), USA: Quorum books.
Baker, A.C., Jensen, P.J. and Kolb, D.A. (1997) 'In conversation: Transforming experience into learning', *Simulation and Gaming*, Vol. 28(1), pp. 6–12.
Baker, A.C., Jensen, P.J. and Kolb, D.A. (2002) 'Preface, and Learning and conversation', in A.C. Baker, P.J. Jensen and D.A. Kolb (Eds.), *Conversational Learning: An Experiential Approach to Knowledge Creation* (pp. ix–13), USA: Quorum books.
Bandura, A. (1977) *Social Learning Theory*, USA: Prentice-Hall.
Barker, M. and Neailey, K. (1999) 'From individual learning to project team learning and innovation: A structured approach', *Journal of Workplace Learning*, Vol. 11(2), pp. 60–7.
Baumard, P. (1999) *Tacit Knowledge in Organizations*, Great Britain: Sage Publications Ltd.
Beard, C. and Wilson, J.P. (2002) *The Power of Experiential Learning: A Handbook for Trainers and Educators*, London: Kogan Page Limited.
Billett, S. (2000) 'Guided learning at work', *Journal of Workplace Learning: Employee Counselling Today*, Vol. 12(7), pp. 272–85.
Billett, S. (2001a) 'Learning through work: Workplace affordances and individual engagement', *Journal of Workplace Learning*, Vol. 13(5), pp. 209–14.
Billett, S. (2001b) *Learning in the Workplace: Strategies for Effective Practice*, Australia: Allen and Unwin.

Billett, S. (2004) 'Workplace participatory practices: Conceptualising workplaces as learning environments', *Journal of Workplace Learning*, Vol. 16(6), pp. 312–24.
Björkegren, C. (1999) *Learning for the Next Project: Bearers and Barriers in Knowledge Transfer within an Organization*, Licentiate thesis No. 32 from the International Graduate School of Management and Industrial Engineering, Institute of Technology, Linköpings Universitet, Linköping, Sweden.
Blackler, F. (1995) 'Knowledge, knowledge work and organisations: An overview and interpretation', *Organization Studies*, Vol. 16(6), pp. 1021–47.
Block, R. (1983) *The Politics of Projects*, New York: Yourdon Press.
Blomquist, T. and Packendorff, J. (1998) 'Learning from renewal projects: Content, context and embeddedness', in R.A. Lundin and C. Midler (Eds.), *Projects as Arenas for Renewal and Learning Processes* (pp. 37–46), USA: Kluwer Academic Publishers.
Boddy, D. (2002) *Managing Projects: Building and Leading the Team*, Great Britain: Pearson Education Limited.
Borda, O.F. (2001) 'Participative (action) research in social theory: Origins and challenges', in P. Reason and H. Bradbury (Eds.), *Handbook of Action Research: Participative Inquiry and Practice* (pp. 27–37), London: Sage Publications Ltd.
Boud, D. (1991) *Experience and Learning: Reflection at Work*, Australia: Deakin University.
Boud, D. (2006) 'Creating the space for reflection at work', in D. Boud, P. Cressey and P. Docherty (Eds.), *Productive Reflection at Work: Learning for Changing Organizations* (pp. 158–69), Great Britain: Routledge.
Boud, D., Cressey, P. and Docherty, P. (2006) 'Setting the scene for productive reflection', in D. Boud, P. Cressey and P. Docherty (Eds.), *Productive Reflection at Work: Learning for Changing Organizations* (pp. 3–10), Great Britain: Routledge.
Boud, D. and Garrick, J. (1999) 'Understandings of workplace learning', in D. Boud and J. Garrick (Eds.), *Understanding Learning at Work* (pp. 1–12), Great Britain: Routledge.
Boudès, T., Charue-Duboc, F. and Midler, C. (1998) 'Project management learning: A contingent approach', in R.A. Lundin and C. Midler (Eds.), *Projects as Arenas for Renewal and Learning Processes* (pp. 61–70), USA: Kluwer Academic Publishers.
Bourne, L. and Walker, D.H.T. (2004) 'Advancing project management in learning organizations', *The Learning Organization*, Vol. 11(3), pp. 226–43.
Bresnen, M., Edelman, L., Newell, S., Scarbrough, H. and Swan, J. (2003) 'Social practices and the management of knowledge in project environments', *International Journal of Project Management*, Vol. 21(3), pp. 157–66.
Briner, W., Hastings, C. and Geddes, M. (1996) 2nd edition, *Project Leadership*, Great Britain: Gower Publishing Limited.
Brookes, N.J., Morton, S.C., Dainty, A.R. and Burns, N.D. (2006) 'Social processes, patterns and practices and project knowledge management: A theoretical framework and an empirical investigation', *International Journal of Project Management*, Vol. 24(6), pp. 474–82.
Brown, J.S. and Duguid, P. (1991) 'Organizational learning and communities-of-practice: Toward a unified view of working, learning, and innovation', *Organization Science*, Vol. 2(1), pp. 40–57.

Brown, J.S. and Duguid, P. (2000) *The Social Life of Information*, Boston: Harvard Business School Press.
Brunas-Wagstaff, J. (1998) *Personality: A Cognitive Approach*, Great Britain: Routledge.
Bryans, P. and Smith, R. (2000) 'Beyond training: Reconceptualizing learning at work', *Journal of Workplace Learning*, Vol. 12(6), pp. 228–35.
Buchanan, D. and Badham, R. (1999) *Power, Politics, and Organizational Change: Winning the Turf Game*, London: Sage Publications Ltd.
Burrell, G. and Morgan, G. (1979) *Sociological Paradigms and Organisational Analysis: Elements of the Sociology of Corporate Life*, England: Gower Publishing Company Ltd.
Busby, J.S. (1999) 'An assessment of post project reviews', *Project Management Journal*, Vol. 30(3), pp. 23–9.
Calhoun, M.A. and Starbuck, W.H. (2003) 'Barriers to creating knowledge', in M. Easterby-Smith and M.A. Lyles (Eds.), *The Blackwell Handbook of Organizational Learning and Knowledge Management* (pp. 473–92), Oxford: Blackwell Publishing Ltd.
Carr, W. and Kemmis, S. (1986) *Becoming Critical: Education, Knowledge and Action Research*, Victoria: Deakin University.
CC Working Party (2001) *The Coke Guide: Phase 1*, Internal company document.
Chein, I., Cook, S.W. and Harding, J. (1948) 'The field of action research', *American Psychologist*, Vol. 3, pp. 43–50.
Choo, C.W. (1998) *The Knowing Organization: How Organizations use Information to Construct Meaning, Create Knowledge and Make Decisions*, USA: Oxford University Press.
Cicmil, S. (2005) 'Reflection, participation and learning in project environments: A multiple perspective agenda', in P. Love, P. Fong and Z. Irani (Eds.) (2005) *Management of Knowledge in Project Environments* (pp. 155–80), Great Britain: Elsevier Butterworth-Heinemann.
Cleland, D.I. (1999) 3rd edition, *Project Management: Strategic Design and Implementation*, USA: McGraw-Hill Companies Inc.
Collier, B., DeMarco, T. and Fearey, P. (1996) 'A defined process for project postmortem review', *IEEE Software*, July, pp. 65–72.
Cook, S.D.N. and Yanow, D. (1993) 'Culture and organizational learning', *Journal of Management Inquiry*, Vol. 2(4), pp. 373–90.
Coombs, S.J. and Smith, I.D. (1998) 'Designing a self-organized conversational learning environment', *Educational Technology*, May–June, pp. 17–28.
Coop, A.H. and Sigel, I.E. (1971) 'Cognitive style: Implications for learning and instruction', *Psychology in the Schools*, Vol. 2, pp. 152–61.
Coopey, J. and Burgoyne, J. (2000) 'Politics and organizational learning', *Journal of Management Studies*, Vol. 37(6), pp. 869–85.
Crossan, M.M., Lane, H.W. and White, R.E. (1999) 'An organizational learning framework: From intuition to institution', *Academy of Management Review*, Vol. 24(3), pp. 522–37.
Crouch, A. (2001) 'Behaviour of people in organisations', in D. Samson (Ed.), 3rd edition, *Management for Engineers* (pp. 177–201), Australia: Pearson Education Australia Pty Ltd.
Cunningham, J.B. (1993) *Action Research and Organizational Development*, USA: Praeger Publishers.

Curry, L. (1983a) *Learning Styles in Continuing Medical Education*, Ottowa: Canadian Medical Association.

Curry, L. (1983b) 'An organisation of learning styles theory and constructs', *ERIC Document*, 235: 185.

Daft, R.L. and Weick, K.E. (1984) 'Toward a model of organizations as interpretation systems', *Academy of Management Review*, Vol. 9(2), pp. 284–95.

Davenport, T.H. and Prusak, L. (1998) *Working Knowledge: How Organizations Manage What They Know*, USA: Harvard Business School Press.

Dawson, P. (1997) 'In the deep end: Conducting processual research on organisational change', *Scandinavian Journal of Management*, Vol. 13(4), pp. 389–405.

DeFillipi, R.J. (2001) 'Introduction: Project-based learning, reflective practices and learning outcomes', *Management Learning*, Vol. 32(1), pp. 5–10.

Denscombe, M. (1998) *The Good Research Guide: For Small-scale Social Research Projects*, Great Britain: Open University Press.

Denton, J. (1998) *Organisational Learning and Effectiveness*, Great Britain: Routledge.

Dewey, J. (1938) *Experience and Education*, USA: Collier Macmillan Publishers.

Dickens, L. and Watkins, K. (1999) 'Action research: Rethinking Lewin', *Management Learning*, Vol. 30(2), pp. 127–40.

Dixon, N. (1999) 2nd edition, *The Organizational Learning Cycle: How We Can Learn Collectively*, England: Gower.

Dodgson, M. (1991) 'Technology learning, technology strategy and competitive strategies', *British Journal of Management*, Vol. 2(3), pp. 132–49.

Dodgson, M. (1993) 'Organizational Learning: A review of some literatures', *Organization Studies*, Vol. 14(3), pp. 375–89.

Dunphy, D., Turner, D. and Crawford, M. (1997) 'Organizational learning as the creation of corporate competencies', *Journal of Management Development*, Vol. 16(4), pp. 232–44.

Easterby-Smith, M. (1997) 'Disciplines of organizational learning: Contributions and critiques', *Human Relations*, Vol. 50(9), pp. 1085–113.

Easterby-Smith, M., Crossan, M. and Nicolini, D. (2000) 'Organizational learning: Debates past, present and future', *Journal of Management Studies*, Vol. 37(6), pp. 783–96.

Elkjaer, B. (2001) Book review, 'The dance of change: The challenges of sustaining momentum in learning organizations', *Management Learning*, Vol. 32(1), pp. 153–6.

Ellinger, A.D., Ellinger, A.E., Yang, B. and Howton, W. (2002) 'The relationship between the learning organization concept and firms' financial performance: An empirical assessment', *Human Resource Development Quarterly*, Vol. 13(1), pp. 5–21.

Ellström, P.E. (2006) 'The meaning and role of reflection in informal learning at work', in D. Boud, P. Cressey and P. Docherty (Eds.), *Productive Reflection at Work: Learning for Changing Organizations* (pp. 43–53), Great Britain: Routledge.

Englehardt, C.S. and Simmons, P.R. (2002) 'Creating an organizational space for learning', *The Learning Organization*, Vol. 9(1), pp. 39–47.

Entwistle, N.J. (1988) *Styles of Learning and Teaching*, London: David Fulton.

Eskerod, P. and Skiver, H.J. (2001) 'Creative ways to enhance knowledge transfer/learning between project managers', in Proceedings of the 'IPMA International Symposium and Nordnet 2001 – Project Management Creativity Conference', May/June, Stockholm, Sweden, pp. 169–78.

Eskerod, P. and Skiver, H.J. (2007) 'Organizational culture restraining in-house knowledge transfer between project managers – A case study', *Project Management Journal*, Vol. 38(1), pp. 110–22.

Fernie, S., Green, S.D., Weller, S.J. and Newcombe, R. (2003) 'Knowledge sharing: Context, confusion and controversy', *International Journal of Project Management*, Vol. 21(3), pp. 177–87.

Field, L. (2002) 'Organisational learning and competing interests', in J. Teicher, P. Holland and R. Gough (Eds.), *Employee Relations Management: Australia in a Global Context* (pp. 110–32), Malaysia: Pearson education Australia.

Fiol, C.M. and Lyles, M.A. (1985) 'Organizational learning', *Academy of Management Review*, Vol. 10(4), pp. 803–13.

Flyvbjerg, B. (2001) *Making Social Science Matter: Why Social Inquiry Fails and How It Can Succeed Again*, Cambridge: Cambridge University Press.

Fong, P. (2003) 'Knowledge creation in multidisciplinary project teams: An empirical study of the processes and their dynamic interrelationships', *International Journal of Project Management*, Vol. 21(7), pp. 479–86.

Fox, S. (1997) 'From management education and development to the study of management learning', in J. Burgoyne and M. Reynolds (Eds.), *Management Learning: Integrating Perspectives in Theory and Practice* (pp. 21–37), London: Sage Publications Ltd.

Fox, S. (2000) 'Communities of practice, Foucault and actor-network theory', *Journal of Management Studies*, Vol. 37(6), pp. 853–67.

Frame, J.D. (1994) *The New Project Management: Tools for an Age of Rapid Change, Corporate Reengineering, and Other Business Realities*, San Francisco: Jossey-Bass Publishers.

Frame, J.D. (1995) *Managing Projects in Organizations: How to Make the Best Use of Time, Techniques, and People*, San Francisco: Jossey-Bass Publishers.

Frame, J.D. (1998) 'Closing out the project', in J.K. Pinto (Ed.), *The Project Management Institute: Project Management Handbook* (pp. 237–46), San Francisco: Jossey-Bass Publishers.

Frame, J.D. (1999) *Project Management Competence: Building Key Skills for Individuals, Teams, and Organizations*, San Francisco: Jossey-Bass Publishers.

Fulmer, R., Gibbs, P. and Keys, J.B. (1998) 'The second generation learning organizations: New tools for sustaining competitive advantage', *Organizational Dynamics*, Vol. 27(2), pp. 7–20.

Furnham, A., Jackson, C. and Miller, T. (1999) 'Personality, learning style and work performance', *Personality and Individual Differences*, Vol. 27, pp. 1113–22.

Galer, G. and Van Der Heijden, K. (1992) 'The learning organization: How planners create organizational learning', *Marketing Intelligence & Planning*, Vol. 10(6), pp. 5–16.

Galotti, K.M., Drebus, D.W. and Reimer, R.L. (2001) 'Ways of knowing as learning styles: Learning MAGIC with a partner', *Sex Roles*, Vol. 44(7/8), pp. 419–36.

Garrety, K., Robertson, P.L. and Badham, R.J. (2004) 'Integrating communities of practice in technology development projects', *International Journal of Project Management*, Vol. 22(5), pp. 351–8.

Garrick, J. (1998) 'Informal learning in corporate workplaces', *Human Resource Development Quarterly*, Vol. 9(2), pp. 129–44.

Garrison, D.R. (1991) 'Critical thinking and adult education: A conceptual model for developing critical thinking in adult learners', *International Journal of Lifelong Education*, Vol. 10(4), pp. 287–303.

Garvin, D.A. (1993) 'Building a learning organization', *Harvard Business Review*, July–August, pp. 78–91.

Gephart, M.A., Marsick, V.J., Van Buren, M.E. and Spiro, M.S. (1996) 'Learning organizations come alive', *Training and Development*, Vol. 50(12), pp. 34–46.

Gherardi, S. (1999) 'Learning as problem-driven or learning in the face of mystery?*', *Organization Studies*, Vol. 20(1), pp. 101–24.

Gherardi, S. (2001) 'From organizational learning to practice-based knowing' *Human Relations*, Vol. 54(1), pp. 131–9.

Gherardi, S. and Nicolini, D. (2000) 'To transfer is to transform: The circulation of safety knowledge', *Organization*, Vol. 7(2), pp. 329–48.

Gherardi, S., Nicolini, D. and Odella, F. (1998) 'Toward a social understanding of how people learn in organizations', *Management Learning*, Vol. 29(3), pp. 273–97.

Gido, J. and Clements, J.P. (1999) *Successful Project Management*, USA: South-Western College Publishing.

Gido, J. and Clements, J.P. (2003) 2nd edition, *Successful Project Management*, USA: South-Western College Publishing.

Goffman, E. (1974) *Frame Analysis: An Essay on the Organization of Experience*, Great Britain: Penguin Books Ltd.

Gold, J. (1997) 'Learning and story-telling: The next stage in the journey for the learning organization', *Journal of Workplace Learning*, Vol. 9(4), pp. 133–41.

Gray, C.F. and Larson, E.W. (2000) *Project Management: The Managerial Process*, Boston: Irwin/McGraw-Hill.

Gray, C.F. and Larson, E.W. (2002) 2nd edition, *Project Management: The Managerial Process*, Boston: Irwin/McGraw-Hill.

Gummesson, E. (1991) *Qualitative Methods in Management Research*, Newbury Park: Sage Publications Inc.

Hager, P. (2001) 'Workplace judgement and conceptions of learning', *Journal of Workplace Learning*, Vol. 13(7/8), pp. 352–9.

Hampson, S.E. (1995) 'The construction of personality', in S.E. Hampson and A.M. Colman (Eds.), *Individual Differences and Personality* (pp. 20–39), USA: Longman.

Hansen, M.T., Nohria, N. and Tierney, T. (1999) 'What's your strategy for managing knowledge?', *Harvard Business Review*, Vol. 77(2), pp. 106–15.

Hartman, F. and Lundin, R.A. (2000) 'Business in the future and the nature of projects – research issues', in R.A. Lundin and F. Hartman (Eds.), *Projects as Business Constituents and Guiding Motives* (pp. 229–38), USA: Kluwer Academic Publishers.

Hayes, J. and Allinson, C.W. (1994) 'Cognitive style and its relevance for management practice', *British Journal of Management*, Vol. 5(1), pp. 53–71.

Hayes, J. and Allinson, C.W. (1996) 'The implications of learning styles for training and development: A discussion of the matching hypothesis', *British Journal of Management*, Vol. 7(1), 63–73.

Hayes, J. and Allinson, C.W. (1998) 'Cognitive style and the theory and practice of individual and collective learning in organizations', *Human Relations*, Vol. 51(7), pp. 847–71.
Hedberg, B. (1981) 'How Organizations learn and unlearn', in P.C. Nystrom and W.H. Starbuck (Eds.), *Handbook of Organizational Design: Volume 1, Adapting Organizations to Their Environments* (pp. 3–27), Oxford: Oxford University Press.
Heron, J. and Reason, P. (2001) 'The practice of co-operative inquiry: Research "with" rather than "on" people', in P. Reason and H. Bradbury (Eds.), *Handbook of Action Research: Participative Inquiry and Practice* (pp. 179–88), London: Sage Publications Ltd.
Hickcox, L.K. (1995) 'Learning styles: A survey of adult learning style inventory models', in R.R. Sims and S.J. Sims (Eds.), *The Importance of Learning Styles: Understanding the Implications for Learning, Course Design, and Education* (pp. 25–48), USA: Greenwood Press.
Hildreth, P., Kimble, C. and Wright, P. (2000) 'Communities of practice in the distributed international environment', *Journal of Knowledge Management*, Vol. 4(1), pp. 27–38.
Holman, D., Pavlica, K. and Thorpe, R. (1997) 'Rethinking Kolb's theory of experiential learning in management education: The contribution of social constructionism and activity theory', *Management Learning*, Vol. 28(2), pp. 135–48.
Honey, P. and Mumford, A. (1992) *The Manual of Learning Styles*, Berkshire: Peter Honey.
Hong, J. (1999) 'Structuring for organizational learning', *The Learning Organization*, Vol. 6(4), pp. 173–85.
Huang, J.C. and Newell, S. (2003) 'Knowledge integration processes and dynamics within the context of cross functional projects', *International Journal of Project Management*, Vol. 21(3), pp. 167–76.
Huber, G.P. (1991) 'Organizational learning: The contributing processes and the literatures', *Organization Science*, Vol. 2(1), pp. 88–115.
Huemann, M. and Winkler, G. (1998) 'Project management-benchmarking: An instrument of learning', in R.A. Lundin and C. Midler (Eds.), *Projects as Arenas for Renewal and Learning Processes* (pp. 71–8), USA: Kluwer Academic Publishers.
Hurst, D.K., Rush, J.C. and White, J.E. (1989) 'Top management teams and organisational renewal', *Strategic Management Journal*, Vol. 10, pp. 87–105.
Ingelgård, A., Roth, J., Shani, A.B. and Styhre, A. (2002) 'Dynamic learning capability and actionable knowledge creation: Clinical R&D in a pharmaceutical company', *The Learning Organization*, Vol. 9(2), pp. 65–77.
Internal company report (2000) 'Sociotechnical analysis of Antarctic Steel Cokemaking Department'.
Järvinen, A. and Poikela, E. (2001) 'Modelling reflective and contextual learning at work', *Journal of Workplace Learning*, Vol. 13(7/8), pp. 282–89.
Jonassen, D.H. and Grabowski, B.L. (1993) *Handbook of Individual Differences, Learning and Instruction*, USA: Lawrence Erlbaum Associates.
Jones, A. and Hendry, C. (1992) 'How learning organizations are created', *Target Management Development Review*, Vol. 5(4), pp. 10–17.
Jung, C. (1923) *Psychological Types*, New York: Harcourt Brace.
Kanter, R.M. (1994) 'Dilemmas of teamwork', in C. Mabey and P. Iles (Eds.), *Managing Learning* (pp. 173–80), Great Britain: Routledge.

Kasl, E., Marsick, V.J. and Dechant, K. (1997) 'Teams as learners: A research-based model of team learning', *The Journal of Applied Behavioral Science*, Vol. 33(2), pp. 227–46.

Kasvi, J.J., Vartiainen, M. and Hailikari, M. (2003) 'Managing knowledge and knowledge competencies in projects and project organisations', *International Journal of Project Management*, Vol. 21(8), pp. 571–82.

Keegan, A. and Turner, J.R. (2001) 'Quantity versus quality in project based learning practices', *Management Learning*, Vol. 32(1), pp. 77–98.

Keeling, R. (2000) *Project management: An International Perspective*, Great Britain: Macmillan Press Ltd.

Kerzner, H. (2001) 7th edition, *Project Management: A Systems Approach to Planning, Scheduling and Controlling*, USA: John Wiley and Sons Inc.

Kezsbom, D. and Edward, K. (2001) 2nd edition, *The New Dynamic Project Management: Winning Through the Competitive Advantage*, USA: John Wiley and Sons Inc.

Kim, D.H. (1993) 'The link between individual and organizational learning', *Sloan Management Review* (Fall), pp. 37–50.

King, I. and Rowe, A. (1999) 'Space and the not-so-final frontiers: Re-presenting the potential of collective learning for organizations', *Management Learning*, Vol. 30(4), pp. 431–48.

Kirton, M.J. (1989) 'A theory of cognitive style', in M.J. Kirton (Ed.), *Adaptors and Innovators: Styles of Creativity and Problem Solving*, London: Routledge.

Kolb, D.A. (1984) *Experiential Learning: Experience as the Source of Learning and Development*, USA: Prentice-Hall Inc.

Kolb, D.A., Baker, A.C. and Jensen, P.J. (2002) 'Conversation as experiential learning', in A.C. Baker, P.J. Jensen and D.A. Kolb (Eds.), *Conversational Learning: An Experiential Approach to Knowledge Creation* (pp. 51–66), USA: Quorum books.

Kotnour, T. (1999) 'A learning framework for project management', *Project Management Journal*, Vol. 30(2), pp. 32–8.

Lave, J. and Wenger, E. (1991) *Situated Learning: Legitimate Peripheral Participation*, USA: Cambridge University press.

Lechler, T. (2000) 'Empirical evidence of people as determinants of project success', in R.A. Lundin and F. Hartman (Eds.), *Projects as Business Constituents and Guiding Motives* (pp. 217–27), USA: Kluwer Academic Publishers.

Leonard-Barton, D. (1992) 'The factory as a learning laboratory', *Sloan Management Review*, Fall, pp. 23–38.

Leonard-Barton, D. (1995) *Wellsprings of Knowledge: Building and Sustaining the Sources of Innovation*, USA: Harvard Business School Press.

Lewin, K. (1946) 'Action research and minority problems', *The Journal of Social Issues*, Vol. II(4), pp. 34–46.

Lewis, J.P. (1998) *Team-based Project Management*, New York: American Management Association.

Lewis, J.P. (2003) *Project Leadership*, New York: McGraw-Hill.

Lientz, B.P. and Rea, K.P. (1995) *Project Management for the 21st Century*, USA: Academic Press.

Lim, L.E. (2002) 'Learning beyond mentoring: The Singapore experience', *The International Journal of Educational Management*, Vol. 16(4), pp. 185–9.

Linde, C. (2001) 'Narrative and social tacit knowledge', *Journal of Knowledge Management*, Vol. 5(2), pp. 160–70.

Lindkvist, L. (2005) 'Knowledge communities and knowledge collectivities: A typology of knowledge work in groups', *Journal of Management Studies*, Vol. 42(6), pp. 1189–210.

Lock, D. (1996a) 6th edition, *Project Management*, England: Gower Publishing Limited.

Lock, D. (1996b) *The Essentials of Project Management*, England: Gower Publishing Limited.

Love, P., Fong, P. and Irani, Z. (2005) (Eds.) *Management of Knowledge in Project Environments*, Great Britain: Elsevier Butterworth-Heinemann.

Lundin, R.A. and Hartman, F. (2000) 'Pervasiveness of projects in business', in R.A. Lundin and F. Hartman (Eds.), *Projects as Business Constituents and Guiding Motives* (pp. 1–10), USA: Kluwer Academic Publishers.

Lundin, R.A. and Midler, C. (1998a) 'Evolution of project as empirical trend and theoretical focus', in R.A. Lundin and C. Midler (Eds.), *Projects as Arenas for Renewal and Learning Processes* (pp. 1–9), USA: Kluwer Academic Publishers.

Lundin, R.A. and Midler, C. (1998b) 'Emerging convergences or debates', in R.A. Lundin and C. Midler (Eds.), *Projects as Arenas for Renewal and Learning Processes* (pp. 231–41), USA: Kluwer Academic Publishers.

Lundin, R.A. and Söderholm, A. (1998) 'Managing the black boxes of the project environment', in J.K. Pinto (Ed.), *The Project Management Institute: Project Management Handbook* (pp. 41–54), San Francisco: Jossey-Bass Publishers.

MacIntosh, R. (2001) 'Practice based research: Understanding the role of the academic', in Proceedings of the European Group for Organizational Studies (EGOS) conference, July, Lyon, France.

Mantel, Jr S.J., Meredith, J.R., Schafer, S.M. and Sutton, M.M. (2001) *Project Management in Practice*, USA: John Wiley and Sons, Inc.

March, J.G. (1991) 'Exploration and exploitation in organizational learning', *Organization Science*, Vol. 2(1), pp. 71–87.

March, J.G. and Olsen, J.P. (1975) 'The uncertainty of the past: Organizational learning under ambiguity', *European Journal of Political Research*, Vol. 3(2), pp. 147–71.

Marsick, V.J. (1987), 'New paradigms for learning in the workplace', in V. Marsick (Ed.), *Learning in the Workplace* (pp. 11–30), USA: Croom Helm.

Marsick, V.J. and Watkins, K. (1990) *Informal and Incidental Learning in the Workplace*, London: Routledge.

Marsick, V.J. and Watkins, K. (1999) 'Envisioning new organizations for learning', in D. Boud and J. Garrick (Eds.), *Understanding Learning at Work* (pp. 199–215), Great Britain: Routledge.

Mårtensson, M. (2000) 'A critical review of knowledge management as a management tool', *Journal of Knowledge Management*, Vol. 4(3), pp. 204–16.

Matthews, P. (1999) 'Workplace learning: Developing an holistic model', *The Learning Organization*, Vol. 6(1), pp. 18–29.

Matthews, J.H. and Candy, P.C. (1999) 'New dimensions in the dynamics of learning and knowledge', in D. Boud and J. Garrick (Eds.), *Understanding Learning at Work* (pp. 47–64), Great Britain: Routledge.

McKenna, S. (1999) 'Storytelling and "real" management competence', *Journal of Workplace Learning*, Vol. 11(3), pp. 95–104.

McLellan, H. (1996) 'Situated learning: Multiple perspectives', in H. McLellan (Ed.), *Situated Learning Perspectives* (pp. 5–17), New Jersey: Educational Technology Publications.

McNiff, J. (1988) *Action Research: Principles and Practice*, Great Britain: Routledge.

McTaggart, R. (1997) 'Reading the collection, and, Guiding principles for participatory action research', in R. McTaggart (Ed.), *Participatory Action Rresearch: International Contexts and Consequences* (pp. 1–44), Albany: State University of New York Press.

Mead, G.H. (1934) *Mind, Self and Society: From the Standpoint of a Social Behaviorist*, Chicago: University of Chicago Press.

Messick, S. (1976) 'Personality consistencies in cognition and creativity', in S. Messick and associates (Eds.), *Individuality in Learning*, San Francisco: Jossey-Bass Publishers.

Messick, S. (1984) 'The nature of cognitive styles: Problems and promise in educational practice', *Educational Psychologist*, Vol. 19(2), pp. 59–74.

Miettinen, R. (2000) 'The concept of experiential learning and John Drewey's theory of reflective thought and action', *International Journal of Lifelong Learning*, Vol. 19(1), pp. 54–72.

Miner, A. and Mezias, S. (1996) 'Ugly duckling no more: Pasts and futures of organizational learning research', *Organization Science*, Vol. 7(1), pp. 88–99.

Mintzberg, H. (1976) 'Planning on the left side and managing on the right', *Harvard Business Rreview*, July–August, pp. 49–58.

Mitki, Y., Shani, A.B. and Meiri, Z. (1997) 'Organizational learning mechanisms and continuous improvement', *Journal of Organizational Change Management*, Vol. 10(5), pp. 426–46.

Mohrman, S.A., Cohen, S. and Mohrman, Jr A. (1995) *Designing Team Based Organizations: New Forms for Knowledge Work*, San Francisco, Jossey Bass Publishers.

Mohrman, S.A. and Cummings, T.G. (1989) *Self-designing Organizations: Learning How to Create High Performance*, USA: Addison-Wesley Publishing.

Morris, P.W.G. (1994) *The Management of Projects*, London: Thomas Telford Services Ltd.

Morris, P.W.G. (1998) 'Key issues in project management', in J.K. Pinto (Ed.), *The Project Management Institute: Project Management Handbook* (pp. 3–26), San Francisco: Jossey-Bass Publishers.

Morris, P.W.G. (2002) 'Managing project management knowledge for organizational effectiveness', in Proceedings of PMI® Research Conference, July, Seattle, USA, pp. 77–87.

Müllern, T. and Östergren, K. (1998) 'Managing renewal projects in different learning cultures', in R.A. Lundin and C. Midler (Eds.), *Projects as Arenas for Renewal and Learning Processes* (pp. 115–21), USA: Kluwer Academic Publishers.

Mumford, A. (1994) 'Individual and organizational learning: The pursuit of change', in C. Mabey and P. Iles (Eds.), *Managing Learning* (pp. 77–86), Great Britain: Routledge.

Mumford, A. (2000) 'A learning approach to strategy', *Journal of Workplace Learning: Employee Counselling Today*, Vol. 12(7), pp. 265–71.

Murrell, K.L. and Bishop, R.W. (1995) 'The learning model for managers: A tool to facilitate learning', in R.R. Sims and S.J. Sims (Eds.), *The Importance of Learning Styles: Understanding the Implications for Learning, Course Design, and Education* (pp. 179–91), USA: Greenwood Press.

Myers, I.B. (1993) 5th edition, *Introduction to Type*, Palo Alto CA: Consulting Psychologists Press.

Myers, I.B. and McCaulley, M.H. (1985) *Manual: A Guide to the Development and Use of the Myers-Briggs Type Indicator*, Palo Alto CA: Consulting Psychologists Press.

Myers, I.B. and Myers, P.B. (1980) *Gifts Differing*, Palo Alto CA: Consulting Psychologists Press.

Nicolini, D. and Meznar, B. (1995) 'The social construction of organizational learning: Conceptual and practical issues in the field', *Human Relations*, Vol. 48(7), pp. 727–40.

Nonaka, I. and Konno, N. (1998) 'The concept of "Ba": Building a foundation for knowledge creation', *California Management Review*, Vol. 40(3), pp. 40–54.

Nonaka, I. and Takeuchi, H. (1995) *The Knowledge Creating Company: How Japanese Companies Create the Dynamics of Innovation*, USA: Oxford University Press.

Oswick, C., Anthony, P., Keenoy, T., Mangham, I. and Grant, D. (2000) 'A dialogic analysis of organizational learning', *Journal of Management Studies*, Vol. 37(6), pp. 887–901.

Park, P. (1999) 'People, knowledge, and change in participatory research', *Management Learning*, Vol. 32(2), pp. 141–57.

Pasmore, W. (2001) 'Action research in the workplace: The socio-technical perspective', in P. Reason and H. Bradbury (Eds.), *Handbook of Action Research: Participative Inquiry and Practice* (pp. 38–47), London: Sage Publications Ltd.

Pawlowsky, P. (2001) 'The treatment of organizational learning in management science', in A.B. Antal, M. Dierkes, J. Child and I. Nonaka (Eds.), *Handbook of Organizational Learning and Knowledge* (pp. 61–88), New York: Oxford University Press.

Peansupap, V. and Walker, D.H.T. (2005) 'Diffusion of information and communication technology: A community of practice perspective', in A.S. Kazi (Ed.), *Knowledge Management in the Construction Industry: A Socio-technical Perspective* (pp. 90–111), USA: Idea Group Publishing.

Pearn, M., Wood, R., Fullerton, J. and Roderick, C. (1994) 'Becoming a learning organization: How to as well as why', in J. Burgoyne, M. Pedler and T. Boydell, (Eds.), *Towards the Learning Company: Concepts and Practices* (pp. 186–99), Great Britain: McGraw-Hill Book Company Europe.

Pedler, M., Boydell, T. and Burgoyne, J. (1989) 'Towards the learning company', *Management Education and Development*, Vol. 20(1), pp. 1–8.

Pfeffer, J. (1992) *Managing with Power: Politics and Influence in Organizations*, USA: Harvard Business School Press.

Phillips, A. (1994) 'Creating space in the learning company', in J. Burgoyne, M. Pedler and T. Boydell (Eds.), *Towards the Learning Company: Concepts and Practices* (pp. 98–109), Great Britain: McGraw-Hill Book Company Europe.

Piaget, J. (1953) *The Origin of Intelligence in the Child*, Great Britain: Routledge and Kegan Paul Ltd.

Pinto, J.K. (1998a) *Power and Politics in Project Management*, USA: Project Management Institute.

Pinto, J.K. (1998b) 'Power, politics, and project management', in J.K. Pinto (Ed.), *The Project Management Institute: Project Management Handbook* (pp. 256–66), San Francisco: Jossey-Bass Publishers.

Pinto, J.K. (2000) 'Understanding the role of politics in successful project management', *International Journal of Project Management,* Vol. 18(2), pp. 85–91.
Pinto, J.K. and Millet, I. (1999) *Successful Information System Implementation: The Human Side,* USA: Project Management Institute.
Pinto, J.K. and Slevin, D.P. (1998) 'Critical success factors', in J.K. Pinto (Ed.), *The Project Management Institute: Project Management Handbook* (pp. 379–95), San Francisco: Jossey-Bass Publishers.
PMI® (1996) *A Guide to the Project Management Body of Knowledge,* USA: Project Management Institute.
Polanyi, M. (1966) *The Tacit Dimension,* Great Britain: Routledge and Kegan Paul Ltd.
Posner, B.Z. and Kouzes, J.M. (1998) 'The project manager', in J.K. Pinto (Ed.), *The Project Management Institute: Project Management Handbook* (pp. 249–55), San Francisco: Jossey-Bass Publishers.
Probst, G. and Buchel, B. (1997) *Organizational Learning: The Competitive Advantage of the Future,* London: Prentice-Hall.
Raelin, J.A. (1998) 'Work-based learning in practice', *Journal of Workplace Learning,* Vol. 10(6/7), pp. 280–3.
Raelin, J.A. (2000) *Work Based Learning: The New Frontier of Management Development,* USA: Prentice Hall Inc.
Raelin, J.A. (2001) 'Public reflection as the basis of learning', *Management Learning,* Vol. 32(1), pp. 11–30.
Reason, P. (1994) 'Three approaches to participative inquiry', in N.K. Denzin and Y.S. Lincoln (Eds.), *Handbook of Qualitative Research* (pp. 324–39), USA: Sage Publications Inc.
Reason, P. (1999) 'Integrating action and reflection through co-operative inquiry', *Management Learning,* Vol. 30(2), pp. 207–26.
Rezaei, A.R. and Katz, L. (2004) 'Evaluation of the reliability and validity of the cognitive styles analysis', *Personality and Individual Differences,* Vol. 36(6), pp. 1317–27.
Richter, I. (1998) 'Individual and organizational learning at the executive level: Towards a research agenda', *Management Learning,* Vol. 29(3), pp. 299–316.
Riding, R.J. (1991) *Cognitive Styles Analysis,* Birmingham: Learning and Training Technology.
Riding, R.J. (2003) 'On the assessment of cognitive style: A commentary on Peterson, Deary, and Austin', *Personality and Individual Differences,* Vol. 34, pp. 893–7.
Riding, R.J. and Cheema, I. (1991) 'Cognitive styles – An overview and integration, *Educational Psychology,* Vol. 11(3&4), pp. 193–215.
Riding, R.J. and Raynor, S. (1998) *Cognitive Styles and Learning Strategies,* London: David Fulton.
Rifkin, W. and Fulop, L. (1997) 'A review and case study on learning organizations', *The Learning Organization,* Vol. 4(4), pp. 135–48.
Ruggles, R. (1998) 'The state of the notion: Knowledge management in practice', *California Management Review,* Vol. 40(3), pp. 80–9.
Sadler-Smith, E. (1996) 'Learning styles: A holistic approach', *Journal of European Industrial Training,* Vol. 20(7), pp. 29–36.

Sadler-Smith, E. (1998) 'Cognitive style: Some human resource implications for managers', *The International Journal of Human Resource Management*, Vol. 9(1), pp. 185–202.

Sadler-Smith, E. (1999) 'Intuition-analysis cognitive style and learning preferences of business and management students: A UK exploratory study', *Journal of Managerial Psychology*, Vol. 14(1), pp. 26–38.

Sadler-Smith, E. (2001a) 'A reply to Reynolds's critique of learning style', *Management Learning*, Vol. 32(3), pp. 291–304.

Sadler-Smith, E. (2001b) 'The relationship between learning style and cognitive style', *Personality and Individual Differences*, Vol. 30, pp. 609–16.

Sadler-Smith, E., Allinson, C.W. and Hayes, J. (2000) 'Learning preferences and cognitive style: Some implications for continuing professional development', *Management Learning*, Vol. 31(2), pp. 239–56.

Sadler-Smith, E. and Badger, B. (1998) 'Cognitive style, learning and innovation', *Technology Analysis and Strategic Management*, Vol. 10(2), pp. 247–65.

Saint-Onge, H. and Wallace, D. (2002) *Leveraging Communities of Practice for Strategic Advantage*, Amsterdam: Butterworth-Heinemann.

Salaman, G. and Butler, J. (1994) 'Why managers won't learn', in C. Mabey and P. Iles (Eds.), *Managing Learning* (pp. 34–42), Great Britain: Routledge.

Scarbrough, H., Swan, J. and Preston, J. (1999) *Knowledge Management and the Learning Organization*, London: IPD.

Schein, E.H. (1993) 'How can organizations learn faster? The challenge of entering the green room', *Sloan Management Review*, Winter, pp. 85–92.

Schindler, M. and Eppler, M. (2003) 'Harvesting project knowledge: A review of project learning methods and success factors', *International Journal of Project Management*, Vol. 21(3), pp. 219–28.

Schmeck, R.R. (1988a) 'An introduction to strategies and styles of learning', in R.R. Schmeck (Ed.), *Learning Strategies and Learning Styles* (pp. 3–20), New York: Plenum Press.

Schmeck, R.R. (1988b) 'Strategies and styles of learning: An integration of varied perspectives', in R.R. Schmeck (Ed.), *Learning Strategies and Learning Styles* (pp. 317–48), New York: Plenum Press.

Schön, D.A. (1987) *Educating the Reflective Practitioner: Toward a New Design for Teaching and Learning in the Professions*, USA: Jossey-Bass Inc. Publishers.

Schwandt, T.A. (1994) 'Constructivist, interpretivist approaches to human inquiry', in N.K. Denzin and Y.S. Lincoln (Eds.), *Handbook of Qualitative Research* (pp. 118–37), USA: Sage Publications Inc.

Seibert, K.W. and Daudelin, M.W. (1999) *The Role of Reflection in Managerial Learning: Theory, Research, and Practice*, USA: Quorum Books.

Senge, P.M. (1990) *The Fifth Discipline: The Art and Practice of the Learning Organization*, Sydney: Random House Australia.

Senge, P.M., Kleiner, A., Roberts, C., Ross, R., Roth, G. and Smith, B. (1999) *The Dance of Change: The Challenges of Sustaining Momentum in Learning Organizations*, London: Nicholas Brealey Publishing.

Senge, P.M. and Scharmer, O. (2001) 'Community action research: Learning as a community of practitioners, consultants and researchers', in P. Reason and H. Bradbury (Eds.), *Handbook of Action Research: Participative Inquiry and Practice* (pp. 238–49), London: Sage Publications Ltd.

Sense, A.J. (2003a) 'A model of the politics of project leader learning', *International Journal of Project Management*, Vol. 21(2), pp. 107–14.
Sense, A.J. (2003b) 'Learning generators: Project teams re-conceptualized', *Project Management Journal*, Vol. 34(3), pp. 4–12.
Sense, A.J. (2004) 'An architecture for learning in projects?', *Journal of Workplace Learning*, Vol. 16(3), pp. 123–45.
Sense, A.J. (2005a) 'Facilitating conversational learning in a project team practice', *Journal of Workplace Learning*, Vol. 17(3), pp. 178–93.
Sense, A.J. (2005b) *Cultivating Situated Learning Within Project Management Practice: A Case Study Exploration of the Dynamics of Project Based Learning*, PhD Thesis, Macquarie University, Australia.
Sense, A.J. (2006a) 'Project learning relationships and situated learning: Defensive deflection and protective veneers', *International Journal of Learning and Change*, Vol. 1(3), pp. 345–61.
Sense, A.J. (2006b) 'Driving the bus from the rear passenger seat: Control dilemmas of participative action research', *International journal of social research methodology: Theory and practice*, Vol. 9(1), pp. 1–13.
Sense, A.J. (2007a) 'Learning within project practice: Cognitive styles exposed', *International Journal of Project Management*, Vol. 25(1), pp. 33–40.
Sense, A.J. (2007b) 'Stimulating situated learning within projects: Personalizing the flow of knowledge', *Knowledge Management Research and Practice*, Vol. 5(1), pp. 13–21.
Sense, A.J. and Antoni, M. (2003) 'Exploring the politics of project learning', *International Journal of Project Management*, Vol. 21(7), pp. 487–94.
Sense, A.J. and Badham, R.J. (2006) 'Educating bricoleurs: Nurturing a situated learning environment in technology projects', *International Journal of Continuing Engineering Education and Life-long Learning*, Vol. 16(6), pp. 466–81.
Shani, A.B. and Docherty, P. (2003) *Learning by Design: Building Sustainable Organizations*, Oxford: Blackwell Publishing Ltd.
Shrivastava, P. (1983) 'A typology of organizational learning systems', *Journal of Management Studies*, Vol. 20(1), pp. 7–28.
Sims, R.R. and Sims, S.J. (1995a) 'Learning enhancement in higher education', in R.R. Sims and S.J. Sims (Eds.), *The Importance of Learning Styles: Understanding the Implications for Learning, Course Design, and Education* (pp. 1–24), USA: Greenwood Press.
Sims, S.J. and Sims, R.R. (1995b) 'Learning and learning styles: A review and look to the future', in R.R. Sims and S.J. Sims (Eds.), *The Importance of Learning Styles: Understanding the Implications for Learning, Course Design, and Education* (pp. 193–210), USA: Greenwood Press.
Smith, K.A. (2000) *Project Management and Teamwork*, USA: McGraw-Hill Higher Education.
Smith, E.A. (2001) 'The role of tacit and explicit knowledge in the workplace', *Journal of Knowledge Management*, Vol. 5(4), pp. 311–21.
Smith, B. and Dodds, B. (1997) *Developing Managers Through Project Based Learning*, England: Gower Publishing Limited.
Smith, P.A.C. and Saint-Onge, H. (1996) 'The evolutionary organization: Avoiding a titanic fate', *The Learning Organization*, Vol. 3(4), pp. 4–21.

Solomon, N. (1999) 'Culture and difference in workplace learning', in D. Boud and J. Garrick (Eds.), *Understanding Learning at Work* (pp. 119–31), Great Britain: Routledge.
Starkey, K. (1998) 'The organizational learning cycle: How we can learn collectively', *Human Relations,* Vol. 51(4), pp. 531–46.
Steiner, L. (1998) 'Organizational dilemmas as barriers to learning', *The Learning Organization,* Vol. 5(4), pp. 193–201.
Sternberg, R.J. (1988) 'Mental self-government: A theory of intellectual styles and their development, *Human Development,* Vol. 31, pp. 197–224.
Sternberg, R.J. (1995) 'Intelligence and cognitive styles', in S.E. Hampson and A.M. Colman (Eds.), *Individual Differences and Personality* (pp. 1–19). USA: Longman.
Sternberg, R.J. (1997) *Thinking Styles,* USA: Cambridge University Press.
Sternberg, R.J. and Grigorenko, E.L. (1997) 'Are cognitive styles still in style?', *American Psychologist,* Vol. 52(7), pp. 700–12.
Story, J. and Barnett, E. (2000) 'Knowledge management initiatives: Learning from failure', *Journal of Knowledge Management,* Vol. 4(2), pp. 145–56.
Sun, P.Y.T. and Scott, J.L. (2003) 'Exploring the divide – organizational learning and learning organization', *The Learning Organization,* Vol. 10(4), pp. 202–15.
Swan, J., Newell, S., Scarbrough, H. and Hislop, D. (1999) 'Knowledge management and innovation: Networks and networking', *Journal of Knowledge Management,* Vol. 3(4), pp. 262–75.
Teare, R., and Monk, S. (2002) 'Learning from change', *International Journal of Contemporary Hospitality Management,* Vol. 14(7), pp. 334–41.
Tenkasi, R.V. and Mohrman. S.A. (1999) 'Global change as contextual-collaborative knowledge creation', in D.L. Cooperrider and J.E. Dutton (Eds.), *Organizational Dimensions of Global Change: No Limits to Cooperation* (pp. 114–36), Newbury Park: Sage.
Thomas, J.L. (2000) 'Making sense of project management', in R.A. Lundin and F. Hartman (Eds.), *Projects as Business Constituents and Guiding Motives* (pp. 25–43), USA: Kluwer Academic Publishers.
Thompson, M. (2005) 'Structural and epistemic parameters in communities of practice', *Organization Science,* Vol. 16(2), pp. 151–64.
Tsang, E.W.K. (1997) 'Organizational learning and the learning organization: A dichotomy between descriptive and prescriptive research', *Human Relations,* Vol. 50(1), pp. 73–89.
Turner, J.R. (1999) 2nd edition, *The Handbook of Project-based Management,* UK: McGraw-Hill Publishing Company.
Turner, J.R. and Müller, R. (2003) 'On the nature of the project as a temporary organization', *International Journal of Project Management,* Vol. 21(1), pp. 1–8.
Van Der Merwe, A.P. (1997) 'Multi-project management–organizational structure and control', *International Journal of Project Management,* Vol. 15(4), pp. 223–33.
Verma, V.K. (1995) *The Human Aspects of Project Management: Organizing Projects for Success,* USA: Project Management Institute.
von Krogh, G. (2003) 'Knowledge sharing and the communal resource', in M. Easterby-Smith and M.A. Lyles (Eds.), *The Blackwell Handbook of Organizational Learning and Knowledge Management* (pp. 372–92), Oxford: Blackwell Publishing Ltd.

Watkins, K.E. and Cervero, R.M. (2000) 'Organizations as contexts for learning: A case study in certified accountancy', *Journal of Workplace Learning*, Vol. 12(5), pp. 187–94.
Watkins K.E. and Marsick, V.J. (1996) *In Action: Creating the Learning Organization*, Alexandria, VA: American Society for Training and Development.
Weick, K.E. (1995) *Sensemaking in Organizations*, USA: Sage Publications Inc.
Weick, K.E. (2001) *Making Sense of the Organization*, United Kingdom: Blackwell Publishing Ltd.
Weick, K.E. and Westley, F. (1996) 'Organizational learning: Affirming an oxymoron', in S.R. Clegg, C. Hardy and W.R. Nord (Eds.), *Handbook of Organization Studies* (pp. 440–58), Great Britain: Sage publications Ltd.
Wenger, E. (1998) *Communities of Practice: Learning, Meaning and Identity*, USA: Cambridge University Press.
Wenger, E. (2003) 'Communities of practice and social learning systems', in D. Nicolini, S. Gherardi and D. Yanow (Eds.), *Knowing in Organizations: A Practice-based Approach* (pp. 76–99), USA: M.E. Sharpe Inc.
Wenger, E., McDermott, R. and Snyder, W.M. (2002) *Cultivating Communities of Practice: A Guide to Managing Knowledge*, USA: Harvard Business School Press.
Wenger, E. and Snyder, W. (2000) 'Communities of practice: The organizational frontier', *Harvard Business Review*, January–February, pp. 139–45.
Wheatley, M.J. (1999) *Leadership and the New Science: Discovering Order in a Chaotic World*, USA: Berrett-Koehler Publishers.
Wheelwright, S.C. and Clark, K.B. (1992) *Revolutionizing Product Development: Quantum Leaps in Speed, Efficiency, and Quality*, USA: The Free Press.
Whyte, W.F. (1991a) 'Introduction', in W.F. Whyte (Ed.), *Participatory Action Research* (pp. 7–15), USA: Sage Publications Inc.
Whyte, W.F., Greenwood, D.J. and Lazes, P. (1991) 'Participatory action research: Through practice to science in social research', in W.F. Whyte (Ed.), *Participatory Action Research* (pp. 19–55), USA: Sage Publications Inc.
Wilemon, D. (1998) 'Cross-functional cooperation', in J.K. Pinto (Ed.), *The Project Management Institute: Project Management Handbook* (pp. 279–99), San Francisco: Jossey-Bass Publishers.
Willmott, H. (2000) 'From knowledge to learning', in C. Pritchard, R. Hull, M. Chumer and H. Willmott (Eds.), *Managing Knowledge: Critical Investigations of Work and Learning* (pp. 216–22), Basingstoke: Macmillan Press Ltd.
Witkin, H.A., Moore, C.A., Goodenough, D.R. and Cox, P.W. (1977) 'Field dependent and field independent cognitive styles and their educational implications', *Review of Educational Research*, Vol. 47, pp. 1–64.
Yin, R.K. (1994) 2nd edition, *Case Study Research: Design and Methods*, USA: Sage Publications Inc.

Index

action research, 8–9
ambiguity, 121–5
  about project roles, 122–4, 134, 171
  about the project process, 124–5, 134, 171
  about the topic of learning, 121, 134, 171
authorities accumulated, 108–10, 112, 115, 170–1
  see also politics and power in projects, described
authority
  bureaucratic, 108, 126
  charismatic, 108
  crisis, 108
  formal, 108, 111, 170–1
  technical, 108, 119
authority issues, cultural, 106, 129
  see also deference to higher authority
authority, latent of, core participants, 116–20

boundary objects, in COPs, 39, 60
bricoleurs, in the research process, 34, 175
brokering, in COPs, 39, 60
business issues, short term effects on learning, 162–4, 166, 172

case study, details, 10–14
co-location, of project participants, 158–9
coaching, 105–7, 133, 170
codification, of information, 141, 143
cognitive learning, 25–30
  see also learning, cognitive dimension of
cognitive style and knowledge management, 140
cognitive style assessment, 71–84
cognitive style conditioners, 85–90

cognitive style, 66–92
  Adaptor type, 74–7
  Analyst type, 72–4
  Innovator type, 74–7
  Intuitive type, 72–4
  Verbalizer-Imager type, 79–80
  Wholist-Analytical type, 78–9
cognitive style, definition, 68
commitment to learn
  organizational, 151–2
  project participant, 152–3
common practice, development of, see under situated learning theory
commonly held information, see shared information
communities of practice (COPs), 35–40
conceptions of project teams
  learning perspective, 59–63
  traditional perspective, 57–9
conceptual architecture, see pentagon of project situated learning behaviour

defensive deflection, 99–101
defensive routines, 6, 29, 98–9, 170
deference to higher authority, 119–20, 124, 126, 134, 171

environmental stimulus, to encourage learning, 159–62
expertise knowledge, distribution of, 119–20, 148–9, 165
explicit knowledge, 141

heuristics for learning, see pentagon of project situated learning behaviour
hierarchy dependence, see deference to higher authority

infrastructural constraint/enabler elements, 136–7
infrastructures to learn, physical and social, 153–9
intra-project learning, importance of, 2–7

knowing in action, *see* tacit knowledge
knowledge exchange venues, project teams as, 60–1
knowledge flow, formal/informal channels for, 147–8
knowledge management, 137–49
  definition, 140
  social dimension, 137–40, 142–3
  technical dimension, 137–9, 141
Kolb's experiential learning cycle, 26–8

learning experiments, projects as, 48
learning generators, project teams as, 62
learning-how-to-learn, 1
learning libido, 7–8
learning organization, 19–20
learning relationships, 94–108
learning relationships, definition, 95
learning spaces, 155–7
learning styles, relation to cognitive styles, 69–71
learning workshops, 154
learning, cognitive dimension of, 25–30
learning, conversational, 23–4
learning, double-loop, 21, 29, 104
learning, relationship between individual and organizational learning, 23–5
learning, single-loop, 29, 74
learning, situated dimension of, 30–42
learning, triple-loop, *see* learning-how-to-learn
legitimate peripheral participation (LPP), 40–2

mental models, 29
mentoring, 106–7

Model I / Model II Theory of Action, 29–30
Myer-Briggs Type Indicator (MBTI), 80–1

organizational learning, 17–23
  behavioural, 21
  cognitive, 20–1
  sociological, 21–3
organizational setting
  description, 11
  stimulating participants to learn, 159–62

participative action research, 9–10, 173–5
participative action research, dilemmas, 173–5
past organizational authority, exercise of, *see* authority, latent of, core participants
pentagon of project situated learning behaviour, 63–5
personal matters, exposure thereof, 98–103
personality, 70
personality style types, *see under* Myers-Briggs Type Indicator(MBTI)
personalization approach, to knowledge management, 142–3
political accommodation, of alternate views, 112–13
political influence, exercise of, 108–9, 111–13
politics and learning, in projects, 113–15
politics and power in projects, described, 110–1
post completion reviews, *see* project end reviews
powerlessness, feeling of, *see* deference to higher authority
practical aspects of learning, *see* situated learning theory
project audit processes, *see* project end reviews
project context, description, *see* case study, details

project end reviews, 5–7, 51
project goals, 14, 122
project hegemony, 130–2
project information processing demands, 85–8, 91
project learning strategy/intention to learn, 151–3
project learning trajectory, 61–2
project management, definition, 57–8
project sponsor, 126–30
  discernable authority, 128–9
  latent authority, 126
project teams, definition of, 58–9
projects, definition of, 57–8
psychological types, *see under* Myers-Briggs Type Indicator(MBTI)
public exposition, of constraint/enabler elements, 1, 169, 179
pyramid of authority, 108–32
  definition of, 109–10

rankings, applied to knowledge sources, 148–9
reflection in action, 34
reflection, communal, on constraint/enabler elements, 1, 169, 179
reflective practitioners, 53, 56, 151

relationship frameworks, challenge thereof, 103–7
relationships, project to project, *see* project hegemony

seeding structures, *see* pentagon of project situated learning behaviour
self-design, of learning activities, *see* pentagon of project situated learning behaviour
Senge's five disciplines of organizational learning, 28–9
sensemaking, 22
shared information, 145–6
shared practice, of COPs, 40
shared world view, of COPs, 40–2
situated learning, *see* learning, situated dimension of
situated learning theory, 30–5
situational context, 149–64
  definition, 150
social aspects of learning, *see* situated learning theory
social reproduction of COPs, 40
storytelling, 23–4

tacit knowledge, 142, 144–5
team parameters affecting knowledge flow, 145–7
time, for learning, 6–7, 53, 157